KB090428

ENIE 지침서

영어야, 논술로 말할래?

박창석 지음

PACKSAN Publishing Co.
백산 출판사

ENIE MUST FOR WRITING, SPEAKING!

Question 1: Can you explain the meaning of "오비이락 (烏飛梨落)" in nglish?

uestion 2: How can you explain phones in English for African es who have never seen mobile s?

e are among questions asked licants to enter LG Electron- of Korea's leading electron- panies, in recent corporate examinations. Among simi- ons are "조삼모사 (朝三暮 양난 (進退兩難)" "침소봉대 " all meaningful phrases hinese letters.

tions are entirely differ- s from ones previously companies which have f their English tests in

change is not confined to company tests. TOEFL, transformed into Inter- net-based test (iBT), has changed much in such a way as to give greater

Park Chang-seok

경희대 ENIE교수 / 에듀타임즈 편집인 · 주필

weight on testing speaking and writing proficiency in place of grammar tests previously applied in computer-based test (CBT) or paper-based test

Asian nations in ability to make themselves understood in English.

The altered tests focus on skills in speaking and writing based on logi- cal structure. Essay writing and con- versations practices through tele- phone talking are gaining popularity at hagwons

English teaching (learning) meth- ods have been put into practice in various forms. A number of hagwons and English immersion-program vil- lages nationwide are now teaching students English "very earnestly."

We have made a lot English

S Put on Highest A

"영어야, 논술로 말할래?" 출간에 부쳐...

이번에 출간되는 "영어야, 논술로 말할래?"는 2001년 12월 출간된 "영어야, 뉴스로 말할래?"의 증보판이다. 필자가 한국외국어대학교 언론정보학부의 "영문기사작성"과 경희대학교 언론정보학부 "영문 미디어작문" 강의 교재로 사용하고 있는 "영어야, 뉴스로 말할래?"의 내용을 수정 보완한 책이다. 신문 방송 홍보 광고 분야 등의 언론분야 또는 유사계열 진출을 희망하는 예비 언론인 지망 학생들과 어문계열 학생들에게 ENIE(English Newspaper in Education)교재로 쓰이고 있다. 한양대학교 행정자치 대학원의 성인 학생들에게는 시사영어교재로 이용되고 있다. 학부 학생들에게는 실용영어 실력을 요구하는 취직시험과 유학시험 안내서로, 직장인 대학원 학생들에게는 승급시험 대비 준비서로 활용되고 있다.

미국대학 지원유학생에게 실시되는 영어 학력 테스트인 TOEFL(Test of English as a Foreign Language)이 한국에서는 Internet-based test(iBT)로 바뀌면서 에세이(essay) 시험의 비중이 높아 졌다. "찍기 영어"에 길들여진 한국 학생들에게 비상이 걸린 셈이다. 제한된 시간에 주어진 주제에 대해 글쓰기가 출제 되어 문법위주의 공부에 전력을 다한 한국학생들에게는 엄청난 부담이 아닐 수 없다.

좋은 영문 작성은 정확하고(Accurate), 간결하고(Simple), 논리적(Logical)이어야 한다.

이 같은 원칙은 유형이 바뀐 TOEFL 시험과 취직시험에 기본이 되고 있다. 오프라인, 온라인상의 모든 영어신문, 홈페이지, 에세이 작성에도 같은 원칙이 적용되고 있다.

논리적인 문장, 간결한 헤드라인, 정교한 사진설명 (caption) 쓰기 훈련이 Essay Writing의 필수 실습 과정이다.Writing 이론과 개념은 기존의 미디어 관련 외국서적과 저널에서 인용하였고 응용예문은 국내외 신문, 통신사에서 발행된 문장들을 인용 발췌하였다. 독자들이 이론과 실제를 비교 습득할 수 있도록 했다.

박찬호 파이팅!

Los Angeles Dodgers의 박찬호가 선발투수로 뛰고 있는 미국의 야구 경기장.

교포와 어학 연수간 한국학생들이 관중석에서 '박찬호 파이팅!'을 연발한다. 'Park Chan Ho, Fighting!'이라고 쓴 플래카드도 여기저기 보인다.

'Fighting, Fighting'영어 같기도 한데 무슨 뜻인지 몰라 주위의 미국인들이 어리둥절해 한다.

'Park Chan Ho, Fighting!'이 아니고 'Park Chan Ho, Go!'가 올바른 표현이다.

최근 어느 영어신문사의 견습기자 채용시험에 '한국, 파이팅'을 번역하라는 간단한 문제가 나왔다. 많은 수험생들이 'Korea, Fighting'이라고 썼다. 'Korea, Go'가 정답이다.

필자는 30년 가까이 영어신문 현장에서 일해 왔다.

저자가 견습기자로 코리아타임스에 입사한 며칠 후 에디터는 간단한 교통사고기사를 처리하라고 국문으로 된 통신을 건네주었다.

'택시가 핸들고장으로 마주 오던 버스와 정면충돌 하여 택시 승객 3명이 그 자리에서 숨졌다…. [중략]'이라는 내용의 기사였다.

복병은 '핸들'에 있었다. 필자는 무심코 'handle'이라고 썼다. 미국인 copy editor는 'steering wheel'이라고 고쳤다. handle은 문, 망치 따위의 손잡이를 말하며 자동차의 운전대는 'steering wheel'이라고 써야 한다.

시행착오는 한두 개가 아니며 부끄러운 순간이 한두 번이 아니었다. 오랫동안 영어문장을 다루어 오면서 저자에게 있었던 실수와 오류가 다른 사람들에게도 비슷한 빈도로 일어나고 있음을 알게 되었다. 영어를 모국어로 사용하지 않는 사람들이 겪는 어려움이라고 생각된다.

말을 정확하게 구사하기란 어려운 일이다. 더욱이 정확한 글을 쓰기란 어려운 일이며 더더욱 어려운 일은 그것을 정확한 외국어로 표현하는 것이다.

인터넷의 발달로 영어는 미국, 영국의 '민속어'가 아니고, '인류의 표준어', '세계어'가 되었다. 전 세계에서 이용되고 있는 인터넷 내용물의 80% 정도가 영어로 되어 있다.

인터넷보급의 확산과 세계화물결에 편승하여 정부기관, 지방자치단체, 공공단체, 학교, 기업체, 병원, 군, 경찰, NGO를 포함한 각종 사회단체가 영문 홈페이지를 만들고 있다.

기존의 영어신문은 물론이고 한국어로 제작되는 신문들도 온라인 영문뉴스를 제공하고 있다.

한마디로 말하자면 사회를 구성하는 주요기관 들이 모두 영어신문을 발행한다 해도 과언이 아니다. 그러나 적지 않은 곳에서 오류가 발견되어 국제적 망신을 당한 홈페이지들이 여러 차례 보도된 바 있다.

2001년 '한국 방문의 해', '2002 World Cup'과 때를 같이해 영문 홈페이지 작성은 정점을 이루었고 지금은 1인 미디어 시대다. Blog, UCC등 개인은 단순한 콘텐츠 사용자가 아니라

생산자가 되었다. 영어 홈페이지 작성은 이제 생활의 일부가 되었다. Prosumer 시대에 누구나 논리적 기사 작성의 기본을 익혀야 할 새로운 숙제가 우리 앞에 놓여지게 되었다.

Offline(오프라인), Online(온라인)상에서 발행되는 모든 영어신문, 홈페이지 등은 좋은 글, 좋은 헤드라인, 좋은 Lead 쓰는 요령으로 구성될 때 훌륭한 지식상품이 될 수 있다. 어떻게 하면 Good Writing, Good Headline, Good Lead를 유지할 것인가? 이러한 물음에 조금이나마 도움이 되는 해답을 제시코자 본서를 쓰게 되었다.

본서에서는 특히 한국어의 직역에서 오는 오류, 그리고 내국인, 원어민(native speaker) 모두가 겪는 common errors들을 정리해 보았다. 이는 일선에서 영문기사를 다루는 writer는 물론 copy reader들의 news editing 실무에도 도움이 되도록 하였다.

실용 예문은 가급적 한국의 정치, 경제, 사회, 문화, 체육 분야에 관련된 뉴스 중에서 상식적으로 알아둘 필요가 있는 사항을 중점적으로 다루었다. 예를 들어 남북정상회담, 미국의 테러전쟁, 박세리의 골프우승, 이봉주의 마라톤우승 같은 뉴스를 다룸으로서 독자들의 지식을 동시에 넓힐 수 있도록 했다.

또한 영어신문, 전자신문, 홈페이지에서 혼란스럽게 사용되고 있는 전문 용어, 기관들의 고유명칭을 정리하여 참고가 되도록 했다.

한글의 로마자 표기법에 대해서는 현재 병용되고 있는 McCune-Reischauer System과 2000년 개정 발표한 문화관광부 안을 동시에 수록하여 비교 참고토록 했다. 지명, 도로 표시, 사람 이름 등에 아직도 많은 곳에서 McCune-Reischauer, 문화관광부안 표기법이 혼용되고 있어 틀리기 쉬운 표기를 예를 들어 설명하였다.

영어가 신분상승의 비상구로 인식되면서 영어라고 하는 "문화유산"을 자녀에게 물려주기 위해 태아 교육 조기유학, 조기이민의 "조기병"이 불고 있다. 영어는 이제 자본이자 권력이 되어 가고 있다. 영어는 부자 아빠, 부자 아들, 딸을 만들 수 있다는 인식이 팽배하다.

영어가 정보화 시대에 "digital divide" 못지않게 "English divide"의 양극화 현상을 일으키게 하고 있으며 이는 다시 "wealth divide"현상으로 이어진다.

세계화 시대의 국제무대에서 국가홍보, 단체홍보, 기업체홍보, 학교홍보를 제대로 하는 것만이 국제경쟁력을 키우는 것이다.

정확한 영문구성을 통한 정보의 효율적인 전달이 세계시장 소비자들의 이해를 높이는 최선의 홍보요, 생존의 수단이다.

"English divide"의 우위를 유지하는 것이 "wealth divide"의 큰 파이를 보장 받는 것이다.

본서의 증보판을 출간함에 있어 어려운 시기에도 교육적 사명을 다하고자 결단을 내려주신 백산출판사 寅製 진욱상 사장님 그리고 편집부 일원들께 감사를 드린다.

유난히도 더웠던 2007년 여름휴가도 없이 원고의 보완과 수정을 하는데 도움을 주었던 나의 가장 친한 친구이자 평생의 반려자인 김경희와 출판의 기쁨을 같이 하고자 한다. 어려운 순간들마다 격려와 용기를 북돋아 주었던 두 아들 준원, 태원의 정신적 지원은 집필하는 데 큰 힘이 되었다.

이 책의 첫판은 2001년 한국언론재단의 연구·저술활동 지원으로 출판되었습니다. 본서를 출간하는데 지원해 주신 재단관계자 여러분들께 감사드립니다.

2007년 7월

지은이 박 창 석

차례

Writing 1

Readability & Legibility

한국말 "태권도", "재벌", "김치"는 영어화 된지 오래다. 간단히 소리나는 대로 "taekwondo", "chaebol", "kimchi"라고 쓰면 된다. 이 단어들은 웹스터 사전과 옥스포드 사전에 이미 영어단어로 올라있다.

과거에는 태권도를 Korean martial art, 재벌을 business group, 또는 business conglomerate, 김치를 pickles made of radish, cabbage, cucumber, spiced with red pepper, garlic, onion, ginger로 설명을 해 표기했었다.

또 "불고기", "과외", "학원" 같은 말도 "pulgogi", "kwaoe", "hakwon" 으로 표기하면 주한 외국인들에게는 의미가 통하는 준 영어가 되었다.

한국 남성들의 음주 문화를 대변하는 "폭탄주"는 정통 영어인 "boilermaker"보다는 "bomb drink"의 "한국산 영어"가 해외에서 발간되는 영문 잡지 등에서 사용되고 있다.

일본어의 경우도 비슷한 케이스가 많다. "가라오케(karaoke)"가 대표적인 예다. 얼마 전 미국의 시사주간지 Time은 "원조 교제"를 일본어 소리나는 대로 "enjokosai"로 표기했다(cf: 금품따위를 뿌리며 젊은 여자를 유혹하는 중년 남자를 미국인들은 "sugar daddy"라고 한다).

시대가 변함에 따라 인간생활의 의식주형태가 바뀌고, 이에 따른 유행의 패턴이 달라지고 있는데 언어도 마찬가지다. 시대의 흐름에 따라 단어가 변하고, 신조어가 많이 생기고 있다.

미래학자 Alvin Toffler의 "변화"에 대한 세계적 3대 명저인 "Future Shock"(1970), "The Third Wave"(1980), "Power Shift"(1990)에서 예견

된 바와 같이, 우리는 산업, 일상생활 전반에 걸쳐 엄청난 변화의 물결 속에서 살고 있다.

산업사회에서 정보통신사회로의 진입은 Marshall McLuhan(1911 - 1980)이 예견한 "Global Village"의 도래를 피부로 느끼며 살고 있는 것이 현실이다.

Digital 서비스와 Internet망의 확충으로 세계는 하나로 연결되고, 정보통신사회에 맞는 신조어들이 무수히 생겨나고 있다.

오프라인, 온라인 신문, 잡지, 그리고 정부기관, 지방자치단체, 학교, 기업체, NGO 등이 만들어내는 홈페이지에 종래에 쓰던 "Citizen", "Telephone", "Airmail" 같은 단어보다는 "Netizen", "Cellular Phone"(또는 "Mobile Phone"), "Email" 등의 용어가 더 많이 쓰이고 있다.

이러한 언어적 변화 속에서도 아직까지 변하지 않는 것이 있는데 바로, 영문작성의 포맷이다. 특히, 시사성사건이나 행사 등을 다루는 뉴스성격의 영문은 몇 십년이 지난 지금도 보수적인 형태를 그대로 유지하고 있다.

신문인 경우 제호(Flag), 편집디자인(Editorial Design), 글자체(Typography), 사진 color화 등의 외형적인 형태는 기술의 발달에 따라 많은 변화를 가져왔다.

그러나 현대 새로운 저널리즘의 3대 요체라고 불리는 WED, 즉 Writing, Editing, Design에 있어 Writing과 Editing만은 보수적인 형태를 그대로 유지하고 있다.

기사의 작성은 '저널리즘의 특성', '글이 읽기 쉬운가(Easy To Read)?', '정확한가(Accurate)?', '논리적인가(Logical)?'에 기초한 "가독성(Readability)"으로 그 가치를 찾기 때문이다.

내용적인 측면을 강조하는 개념의 Readability에 대해 시각적인 면을 강조하는 "가시성(Legibility)"은 인쇄기술과 디자인산업의 발달과 더불어 많은 융통성을 가지고 활자체와 편집면에서 혁신적인 변화를 가져왔다.

예컨대, 가독성은 "읽고 이해하기 쉬움"이란 뜻을 내포하고 있으며 가시성은 "읽기 쉽고 명료한가"라는 외형적인 뜻을 포함하고 있다. 이들 모두가 독이성을 높이는 양대 축이라 할 수 있다.

한마디로 가시성을 높이는 수단은 많은 변화를 가져 왔으나, 그에 비해 가독성을 높이는 문장형식은 전통적인 원칙을 그대로 유지하고 있다고 해도 지나침이 없다.

현행 구미지역을 포함, 세계 곳곳에서 발행되는 모든 신문, 잡지, 대학에서 발행되는 학생 영어신문, 중앙 행정부처, 지방자치단체, NGO 등 민간사회단체 및 기업체가 발행하는 홍보지 등 모든 오프라인성격의 저널, 그리고 이와 병행해서 온라인상에서 제작되는 전자신문, 홈페이지에 사용되는 뉴스를 다루는 영문구성은 시대의 변화에도 불구하고, 몇 십 년 동안 그 포맷이 변하지 않고 일정한 형식을 취하고 있다.

본란에서는 뉴스를 다루는 좋은 영문은 어떻게 쓸 때 가독성을 높일 수 있는가?의 방안에 대해 논해보기로 한다.

좋은 글에 대한 연구

사건, 사고, 행사(정치, 경제, 사회, 문화, 예술, 스포츠 등 각 분야를 망라) 등을 다루는 뉴스성격의 글은 그것이 신문이든, 기관의 홍보지든, 또는 온라인상의 홈페이지든 간에 독자에게 "정보전달"함이 그 목적이다.

정보전달을 위한 글은 기본적으로 3가지 요건이 충족되었을 때 "좋은 글"이 될 수 있다.

"간결(Simplicity)", "명료(Clarity)", "강조(Emphasis)"가 바로 그것인데 글 작성자와 독자간의 거리는 이 세 가지 요건이 충족될 때 좁혀질 수 있으며 공급자와 수용자가 일체감을 이룰 수 있다.

구미의 각 신문사와 AP, UPI, Reuters 등 외국 통신사들은 양질의 기사를 독자들에게 제공하기 위해 부단히 노력하고 있다. 외국 통신사들은 어떻게 하면 가독성을 높일 수 있는 기사를 제공할 것인가의 숙제를 풀기 위해 전문가들에 용역을 주어 연구를 해왔다.

본란에서는 Writing Skill을 익히려는 이들에게 "Flesch Test"를 예로 들어 소개하고자 한다.

Flesch Test

　"The Art of Plain Talk"의 저자 Rudolf Flesch는 The Associated Press(AP)에 기자들이 좋은 글을 쓰기(Good Writing) 위한 4가지 요건을 제시했다.

1) 短文(Short Sentences)으로 써라.

　독자들이 읽기 쉬운 글은 짧은 문장이다. 읽기에 편한 문장은 평균단어(Average Words)수가 16에서 19의 범위다.

2) Simple Words, Direct Words를 사용하라.

　일반적으로 Latin 계통에서 연유한 단어보다는 순수한 Anglo-Saxon Words가 읽고 이해하기 쉬우며 난해한 단어보다는 쉬운 단어를 사용해야 한다. 또 직접 표현방식이 의미전달 속도가 빠르다.

3) 인칭대명사(Personal Pronoun)를 많이 사용하라.

　사람의 이름, 대명사, 인척관계를 표현하는 단어는 읽기에 편하여 독자들이 빠른 속도로 가독할 수 있다.

ex　Tom, Brown, He, She, Me, Aunt, Uncle 등.

4) 구어체 문장(Spoken Sentence)을 사용하라.

인용문, 감탄문, 의문문 등으로 표현되는 Spoken Sentences는 읽기에 평이하다.

Flesch의 제언 이외에도 여타 전문가들의 공통적인 견해는 대체로 ① 중복되는(Redundant) 단어사용의 삼가 ② 추상적이거나 복잡한 단어사용의 절제를 권장한다.

이러한 연구자들의 제언에도 불구하고 현장에서 실제 기사작성을 할 때 기자나 기사체크를 담당하는 사람(Copy Editor)들은 이러한 제언을 잘 지키지 않는다.

기사작성자나 편집실무자 들은 Flesch가 제시한 16~19단어범위의 문장은 너무 간결하여 "어린이용 평이한 문장(Baby Talk)"이 되기 쉽다고 주장한다. 어떤 편집인들은 적어도 한 문장을 작성하는데 있어 50단어까지는 독자들의 가독성을 해치지 않는다고 주장한다.

특히 신문을 포함한 시사성 뉴스의 경우 서구에서 발행되는 많은 신문사들이 견습기자 훈련을 시킬 때 문장 서두의 Lead는 30단어 이내로 단어 수를 제한하고 있다.

이 같은 연구자들의 제언과 실무자들의 주장을 기본으로 하고, 30년 가까이 영문작성을 하면서 시행착오의 경험을 해온 필자의 견해는 한 문장이 꼭 16자에서 19자 사이의 규격화된 포맷을 지키기 보다는 단어 수를 가급적 줄여 간결성을 유지하는 노력이 필요하며, 관계 대명사 등이 여러 번 사용 되어야 할 긴 문장인 경우는 무리하게 늘리지 말고, 과감하게 문장을 나누는 용기가 필요하다고 본다.

구태여 산술적으로 말한다면 한 문장을 구성하는 바람직한 단어 수를 30개 정도로 제시코자 한다.

Flesch Test 실용예문

1) Short Sentences

16~19 단어 사용범위의 문장:

ex 1 Lee Bong-ju of Korea won the Boston Marathon on April 17, 2001, snapping a 10-year win streak for Kenya. Lee came down Boylston Street to finish in 2 hours, 9 minutes, 43 seconds. Kenyans captured the women's race for the second consecutive year.

ex 2 Lotte Group is reportedly considering the takeover of Midopa Department Store. A business source said that if the Lotte Group acquires Midopa, its market share would be rising.

30단어 사용규모의 문장:

ex 1 The National Tax Service(NTS) yesterday launched an extensive tax probe into 155 private moneylenders to investigate the alleged inappropriate profiteering practices by loan sharks.

ex 2 The special tax audit came on reports that many cash-crunched small business owners and citizens in low-income brackets have been suffering from high interest rates demanded by usurers.

✔ 50 단어 규모의 문장:

> *ex* **1** With criticism intensifying over the police's excessive use of force against protesting Daewoo workers, a National Assembly standing committee meeting yesterday turned into a battleground between the ruling and opposition parties over who offered the correct cause of the bloody clash in Inchon, 40 kilometers west of Seoul.

> *ex* **2** At the National Assembly's Government Administration and Home Affairs Committee session, the main opposition Grand National Party(GNP) insisted on the collective resignation of Prime Minister Lee Han-dong, Government Administration-Home Affairs Minister Lee Keun-sik and National Police Agency head Lee Moo-young, saying that the government is to blame for the tragic incident, which left dozens of workers and their lawyer injured.

위 3가지 예문의 가독성을 보자. 분명한 것은 words수가 적을수록 읽기 쉽다는 것을 알 수 있다. Words가 많으면 경우에 따라서는 2번 이상 읽어야 해독이 가능한 경우도 있어 독자들의 수고를 필요이상으로 요구하게 된다.

Point :

Chop Long Sentences Into Readable Lengths!

앞에서 제시한 50단어 규모문장의 *ex* 2는 다음과 같이 둘로 나눌 수 있다.

At the National Assembly's Government Administration and Home Affairs Committee session, the main opposition Grand National Party(GNP) insisted on the collective resignation of Prime Minister Lee Han-dong, Government Administration-Home Affairs Minister Lee Keun-sik and National Police Agency head Lee Moo-young. It said that the government is to blame for the tragic incident, which left dozens of workers and their lawyer injured.

2) Simple Words, Direct Words

난해한 용어, 전문용어, 순수영어가 아닌 라틴어 또는 기타 언어계통의 어휘나, 접두사, 접미사가 붙은 단어들은 문장의 해독을 어렵게 만들어 가독성이 떨어진다. Direct Words를 사용한 직접 표현방식의 의미전달이 빠르다.

Avoidable	8 U.S. dollars per day, 10 miles per hour, income per capita.
Better	8 U.S. dollars a day, 10 miles an hour, personal income.
Avoidable	He got lacerations and contusions.
Better	He got cuts and bruises.
Wordy	The killer suspect managed to make his escape.
Better	The killer suspect escaped.
Wordy	The announcement was made by him.
Better	He announced.

Wordy	She was given a five-year prison sentence.
Better	She was sentenced to five years in prison.

3) Personal Pronoun

사람 이름, 대명사, 인척관계를 표현하는 용어는 가독성을 높여 준다. 문장에서 복잡한 직함을 지속적으로 쓰는 것은 읽기에 불편하며 이름이나 인칭대명사로 대체하면 읽기에 편하다.

Unreadable	Foreign Affairs and Trade Minister Han Seung-soo visited Iran. The minister held a press conference in Tehran.
Readable	Foreign Affairs and Trade Minister Han Seung-soo visited Iran. Han(or He) held a press conference in Tehran.

Unreadable	Ma Ying-jeou, mayor of Taipei, came to Seoul. The mayor attended the World Ceramics Expo in Ichon, Kyonggi-do.
Readable	Ma Ying-jeou, mayor of Taipei, came to Seoul. Ma(or He) attended the World Ceramics Expo in Ichon, Kyonggi-do.

4) Spoken Sentences

인용문, 감탄문, 의문문 등으로 표현되는 구어체 문장은 읽기 쉽다.

ex **1** Is it over yet?

With stock prices now down 20 percent over the last year, a debate rages on Wall Street about whether the worst is over.

ex 2 "Revolution is not a dinner party", former Chinese leader Mao Zedong once warned the people. But the Communist Party's 80th anniversary could pass for a coffee break, or perhaps a wine tasting.

ex 3 Amen!
The real questions(in the Clinton pardon scandal) involve the leveraging of influence by relatives, associates and campaign contributors.

Tips for Good Writing

앞서 말한 바와 같이 "간결(Simplicity)", "명료(Clarity)", "강조(Emphasis)"는 좋은 글이 되기 위한 3가지 중요한 요건이다. Flesch Test는 이들 기본요건을 구체적이며 체계적으로 정리했다.

앞서 인용된 예문들은 Flesch Test에 부합되는 문장을 예로 들면서 장황하게 설명은 하였지만 좋은 글을 쓴다는 것이 그리 쉬운 일은 아니다.

좋은 글을 쓰기 위해서는 남들이 써놓은 좋은 글을 많이 읽어서 자기 것으로 재활용하는 것이 최선의 방법이다.

The easiest and the best way to learn about good writing is through reading. Read as much as you can, and take time to evaluate the writing involved.

본란에서는 지금까지의 연구결과를 토대로 실제로 좋은 글을 쓰기 위한 비법(Tips on Good Journalistic Writing)을 알아보기로 한다.

Tips on Good Writing

Tip 1:   Find the main idea.
Tip 2:   Be accurate, logical.
Tip 3:   Be fair, objective.
Tip 4:   Be short, simple, limiting a sentence to about 30 words.
Tip 5:   Restrict a paragraph to one–three sentences.
Tip 6:   Be direct, active, positive.
Tip 7:   Avoid word–for–word translation.
Tip 8:   Watch out such words as No, Not, Only, Less.
Tip 9:   Shun the editorial "We".
Tip 10:   Avoid the monotonous writing.
Tip 11:   Avoid the double negative.
Tip 12:   Avoid redundancies, unneeded words.
Tip 13:   Use words economically.
Tip 14:   Avoid abstract or complex words.
Tip 15:   Be lucid in explaining sources.

실습 Tip 1: Main Idea

1) 작성과정

① News Writing의 기본요소 원칙인 5W's+1H(Who, What, Where, When, Why, and How) 중 글 작성자 스스로 Who와 What에 관해 우선 질문해 본다.

② 질문에 대답해 본다. 그러면 "누가" 관련된 "무엇에 관한" News의 주제는 무엇인지 방향이 잡힌다.

③ 대답을 조합해 간단한 단문으로 구성해 본다. Main Idea의 그림이 떠오를 것이다.

④ Main Idea를 중심으로 글의 첫 머리에 5W's+1H원칙에 입각, 요약해 'Lead"를 쓴다. 칭호나 장소 등의 세세한 묘사는 Lead 부분에서는 피한다. 문장이 복잡해지기 때문이다. 간단, 명료한 Lead는 포괄적으로 쓰는 것이 좋다. (Lead 부분은 뒤에서 다시 설명)

⑤ Main Idea를 정점으로 세부적인 사항(Supporting Details)을 중요한 순서에 입각, 역피라미트(Inverted Pyramid) 형태로 전개해 나간다.

⑥ 중요한 사항은 Lead 다음의 Paragraph에 바로 이어지도록 하여 편집에서 끝 부분이 잘려 나가도 독자들이 이해하는데 지장이 없게 한다.

⑦ 며칠간, 혹은 몇 달간 지속적으로 발전되는 상황을 연일 보도해야 하는 대형 사건, 사고(지진, 비행기 추락 등에 관한)의 후속기사는 독자가 어느날 기사를 보아도 전체상황을 한눈에 알 수 있도록 기사의 앞부분에 전개과정 기술을 원칙으로 한다.

실습예문

2000년 6월 13~15일 평양에서 열렸던 남북 정상회담에 관한 글을 위에서 열거한 7단계 과정에 따라 작성해 보기로 한다.

기초자료는 남북한정상 들이 3일간의 회담을 마치고 발표한 공동선언문을 기본으로 한다.

작성과정 1~2:

아래 Figure 1의 "6.15 남북공동선언문"을 "자료"로 기사작성을 한다고 가정해보자.

Who(누가)가 What(무엇)에 관한 내용인가에 대한 질문의 답은 한번 읽어서 쉽게 알 수 있다.

▶ *Who?*

남북 정상: (Top) leaders of South and North Korea.
President Kim Dae-jung of South Korea.
National Defense Commission Chairman Kim Jong-il of North Korea.

▶ *What?*

정상회담에서 공동선언에 합의: Agree in Summit.

작성 3: Who와 What에 관한 사항을 단문으로 작성

(Top) leaders of South and North Korea agree in summit.

작성 4: 5W's+1H형 Lead 작성

작성 3의 과정에서 만든 단문에 5W's+1H의 원칙에 의거, 앞뒤로 필요한 단어들을 나열하면서 문법적으로 완벽하게 Lead를 만들어나간다.

The leaders of North and South Korea yesterday agreed in a landmark summit to allow families separated by the partition of the peninsula to meet, and to repatriate political prisoners.
(Financial Times June 15 Report의 Lead)

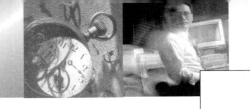

작성 5∼6: Supporting Details

남북의 두 정상을 Lead에서는 "Leaders"로 포괄적으로 표기하고, Second Paragraph에서 Title을 쓰면 문장이 간단, 명료하게 이어진다.

South Korean President Kim Dae-jung described as "successful" his unprecedented talks in Pyongyang with National Defense Commission Chairman Kim Jong-il of North Korea, at which they signed a broad agreement aimed at reconciling the world's last Cold War rivals. (2nd Paragraph)

작성 7: 후속기사

김대중 대통령은 3일간의 평양정상회담을 마치고 6월 16일 서울로 돌아와 도착성명을 발표한다. Financial Times는 김대통령의 도착성명을 후속기사로 쓰면서, 기사 전반부에 3일간의 평양정상회담에 대해서 기술한다.

16일자 신문을 처음으로 접하는 독자라도 이전에 있었던 정상회담에 관한 사항을 개략적으로 알 수 있다.

다음의 1∼3 Paragraph는 15일, 16일 상황을 동시에 알려준다.

South Korean President Kim Dae-jung said yesterday that he was hopeful of a breakthrough on crucial security issues with North Korea including Pyongyang's nuclear and missile programs, which have raised tensions in East Asia to the brink of war. (Lead)

"The dialogue was very fruitful on(security issues), and there were some talks that showed very good prospects", President Kim told a rapturous welcoming crowd on his return from an extraordinary three-day visit to Pyongyang, the North Korean capital. Tens of thousands lined the streets of his route to the presidential Blue House. (2nd Paragraph)

The programs were among issues discussed in his unprecedented summit with Kim Jong-il, the North Korean leader, that exceeded expectations and promised to end 55 years of hostilities across the Cold War's last frontier. The accords, in which the two Koreas "agreed to tackle the reunification issue independently by joining forces", won praise from across the globe. (3rd Paragraph)

6.15 남북공동선언문

조국의 평화적 통일을 염원하는 온 겨레의 숭고한 뜻에 따라 대한민국 김대중 대통령과 조선민주주의인민공화국 김정일 국방위원장은 2000년 6월 13일부터 6월 15일까지 평양에서 역사적인 상봉을 하였으며 정상회담을 가졌다.

남북 정상들은 분단 역사상 처음으로 열린 이번 상봉과 회담이 서로 이해를 증진시키고 남북관계를 발전시키며 평화통일을 실현하는데 중대한 의의를 가진다고 평가하고 다음과 같이 선언한다.

1. 남과 북은 나라의 통일문제를 그 주인인 우리 민족끼리 서로 힘을 합쳐 자주적으로 해결해 나가기로 했다.

2. 남과 북은 나라의 통일을 위한 남측의 연합제안과 북측의 낮은 단계의 연방제안이 서로 공통성이 있다고 인정하고 앞으로 이 방향에서 통일을 지향시켜 나가기로 했다.

3. 남과 북은 올해 8.15에 즈음하여 흩어진 가족, 친척방문단을 교환하며 비전향 장기수 문제를 해결하는 등 인도적 문제를 조속히 풀어나가기로 하였다.

4. 남과 북은 경제협력을 통하여 민족경제를 균형적으로 발전시키고 사회, 문화, 체육, 보건, 환경 등 제반 분야의 협력과 교류를 활성화하여 서로의 신뢰를 다져 나가기로 하였다.

5. 남과 북은 이상과 같은 합의사항을 조속히 실천에 옮기기 위하여 빠른 시일 안에 당국 사이의 대화를 개최하기로 하였다.

김대중 대통령은 김정일 국방위원장이 서울을 방문하도록 정중히 초청하였으며 김정일 국방위원장은 앞으로 적절한 시기에 서울을 방문하기로 하였다.

2000년 6월 15일

대 한 민 국	조선민주주의인민공화국
대 통 령	국방위원장
김 대 중	김 정 일

Figure 1

세계 주요 신문들의 남북정상회담에 대한 6월 15자 보도예문

> Sample 1:

Koreas Reach Accord Seeking Reconciliation After 50 Years

SEOUL, South Korea, Thursday, June 15 — With surprising speed and warmth, the leaders of North and South Korea reached a broad agreement on Wednesday to work for peace and unity on their bitterly divided peninsula, the biggest step by either side to ease tensions in 50 years.

The agreement, which came after more than three hours of talks in the North Korean capital, Pyongyang, on the second day of their first summit meeting, was signed and toasted by President Kim Dae-jung of South Korea and North Korean leader Kim Jong-il, who were shown on South Korean television clinking champagne glasses, shaking hands vigorously and smiling broadly.

The agreement, while deliberately vague, had clearly left both men buoyant. If carried through, the accord would reduce the precarious isolation of the North and address many basic points that have long been seen as keys to ending the Cold War on the heavily fortified peninsula, where the United States still maintains 37,000 troops.

The general points agreed on included the need for reconciliation and unification; the establishment of peace; the commencement in August of exchange visits by members of divided families; and more cultural exchanges.

In addition, it was agreed that Kim Jong-il would visit Seoul "at the earliest appropriate moment". The two sides also discussed the creation of offices in each other's capitals, and establishing a hot line between their leaders.

················ The New York Times, 중략 ················

29

Korean Leaders Sign Pact Offering Hope

SEOUL, South Korea — North Korea and South Korea signed an accord short on specifics but offering hope that the first summit between the countries' top leaders may be a step toward easing the most intractable conflict of the Cold War.

The accord was signed by Kim Jong-il, the paramount leader of Stalinist North Korea, and President Kim Dae-jung of South Korea during his visit to Pyongyang. In it, the two Koreas agreed to "resolve the question of reunification independently". Kim Jong-il promised to visit Seoul, although no firm date was set.

The document also said the two Koreas would increase economic cooperation to bring about a "balanced" economy, which will likely lead to more investment and aid for North Korea from South Korea. And, in a political victory for Kim Dae-jung, North Korea agreed to hold reunions, around Aug. 15, of families separated between the two countries.

The summit ends today, and Kim Dae-jung will return to South Korea by car through the heavily armed border that divides the two countries.

The pact suggests that perhaps North Korea is ready to end its international isolation and begin rebuilding its shattered economy. Kim Jong-il seems keen to change his own image as a reclusive mystery man to one of a world statesman.

·················· The Wall Street Journal, 중략 ··················

Sample 3:

Two Koreas Sign Conciliatory Accord

SEOUL, June 15(Thursday) — North and South Korea stepped back from a half-century of confrontation Wednesday night as their leaders signed an agreement to work toward reunification of the divided peninsula and begin an epochal process of reconciliation.

With handshakes, smiles and a champagne toast, South Korean President Kim Dae-jung and North Korean ruler Kim Jong-il agreed to bring together some of the tens of thousands of families split between North and South by the Korean War of 1950-1953 and to take up the issue of Communist political prisoners being held in the South. The first family reunions were set for Aug. 15, when both nations celebrate their liberation from 40 years of Japanese occupation after World War II.

The two men also agreed to take unspecified economic actions, begin social and cultural exchanges and undertake follow-up governmental contacts to ease cross-border tensions. "An era of conciliation and cooperation has begun", the South Korean President declared, as he praised the "historic agreement". "The hopes and dreams of the people have been realized".

The agreement, which was cast in general terms, will not by itself erase friction on the Korean Peninsula, one of the world's major flash points. Lower-level officials of the two countries had signed agreements previously, but most of them have failed to stick. But the extraordinary three-day summit in Pyongyang, the North Korean capital, has brought the leaders of the two countries together in scenes of friendship and congeniality that millions of Koreans thought impossible.

Whatever the fate of the accord, the summit has permanently

changed the image of Kim Jong-il, leader of the world's last Stalinist regime, who presented an amicable and statesman-like image in pledging his country would work with the South. Kim Jong-il will accept an invitation to visit Seoul "at the appropriate time", the agreement said, a vague but nevertheless unprecedented promise.

·················· The Washington Post, 중략 ·················

Sample 4:

Leaders of two Koreas to let families meet

SEOUL, South Korea — The leaders of North and South Korea yesterday agreed in a landmark summit to allow families separated by the partition of the peninsula to meet, and to repatriate political prisoners.

Kim Dae-jung, the South Korean President, described as "successful" his unprecedented talks with Kim Jong-il, North Korea's leader, at which they signed a broad agreement aimed at reconciling the world's last Cold War rivals.

Park Joon-young, South Korea's presidential spokesman, announcing details of the agreement late last night, said the two sides had agreed to hold reunions around August 15 of families ripped apart half a century ago. The date is when both countries mark the liberation of Korea from Japanese occupation at the end of the second world war.

They also agreed at the end of the second day of the summit in Pyongyang to "resolve as soon as possible humanitarian issues such as the repatriation of long-term political prisoners".

In addition, they pledged to work together towards reunification, promote economic, cultural and sports exchanges and hold early government-level talks on these issues.

·················· Financial Times, 중략 ·················

Sample 5:

Korean Leaders Sign Historic Accord
By Chong Wa Dae Press Corps

PYONGYANG — The leaders of the two Koreas signed a landmark five-point accord which includes a call for the exchange of separated family members on the occasion of the National Liberation Day on August 15.

The joint declaration calls for the two Koreas, who are the main parties on the peninsula, to solve the question of national unification in an independent manner, while pursuing unity on the basis of similar elements of Seoul's "Korea commonwealth unification formula" and Pyongyang's proposal of the loose form of "confederation unification system".

President Kim Dae-jung and North Korean leader Kim Jong-il then agreed to resolve the issue of "long-term Communist prisoners in the South".

They shared the view that the two Koreas must build trust between each other by developing a national economy in a balanced manner through economic cooperation.

The two Koreas agreed to launch dialogue between their authorities at the earliest date to translate the accord into action.

National Defense Commission Chairman Kim Jong-il agreed to visit Seoul at an appropriate date after the invitation of President Kim, according to the agreement.

President Kim and North Korean leader Kim reached the agreement following a marathon meeting which lasted more than three hours and a 40-minute recess at the Paekhwawon State Guest House.

·················· The Korea Times, 중략 ··················

남북 정상회담 공동선언문 전문영역

Full Text of South−North Korea Joint Declaration

In accordance with the sublime aspiration of the Korean people for peaceful unification of the fatherland, Kim Dae-jung, President of the Republic of Korea, and Kim Jong-il, National Defense Commission Chairman of the Democratic People's Republic of Korea, made a historic meeting and held a summit in Pyongyang from June 13 through 15 in 2000.

Evaluating that their get-together and summit, which took place for the first time since national division, is significant in helping promote mutual understanding, develop the inter-Korean relations and realize peaceful unification, the leaders of the two Koreas made the following declaration.

1. The South and the North have agreed to join hands to solve the question of national unification in an independent manner between us, who are the main parties.
2. Acknowledging that the South's "Korea commonwealth unification formula" and the North's proposal of the "loose form of confederation unification system" have similarities, the South and the North decided to pursue unification in this direction.
3. In marking the August 15(Liberation Day) this year, the South and the North decided to exchange delegations of separated families and relatives and seek to resolve humanitarian issues, including the problem of long-serving(North Korean) prisoners who have refused to convert.
4. The South and the North decided to build up trust between each other by developing a national economy in a balanced manner through economic cooperation and by stimulating cooperation and exchanges in such various fields as society, culture, sports, health and the environment.
5. The South and the North have agreed to begin dialogue between the authorities of the two Koreas at the earliest date in order to implement the accord.

President Kim Dae-jung formally and cordially invited National Defense Commission Chairman Kim Jong-il to visit Seoul at an appropriate date, which Defense Commission Chairman Kim formally accepted.

June 15, 2000
The Republic of Korea   The Democratic People's Republic of Korea
President   National Defense Commission Chairman
Kim Dae-jung   Kim Jong-il

Figure 2

Note

Figure 2는 Figure 1의 남북 공동선언문으로 발표된 보도자료를 직역한 영문이다. Figure 2의 직역한 번역문과 5개의 실제기사(Sample 1~5) 예문을 비교해 보면 현격한 차이가 있다. 기사형태는 어느 것이든 강조되는 부분을 Lead로 하고 중요한 순서대로 정렬, Pyramid 형태를 유지하고 있다. 그러나 직역한 영문은 자료문안을 순서대로 쓴 단순한 나열식이다.

실습 Tip 2: Be accurate, logical.

뉴스기사는 정확하고(Accurate), 논리적(Logical)인 것이 생명이다.

ex **1** A court hearing for a killer suspect was set for Aug. 12, 2001.

어느 기자가 위 예문과 같이 기사를 썼다고 가정하자.

위 문장은 정확한 것인가? 한마디로 *ex* 1의 예문은 Inaccurate하다.

언뜻 보아 문법적으로 오류가 없어 보이지만 잘 살펴보면 살인범에 대한 공판은 August 12에 열릴 수가 없다. August 12는 일요일이기 때문이다.

ex **2** A 20-year-old woman was divorced from his husband and has been granted the custody of her 12-year-old son.

위 문장도 문법적으로는 문제가 없어 보인다. 그러나 생각해 보면 논리적 오류를 쉽게 발견할 수 있다. 20살인 여자가 남자와 결혼하고 이혼할 수는 있으나 12살인 아들이 있다는 것은 있을 수 없기 때문이다. *ex* 2의 예문은 Illogical하다.

Illogical	After waiting an hour, a train finally came.
Logical	After waiting an hour, we finally caught a train.
	(waiting an hour의 주어는 "we"인가? "train"인가? 말할 것도 없이 "we"이다)

실습 Tip 3: Be fair, objective.

뉴스를 전달하는 기사형식의 글은 공정성과 객관성이 있어야 한다. writer의 주관적인 생각이나 느낌을 글에 쓰는 것은 금물이다. 개인의 의견을 쓰면 사설이나 "일기장"이 된다.

아래 문장에서 "pretty", "handsome", "special" 같은 수식어는 다분히 주관적인 느낌의 표현이라 할 수 있다.

Avoidable	A pretty woman and a handsome man were killed in a traffic accident.
Right	A woman and a man were killed in a traffic accident.
Avoidable	A special ceremony was held yesterday at a hotel to support needy children.
Right	A ceremony was held yesterday at a hotel to support needy children.

실습 Tip 4: Be short, simple, limiting a sentence to about 30 words.

문장은 짧게, 간단히!

이는 글을 쓰는 모든 사람들에게 금과옥조와 같은 것이다.

한 문장의 단어 수는 30자 내외를 유지하라. 이는 공식은 아니나 지킬 만한 서식이다. 긴 문장은 집중력을 떨어뜨린다.

문장이 길어지면 과감하게 둘로 나눠라.

(Flesch Test 참조)

실습 Tip 5: Restrict a paragraph to one-three sentences.

한 문항(Paragraph)은 1~3의 Sentence를 유지토록 하는 것이 독자들의 지루함을 덜어준다.

> *ex* BERLIN(AP) — During its 28 years of existence, the Berlin Wall divided Europe by ideology. But first it divided families.
>
> Sabine Sprengel remembers waking to pounding on the door at 7:30 a.m. on Aug. 13, 1961, 40 years ago Monday. Neighbors shouted urgently: "They're closing the border! They're closing the border!"
>
> The news was unfathomable. The city had been divided by the four Allied powers since the end of World War II, but the border between East and West Berlin remained open···.

실습 Tip 6: Be direct, active, positive.

- Say in the direct expressions! – 직접 표현으로!
- Say in the positive form! – 긍정문으로!
- Say in the active voice! – 능동태로!

직접 표현, 긍정문, 능동태는 가독성을 높인다.

Good writing makes direct, positive, active-voice statements. Use the word "not" only when the negative idea is emphatic; otherwise express what you want to say in the positive form.

| Indirect | The opposition party did not like the government's reform plan. |
| Direct, Better | The opposition party disliked the government's reform plan. |

| Negative | I did not think the trip would be very interesting. |
| Positive, Better | I thought the trip would be a bore. |

| Passive | A restructuring program was announced by the government. |
| Active, Better | The government announced a restructuring program. |

실습 Tip 7: Avoid word-for-word translation.

정부기관에서 발표하는 한국어로 된 보도자료나 한국어신문에 잘못 사용되는 용어를 직역하여 영문기사를 쓸 경우, 간혹 외국인독자 들은 뜻을 몰라 당황할 때가 있다. 의미를 완전히 파악하고 번역해야 한다.

명예퇴직

한국의 기업, 금융기관에서 시행하는 "명예퇴직" 제도는 당사자에게는 "명예로운(Honorable)" 것이 아니다. 오히려 "명예롭지 못함(Dishonorable)"으로 "조기퇴직(Early Retirement)"이란 표현이 적합하다.

| Wrong | Honorable Retirement. |
| Right | Early Retirement. |

IMF 위기

한국이 1997년 IMF(International Monetary Fund, 국제통화기금)에서 구제금융을 받고 경제가 IMF 관리체제 하에 놓이게 되었다. 그 후

사람들은 거두절미 하고 "IMF 맞았다". "IMF 위기"라는 정체불명의 언어들을 사용하게 되었다.

정확한 표현은 "IMF 위기"가 아니라 "금융위기", 또는 "외환위기"로 표현해야 한다.

Wrong	IMF crisis.
Right	financial crisis, foreign exchange crisis.

> *ex*　Korea borrowed a total of $19.5 billion from the International Monetary Fund(IMF) in the wake of the financial crisis in 1997.

✔ 워크아웃

한국어로 발행되는 신문에서 "워크아웃"이라는 단어를 많이 쓴다.

영어로 "l"과 "r" 발음의 차이를 표기할 길이 없어 "Walkout"과 "Work-out"을 같이 표현하는 것 같다.

"워크아웃"이 "Walkout"(파업, a strike of workers)의 의미로 사용되는 것은 이해할 만 하다.

문제는 "워크아웃"이 "기업체질 개선작업"의 의미로 쓰는 것에 대해 많은 원어민들이 이해하지 못 하는데도 국내에서 종종 사용되고 있다. 아마도 work-out이 갖는 여러 뜻 중 "To improve physical conditions by exercise"에서 유래하지 않았나 생각된다. 재정경제부의 어떤 관리가 처음 사용한 것이 유래가 되었다는 설이 있다. Work-out보다는 "Restructuring"이 뜻이 더 잘 통한다.

Awkward	Several companies are under a massive work-out program.
Better	Several companies are under a massive restructuring program.

정시운행

지하철 노조가 태업수단의 하나로 지하철 운행을 "정시운행" 하겠다고 발표했다.

각 역의 차량 운행시간을 현행 3분에서 5분 간격으로 하겠다는 것이다.

규정에 의하면 운행 간격은 5분이다. 평상시 출퇴근 시간대에 시민의 편의(?)를 위해 운행간격을 3분으로 해 왔던 것이다.

이러한 속사정을 모르는 원어민(Native Speakers)들에게 "정시운행"을 직역하여 "operate trains on regular schedule" 이라고 표현한다면, 어찌 될까?

그들은 묻는다. 정상적인 시간표(on regular schedule)대로 운행(operate trains) 하는 것은 지극히 당연하며 권장할만한 일이지, 어찌 "태업"이 되느냐고?

외국인들에게 태업의 의미를 전달하기 위해서는 "go-slow(strike)" 또는 "slowdown(strike)"으로 표현하는 것이 좋다.

Vague   Subway workers will operate trains on regular schedule.

Clear   Subways workers will start a go-slow(strike), or a slowdown(strike).

폭탄주

맥주에 위스키를 타서 마시는 술(whisky on beer)이 한국인들에게는 "폭탄주"로 통한다. 일부 외국잡지에서 간혹 재미있게 "Bomb Drink"라고 표현한다.

Wrong   Bomb Drink.

Right   Boilermaker.

실습 Tip 8: Watch out such words as No, Not, Only, Less.

"No", "Not", "Only", "Less" 같은 단어는 매우 중요한 어휘로서 글을 강조하지만, 실수로 이런 단어들이 빠질 경우 정반대의 의미가 되어서 때때로 명예훼손 등 송사에 휘말린다.

✔ So Watch Out!

Unsafe   He pleaded not guilty. He was found not guilty.
Safe, Better He pleaded innocent. He was acquitted.

Awkward   Only one person died in a fire.
Fine   One person died in a fire.

실습 Tip 9: Shun the editorial "We".

간접화법에서 "We"의 사용을 삼가라. 사설 같은 성격의 글이 되기 쉽다.

Wrong   He said that we must pay back the remaining debt to the IMF.
Right   He said that Korea must pay back the remaining debt to the IMF.

실습 Tip 10: Avoid the monotonous writing.

글을 쓸 때 단조로움(Monotony)을 피하고 문장의 구조, 단어사용에 있어 다양성을 유지해야 한다.

Monotonous	He opened the car door. He stepped out. He walked toward the store. He tried to remember all the things his wife had told him to buy. He hated shopping!
Varied	Opening the car door, he stepped out and walked toward the store, trying to remember all the things his wife had told him to buy. How he hated shopping!

실습 Tip 11: Avoid the double negative.

이중부정은 긍정을 나타내는데(A double negative makes a positive) 특별한 경우가 아니면 긍정으로 풀어 쓰는 것이 좋다. 이중부정은 실수할 위험이 많다.

Avoidable	I haven't no money left.
Fine	I have money left.

실습 Tip 12~13: Avoid redundant, unneeded words. Use words economically.

단어(Words)사용은 경제적(Economical)으로 해야 한다.

중복되는 단어(Redundant Words)나, 불필요한 단어들(Unneeded Words)을 친절하게(?) 나열하는 글은 초심자들이 저지르기 쉬운 오류다.

특히 형용사의 사용은 문학적인 글을 쓸 때는 문장을 더욱 수려하게 만들 수 있으나, 사실보도에 초점을 맞추어야 할 News Writing인 경우 너무 "친절한" 수식을 위한 형용사의 남용(?)은 문장의 간결성과 신뢰성을 떨어뜨리고 독자에게 진부한 느낌을 준다.

다음은 경험이 부족한 Writer나 Editor들이 저지르기 쉬운 형용사 남용의 예문이다.

다음에 열거한 예문에서 수식어로 사용된 단어(이탤릭체)는 앞뒤에 오는 단어가 수식하려는 의미를 이미 포함하고 있으므로 삭제하는 것이 좋다.

중복되거나 불필요한 단어들

Thorough, Bitter, True, Own, Old, Self, Small, Young, This Morning, Important, Entire, Completely

- □ *Thorough* Investigation
- □ *Bitter* Quarrel
- □ *True* Facts
- □ *Own* Autobiography
- □ *Old* Veterans
- □ *Self*-Confessed
- □ *Small* Child
- □ *Young* Girls
- □ 5 a.m. *This Morning*
- □ *Important* Essentials
- □ *Entire* Monopoly
- □ *Completely* Destroyed

Awkward   The prosecution began a thorough investigation into the bribery scandal.

Better   The prosecution began an investigation into the bribery scandal.

Redundant   He will hold a press conference at 10 a.m. this morning.

Better   He will hold a press conference at 10 a.m. today.

Repetitious   Repeat what you said again.

Better   Repeat what you said.

실습 Tip 14: Avoid abstract or complex words.

추상적인 표현보다는 구체적인 표현이 News Writing에서 설득력이 높다.

Abstract　　　　The lovely sounds of nature woke me.
Better　　　　The wind in the trees and a bird chirping woke me.

실습 Tip 15: Be lucid in explaining sources.

　글을 쓸 때 News의 Source(출처), Origin(근원)을 밝히는 것은 대단히 중요하다.

　News의 Source를 밝히는 것은 독자에게 글의 공정성과 신뢰성을 제고하는데 절대적이다.

　글이 정부기관 발표문에서 나온 것 인지, 인터뷰에서 인용된 것 인지, 소문을 듣고 쓴 것 인지, 글 작성자 개인의 의견인지, 독자들은 알고 싶어한다.

ex **1** The Korean economy will grow 3.5 percent in 2001, the International Monetary Fund(IMF) said in a report. (Source: IMF report)

ex **2** Korea's current economic downturn has been caused by a marked decline in an investor confidence and global growth slowdown, the Organization for Economic Cooperation and Development(OECD) revealed in an economic survey. (Source: OECD)

ex **3** The government will expand its fiscal spending this year, Deputy Prime Minister Jin Nyum announced. (Source: Deputy Prime Minister Jin Nyum)

Lead 2

오프라인, 온라인을 망라, 시사성뉴스를 다루는 영문인 경우 첫머리에 나오는 문장을 Lead라고 한다.

각 문장은 간단, 명료하면서 논리적으로 써야 하는데 특히 Lead는 기사에 있어 독자들의 시선을 끌 수 있는 가장 중요한 대목이다.

Lead는 전체문장의 생명이다. 그런고로 Writer들은 Lead잡는데 많은 고심을 하게 되고 좋은 Lead를 쓰기 위해 많은 시간과 정력을 기울이게 된다.

글은 크게 나누어 객관적인 뉴스를 다루는 Straight Story와 특집기사 성의 Feature Story로 나누어지는데 어느 기사든지 Lead 한 줄을 읽고 글 전체의 개요를 알고 흥미를 끌 수 있도록 구성이 명료해야 한다. 그러기 위해서는 핵심부분이 포괄적으로 요약되도록 하는 News-Peg Lead (뉴스집약)형이 되어야 한다.

좋은 Lead는 한 장의 그림 같아야 하며 기사의 기본 요건인 5 W's and 1 H - Who, What, Where, When, Why and How - 를 기본으로 한다.

좋은 Lead 쓰기

Formula

Formula 1: Key Facts와 Essence에 기초한 News-Peg Lead로 써라.

Formula 2: 문장의 첫 10단어 내외에서 전달하려는 Key Facts가 나타나게 하라.

Formula 3: 30단어 이내에서 간결하게 처리하라. (*cf*: Flesch Test의 16~19 단어)

Formula 4: 흥미 있는 부분을 부각시켜라.

Formula 5: 사람이름, 장소 등의 세세한 부분까지 Lead에 쓰려고 하지 말라.

Formula 6: Feature Lead(특집기사)는 Human-Interest형의 문장으로 구성하라.

Formula 7: "There is(are)…", "At a meeting…", "According to…" 같은 것으로 시작되는 Lead는 삼가하라. (Key Fact가 뒤로 밀리게 된다)

실습 Formula 1: News-Peg Lead(뉴스집약형)

Lead에 뉴스의 핵심이 무엇인가를 파악한 후 Key Facts와 Essence를 기초로 하여 한 문장으로 간략하게 집약한다.

사람, 관련기관 등에 대한 세세한 설명은 2, 3번째 오는 Paragraph에서 다룬다.

Lead의 간결성을 유지하기 위해서다. 복잡한 Lead는 독자들의 주의를 산만하게 한다.

Relegate secondary elements such as authority, identification, and background to the second and third paragraphs!

현대 News Writing에서 가장 많이 쓰는 Lead형식은 News-Peg Lead 지만 초심자들은 Crowded Lead, Buried Lead, Backing Into Lead 같은 형태의 복잡한 문장을 쓰기 쉽다. 다음은 같은 내용의 기사를 News-Peg Lead로 처리한 예문들이다.

ex **1** **Crowded Lead:**

Korean female workers were discovered to earn an average of 954,000 won a month, while male workers were receiving 1.47 million won. Women were found to receive only 64.8 percent of the monthly average wage of male workers in a survey of 5,400 companies conducted by the Labor Ministry. A significant wage difference between male and female workers still persists in most workplaces in Korea, according to the survey.

News-Peg Lead:

A significant wage gap between male and female workers still persists in Korea, a survey revealed.

문장의 핵심은 한국의 남녀간 임금격차가 아직도 심하다는 것이므로 먼저 이 것을 Lead로 쓴다. 구체적으로 남, 여의 임금이 얼마이며 어느 기관에서 몇 명 을 대상으로 조사했는지는 다음 Paragraph에서 쓰면 된다.

ex 2 Crowded Lead:

The Seoul metropolitan government plans to allow taxi fares raises. City officials told reporters that the fare increase plan will be presented to the city's Price Policy Committee for approval. Under the plan, the starting fare will go up from the current 1,300 won to 1,600 won($1.23) for the first 2 kilometers, with an additional 100 won to be charged for every 161 meters, instead of the current 210 meters. The raise, effective August 30, is a 28 percent increase over the current fares.

News-Peg Lead:

Taxi fares in Seoul will rise 28 percent on average on August 30.

시민들에게는 택시요금이 어느 정도로(28 percent), 언제(August 30) 오르느냐 가 제일 중요한 관심사항이다.

실습 Formula 2~3: 첫 10단어 내외에서 전달하려는 Key Facts가 나타나게 하라.

Lead를 포함한 모든 문장은 30단어 정도의 규모가 적합하다. (Formula 3)

이와 같은 원칙은 이미 Flesch Test, Tips for Good Writing에서 설명 을 했기 때문에 중복설명을 피한다.

30단어로 구성된 문장에서 Lead는 Key Facts가 첫 10단어 내외에서 나타나도록 쓰는 것이 정보전달을 신속하게 한다.

ex **1** Fair
A survey of 205 trading companies, conducted by the Korea International Trade Association(KITA), revealed that the Korean goods were losing price competitiveness in the world market.

Better
The Korean goods are losing price competitiveness, according to a survey of 205 trading companies, conducted by the Korea International Trade Association.

ex **2** Fair
A fire ripped through a hotel in downtown Seoul early yesterday morning, killing at least 100 people.

Better
At least 100 people were killed in a fire which ripped through a hotel in downtown Seoul early yesterday morning.

Note

ex 1와 *ex* 2의 "Better" Lead에서는 "한국 상품이 경쟁력이 떨어진다"는 내용과 "화재로 100명이 죽었다"는 내용이 문장 시작 첫 10단어 내에서 나타난다.

실습 Formula 4: 흥미있는 부분을 부각시켜라.

일반적으로 관공서, 기업체, 사회단체 등에서 발표하는 보도자료는 나열식으로 되어 있다. 그 자료를 그대로 번역했다고 가정하자. 참으로 지루하고 재미가 없을 것이다.

자료 가운데 가장 핵심적이면서(Formula 1에서 제시한) 가장 흥미 있는 부분(most interesting aspect of the story)을 부각시키는 것만이 독자들의 눈을 고정시킬 수 있다.

Fair   An international anti-corruption symposium will be held in Seoul Aug 30-31.

To be discussed in the two-day symposium, cosponsored by the Seoul metropolitan government and the United Nations, will be an overall review of policies and achievements of municipal governments in combating corruption, including the operation of online corruption-monitoring system Seoul City has recently developed.

Better   The online corruption-monitoring system, developed by the Seoul metropolitan government, will be discussed in an international anti-corruption symposium in Seoul, scheduled for August 30-31.

Note

전자와 후자의 Lead를 비교할 때 전자는 밋밋한 느낌을 준다. 후자의 Lead는 독자들로 하여금 온라인 corruption-monitoring system에 대해 호기심을 갖게 하고, 지속적으로 다음 문항을 더 읽도록 유인한다.

Good Lead 예문

SUNNINGDALE(AP) — Anika Sorenstam 5, Pak Se-ri 4, Karrie Webb 2.

Not scores on a golf card. Titles won this season on the LPGA Tour by the three dominant players in women's golf. They also hold all four majors between them in a shut out of the American stars.

Pak's standout victory at the Women's British Open on Sunday — closing with a 66 — was the third major title of her developing career and, at age 23, the Korean has a great chance to become the youngest ever player to hold the Grand Slam···

Note

박세리 선수의 Women's British Open 골프대회에서의 우승기사를 쓰는데 단 순히 "Pak Se-ri of South Korea won the Women's British Open…".라고 Lead를 시작하지 않았다. 세계적인 골프선수 Anika Sorenstam, Karrie Webb 과의 성적을 비교시키면서 Lead를 흥미롭게 끌어가고 독자로 하여금 다음 문 장을 계속 읽도록 유인한다.

실습 Formula 5: 사람이름, 장소 등의 세세한 부분까지 Lead에 쓰려하지 말라.

Formula 1에서 부분적으로 설명했듯이 초심자들은 Lead에 Authority(소식통), Identification(신분), Background(배경) 등을 너무 친절(?)하게 상세히 기술함으로서 문장이 어지러워(Cluttered)진다.

Authority, Identification, Background 등은 2번째, 3번째 문장에서 다 룬다.

oint :

Detailed reference or elaborate description of the event weakens a lead.

ex Cluttered Kim Dae-jung, president of the Republic of Korea, and Kim Jong-il, National Defense Commission chairman of the Democratic People's Republic of Korea, yesterday signed a landmark agreement to hold reunions of families separated by the partition of the Korean peninsula on the occasion of the National Liberation Day on August 15, following their marathon meeting which lasted more than three hours at the Paekhwawon State Guest House on

the second day of the summit in Pyongyang, according to a joint declaration which was announced by South Korea's presidential spokesman Park Joon-young.

Improved The leaders of South and North Korea yesterday signed a landmark agreement to hold reunions of families separated by the partition of the Korean peninsula on August 15.

2, 3번째 문장에서 다루어도 좋을 내용들:

Authority, Identification, Background.

▶ Kim Dae-jung, president of the Republic of Korea; Kim Jong-il, National Defense Commission chairman of the Democratic People's Republic of Korea.

▶ on the occasion of the National Liberation Day.

▶ following their marathon meeting which lasted more than three hours at the Paekhwawon State Guest House on the second day of the summit in Pyongyang.

▶ according to a joint declaration which was announced by South Korea's presidential spokesman Park Joon-young.

ex Cluttered Kim Mi-yong, 16, daughter of Kim Kil-dong, a Seoul National University professor, was stabbed to death yesterday by a masked man while she and her father were walking down Mt. Namsan in central Seoul.

Improved   A 16-year-old girl was stabbed to death yesterday by a masked man while she and her father were walking down Mt. Namsan in central Seoul. The girl, identified as Kim Mi-yong, daughter of Kim Kil-dong, a professor at Seoul National University…

실습 Formula 6: Feature Lead(특집기사)는 Human-Interest형의 문장으로 구성하라.

Feature Story는 일반 사건, 사고를 다루는 Straight News와는 달라서 Lead를 쓸 때 무엇보다도 독자들의 시선을 끌 수 있도록 Human-Interest(인간적 흥미를 자아내는)형의 문장으로 시작되는 것이 좋다.

Straight News 보다는 다양성 있게 구성하여 독자들로 하여금 흥미를 가지고 글의 끝부분 까지 읽어 내려갈 수 있도록 재미있게 전개해 나가야 한다.

ex **1** PHILADELPHIA(AP) —Bits of Bach. Bytes of Beethoven. Browsers with Brahms.

Attending a symphony concert in cyberspace could become commonplace under a first-of-its-kind agreement that would allow orchestras to distribute live and recorded music on the Internet.

ex **2** WASHINGTON(AP) — Missile defense? It's time to move ahead even if the science has not been perfected. Global warming? That's different. Needs more scientific study.

President George W. Bush gave diametrically opposing reasons when making separate cases in Europe last week for deploying a missile defense shield and for junking the 1997 Kyoto treaty on climate control.

실습 Formula 7: "There is(are)…", "At a meeting…", "According to…"로 시작되는 Lead는 삼가하라. (Key Fact가 뒤로 밀리게 된다)

Avoidable   There are a total of 3,224 convenience stores nationwide.

Better   The total number of convenience stores nationwide stands at 3,224.

Avoidable   According to business sources, crude oil prices have increased recently.

Better   Crude oil prices have increased recently, according to business sources.

Avoidable   At a meeting, the Cabinet decided to expand fiscal spending.

Better   The Cabinet decided to expand fiscal spending at a meeting.

Bad Lead

Crowded Lead:

과거에 많이 쓰던 문장의 형태로 상황전개에 나타나는 모든 Facts를 장황하게 취합하여 Lead Sentence에 정리해 쓰는 형식으로 문장이 길어지고 복잡해져 독자들이 읽기에 어려움이 있다.

Buried Lead:

초심자들이 News 평가의 미숙으로 기사를 나열식으로 쓰다보니 가장 중요한 Lead 부분에 Key Fact가 명료하게 부각되지 못하는 문장.

Backing Into Lead:

Lead의 중요한 부분이 문장의 시작부분에 나타나야 하는데, 처리미숙으로 끝부분에 나타나는 문장형태.

Headline **3**

Functions of Headlines

① It captures the reader's attention.
② It tells the story.
③ It grades the news.
④ It helps make the newspaper attractive.

    헤드라인은 기사의 요약, 중요도를 나타내며, 독자의 시선을 유인하고, 지면을 구성하는 디자인의 출발점이다.

헤드라인의 유형

    신문, 잡지의 디자인과 마찬가지로 헤드라인도 시간이 흐름에 따라 여러 형태가 생겼다 사라지는 변화를 거쳐 왔다.

    헤드라인은 내용에 따라 부연설명을 위해 부제목을 위에 더 붙일 수도 있고(Kicker), 아래에 붙일 수도(Deck) 있다.

    Colon을 사용해 크게 헤드라인을 둘로 나누는 Slammer형과 주제는 짧고 부제를 길게 처리하는 Hammer형이 있다.

    Feature기사에서 1행의 주제와 2행의 부제로 되는 Tripod, 본문 옆에 제목을 다는 Sidesaddle Head, 여러 단으로 되어있는 기사에서 한쪽 단만을 이용해서 제목을 다는 Raw Wrap 등 여러 가지 특수한 형태도 있다.

    그러나 대략 보편적으로 쓰여 왔던 좌우 칼럼 기준선과의 여백에 따라

다음과 같이 6가지 유형으로 요약된다.

① Crosslines: 칼럼 기준선의 좌우 양측 끝에 균형되게 정렬.
② Steplines: 계단식으로 정렬. 2행에서 첫 행은 왼쪽에 둘째 행은 오른쪽에 붙임. 3행인 경우에는 왼쪽, 중앙, 오른쪽에 붙여 정렬.
③ Inverted Pyramids: 2행 이상인 경우에 역 피라미드 형태로 행을 정렬
④ Hanging Indentions: 2행 이상인 경우에 첫 행은 왼쪽에 붙이고, 나머지 행은 안으로 들여 쓰는 형태.
⑤ Flush Lines: 헤드라인의 행을 Column의 왼쪽 또는 오른쪽 기준자에 붙여 맞추는 정렬.
⑥ Combinations: 여러 가지 형태를 조합해서 쓰는 유형.

1) Writing Headlines

앞서 헤드라인 종류의 유형에 대해 알아보았다. 그러나 이들 중 대부분은 과거 신문 잡지에 사용되었으나 지금은 흔하게 사용되지 않는 것이 대부분이다.

초기의 신문들은 헤드라인 없이 텍스트만 싣는 뉴스레터형식을 취했다.

최초의 미국 신문은 1690년 보스턴에서 발간된 "Public Occurrences" 이다. 초기의 미국 신문들은 팸플릿, 뉴스레터 모양으로 헤드라인 없이 차례로 뉴스 아이템을 늘어놓는 형태를 취했다.

페이지가 늘어나면서 칼럼과 헤드라인의 개념이 생기게 되었다. 이어 편집인들은 지면의 왼쪽에서 오른쪽으로, 위에서 아래로 헤드라인을 넣어 신문을 제작하기 시작하였다.

지난 시절의 신문 헤드라인은 무작위로 혼합된 활자체, 대문자의 사용, 가운데 정렬방식, 좁은 여러 행의 부제목 사용 등 내용전달에만 역점을 두어왔다.

반면 최근 헤드라인은 내용전달의 기능을 넘어 가독성과 디자인의 개념을 고려하게 되었다.

오늘날 신문에 쓰이는 헤드라인은 몇 가지 공통점을 갖고 있다.

오늘날 신문 헤드라인의 추세는 가독성을 의식한 간결성과 소문자 사용의 증대, 디자인 개념을 고려한 통일성, 여백의 활용 등에 역점을 두고 있다.

다음은 최근 구미 여러 신문들에 상용되고 있는 헤드라인의 공통점을 취합, 편집 실무자들이 주목해야 할 "헤드라인 달기 10가지 제안"을 하고자 한다.

그러나 이들 제안도 시간이 흐르면서 독자취향과 디자인산업의 변화에 따라 변할 수 있음을 알려둔다.

---

10 Suggestions for Good Headlines

제안 1:   대문자를 최소한(Downstyle)으로 하라.

제안 2:   기사상단을 전부 덮는 Banner Headline을 활용하라.

제안 3:   칼럼의 왼쪽 끝에 맞추는 형태를 활용하라.

제안 4:   이야기체로 써라.

제안 5:   간결하게 가급적 한 줄로 하라.

제안 6:   현재형으로 써라.

제안 7:   능동형, 긍정문으로 써라.

제안 8:   Be 동사를 생략하라.

제안 9:   약어, 전문용어 사용을 삼가하라.

제안10:   미래형은 "Will…" 대신 "To 부정사…"로 하라.

실전응용

제안 1: 소문자의 확대

헤드라인을 쓸 때 초기에는 힘을 주어 독자의 시선을 끌 수 있다는 취지로 대문자를 많이 사용했다.

그러나 많은 연구에서 단어 하나하나를 전부 대자(Capital Letter or Upper Case)로 하는 것이 소자(Lower Case)로 하는 것보다 가시성 (Legibility)이 떨어진다는 결과가 나왔다.

그 후 신문들은 전 단어, 전 철자 대자(All-Caps Headline)에서 각 단어의 첫 철자(First Spelling)만 대자로 하는 혼합형으로, 헤드라인 문장 첫 단어의 첫 철자만 대자로 하는 형태로 발전하고 있다.

대자 사용이 줄어드는(Downstyle) 추세로 가고 있다. 그러나 특히 강조를 해야 할 부분에서는 요즈음도 전 단어에 대자를 사용한다.

코리아타임스의 경우 각 면 Headline의 모든 명사, 대명사, 동사, 형용사, 부사 등은 첫 자를 대문자로 한다. 그러나 전치사, 접속사는 소문자로 하되, 글자수가 4자 이상이면 대문자로 한다(*ex*: From, Between, Over 등).

"Copy Reading and News Editing", a book authored by Howard B. Taylor and Jacob Scher, says, "Heads in caps and lower case are easier to read than those in caps. Capital letters consist of relatively large blocks that are more difficult to recognize than lower-case letters. Reading habits, conditioned by childhood training, seem to make lower-case letters easier to distinguish".

각 단어 앞머리를 대자로 쓰는 신문

The New York Times, The Asian Wall Street Journal, International Herald Tribune, Los Angeles Times, The Korea Times.

문장 앞머리 대자형 신문

The Daily Telegraph, Taiwan News, The Daily Yomiuri, The Nation(Thailand), Mainichi Daily News, The Korea Herald, Financial Times, USA Today, South China Morning News(Hong Kong), Vietnam News, China Daily(Hong Kong), The Japan Times, Stars and Stripes, Taipei Times.

Note

Figure 1~3은 대문자 헤드라인, 혼합형 헤드라인, 소문자 헤드라인으로의 발전추세를 보여준다.

Figure 1
All-Caps Headline, Courtesy of The NYT

Biotech Crops Moving Rapidly Around Globe

Consumers Now Almost Unable to Avoid Them

By David Barboza
New York Times Service

CHICAGO — Despite persistent concerns about genetically modified crops, they are spreading so rapidly that it has become almost impossible for consumers to avoid them, agriculture experts say.

More than 100 million acres (40 million hectares) of the world's most fertile farmland were planted with genetically modified crops last year, about 25 times more than just four years earlier. Wind-blown pollen, commingled seeds, market plantings have f

perimented with in many other countries, including China, India, Australia and South Africa.

They are even turning up where people least expect them — in countries where they are banned but a black market has developed, in food supplies where they are forbidden or shunned, such as organic products, and even in fields that farmers believe are completely free of genetically modified crops.

The rapid adoption and proliferation scientists and others de- of altering foods' genet cheaper and b

Figure 2
Combination Headline, Courtesy of IHT

Fuel decision deals new blow to California

By Chris Parkes in Los Angeles and Nancy Dunne in Washington

The Bush administration delivered another slap in the face to California yesterday with a move to force the state to use a fuel additive that could increase the cost of a gallon of petrol by 3 cents.

The state – already stung by the highest motor fuel pr the US Washington's

California – has doomed the state to choosing between price rises at the pump and continued pollution of our ground water," said Dianne Feinstein, a California senator.

Oil industry lobbyists say there may not be enough ethanol to meet demand, especially in drought years, and costs will be elevated by the need to t from the mid-west ng states. n of Calif

Figure 3
Lower-Case Headline, Courtesy of Financial Times

제안 2: Banner Headline

Front Page(1면)에서 제호 밑의 상단부에 붙여 횡으로 걸쳐 쓰는 Crossline형 헤드라인을 말한다.

"Streamer", "Ribbon", "Line" 이라고도 불리는 Banner Headline은 칼럼 수에 맞게 다양하게 쓰이며 기사의 비중이 크면 전단(7단~8단)에 걸쳐 쓸 수도 있다.

Banner Head에서 상단부 부제(Kicker), 하단부 부제(Deck)와 함께 쓰일 경우 Kicker와 Deck는 Main Head 글자체의 반 보다 작은 것이 관례이며, 활자형도 Italic체를 사용하는 등 대조적인 조화의 미를 고려하여 쓰는 것이 바람직하다. (Figure 4 참조)

Figure 4
전단에 걸쳐 쓴 Banner Headline (November 9 Issue, 2000, The Korea Times).

제안 3: 왼쪽 끝 맞추기(Flush-Left Headline)

칼럼 양쪽 기준선 중 왼쪽 기준선에 맞추어 헤드라인을 쓰는 형태를 말한다. 오늘날 신문에서 가장 많이 쓰는 형태라 할 수 있다.

The headline is set flush to the left column rule.

특히 한 칼럼인 경우, Figure 5에서 보는 바와 같이 대부분 신문들이 Flush-Left Headline을 사용한다. 이 형식은 전체지면의 통일성을 유지하므로 안정성을 제고한다.

다음으로 많이 쓰는 것이 양쪽 끝 맞추는 형태다. (Set to both column rules) 말하자면 Crossline의 형태로 양쪽 기준선에 균형을 이루는 대칭(Symmetric Position)형태를 말한다. 박스 형태의 1 칼럼 헤드라인, 또는 2칼럼 이상의 다 대칭 칼럼 헤드라인에서 활용된다. (Figure 6 참조)

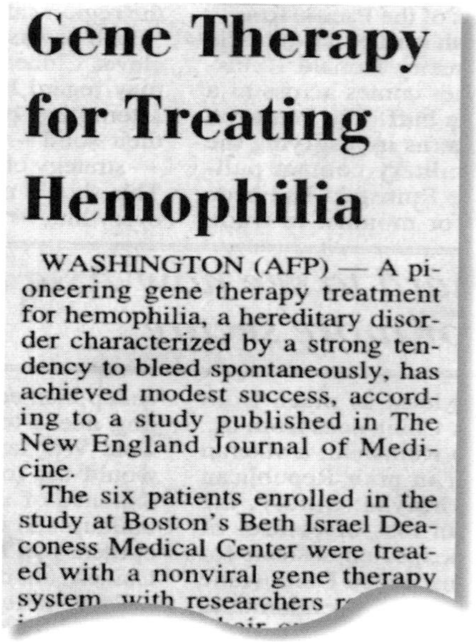

Gene Therapy for Treating Hemophilia

WASHINGTON (AFP) — A pioneering gene therapy treatment for hemophilia, a hereditary disorder characterized by a strong tendency to bleed spontaneously, has achieved modest success, according to a study published in The New England Journal of Medicine.

The six patients enrolled in the study at Boston's Beth Israel Deaconess Medical Center were treated with a nonviral gene therapy system, with researchers r...

Figure 5

Children Used as Fighting Soldiers in 41 Countries

By Susanna Loof

JOHANNESBURG (AP) — More than 300,000 children — some as young as 7 — are fighting as soldiers in 41 countries around the world, according to an international report on child soldiers released Tuesday.

Besides being used as front-line fighters, children are used as minesweepers, spies, porters and sex slaves, according to the report by the Coalition to Stop the Use ... Child Soldiers.

...nents continue to ...

was with 40 other kids. I was fighting for 24 hours. When I saw that only three of my friends were alive, I ran back," said the boy, who was identified with only one name.

Most child soldiers are 15 to 18 years old, but cases of soldiers as young as 7 are listed in the report, the first global survey of its kind.

Child soldiers are often given drugs t... ...m fearless. 14 ...

Figure 6

제안 4~5: 헤드라인의 간결성

오늘날 신문, 잡지, 온라인 홈페이지 할 것 없이 헤드라인이 간결해지는 경향이고 헤드라인은 독자가 이해하기 쉬운 이야기 체로 달고 있다.

내용의 전달에만 역점을 두어 산만하게 달았던 과거신문의 헤드라인과는 달리, 오늘날 신문은 간결한 헤드라인을 선호하고 있다.

특히 Figure 7~10에서 보는 바와 같이 1줄 헤드라인이 유행이다. 부제 Kicker와 Deck를 과감하게 줄이거나 생략하고 있다.

Iran's last reformist newspaper is closed

Iran's conservatives, bolstered by public support from supreme leader Ayatollah Ali Khamenei, yesterday closed the last significant reformist newspaper and mobilised thousands of protesters against press freedom. **Reuters reports from Tehran.**

The hardline Press Court ___ed the immediate ___ion of the popular ___ublished by a ___President

a "fake interview" with parliamentary deputy Ahmad Pournejati, in which he was quoted as saying the reformists would seek a way to introduce a press bill — effectively challenging Mr Khamenei.

The conservative Kayhan newspaper late on Monday cited Mr Pournejati a_ denying the comments proclaiming the pre_ dead. Bahar, fo_ stood by th_

imprisoned, some for long terms. It became one of Iran's best-selling dailies.

The paper, published by Saeed Pourazizi, Mr Khatami's press aide, had had brushes with the Press Court but ___d to surv_

revolution and the Islamic system. "The blood in our veins is a gift to the leader. Our eyes are a gift to the leader," they chanted, many holding portraits of Mr Khamenei.

Many were members of the Basij Islamic university _litia or merchants from _n's central bazaar, a _ld of traditionalist _ threatened by _nisation.

dictatorship," said one conservative student leader.

A US spokesman earlier said Washington had "serious concern" about Mr Khamenei's intervention and called on Iran to respect free speech. Iran promptly denounced the interference.

Some conservative MPs, in the minori__ ___nce the reformis__ electi__

Figure 7 Courtesy of Financial Times

Exploring Brain Chemistry as a Key to Religion

By Shankar Vedantam
Washington Post Service

WASHINGTON — In Philadelphia, a researcher discovers areas of the brain that are activated during meditation.

At universities in San Diego and North Carolina, doctors study how epilepsy and certain hallucinogenic drugs can produce religious epiphani__

And in Canada, a neuroscientist fi_ ___netized helmets that produ_ ___ for the secular

What creates that transcendental feeling of being one with the universe? It could be the decreased activity in the brain's parietal lobe, which helps regulate the sense of self and physical orientation, research suggests.

How does religion prompt divine feelings of love and compassion? Possibly because of changes in the frontal lobe, caused by heightened concentrati__ ___itation.

___ people have a profound ___d their lives? D__

periences and that is why so many people believe in God," he said.

The studies may be the bravest frontier of brain research. But depending on your religious beliefs, it may also be the last straw. For while Mr. Newberg and other scientists say they are trying to bridge the ___ce and religion, many believers are ___n that God is a creation of the ___ the other way around.

___ assumptions and makes ___id Nancey Murphy ___ at Full

Figure 8 Courtesy of IHT

Israeli-Palestinian Violence Flares Again

JERUSALEM (AFP) — Deadly unrest flared in the Palestinian territories Tuesday despite moves to ease tensions ahead of a last-ditch bid by U.S. President Bill Clinton to end the bloodletting and repair the shattered peace process.

___ moves to quell the ___d States named ___national fact-___igate the

was part of the Sharm el-Sheikh understandings of October 17 aimed at putting an end to the violence.

Former U.S. senator George Mitchell, who served as mediator in Northern Ire___ will presi___ panel, ___

Th___

hopes that they will lead to an immediate resumption of peace talks.

"There is no room for excess optimism regarding the meetings about the peace process this week in Washington," Foreign Minister Shlomo Ben Ami was quoted by ___rmy radio as saying.

___inton, anxious to restore ___gion before his

Mubarak and Britain's Prime Minister Tony Blair on Wednesday.

On the ground, the death toll continued to mount, reaching 184, with fierce clashes reported in ___ Bank and

Figure 9 Courtesy of KT

THE KOREA TIMES

Established 1950, No. 15625

www.koreatimes.co.kr

City Edition ★★★
Seoul, Monday, February 5, 2001

Seoul – San Francisco
Daily Nonstop
Reservations (02)757-1691
UNITED AIRLINES

Nationwide 24-hour reservation
1588-2001
KOREAN AIR

Whose Company Is This Anyway?

By Prof. Kang Hee-joon
Indiana University

Rainbow Column

Prof. Kang

BLOOMINGTON, INDIANA — The following are a few "likely" headlines: "Owner of Company Asked to Contribute More Money." "Owner of Bankrupted Company Probed for Wrong Doing." "Former Pacex Corruption Charge."

Who are the owners of those companies? Fortunately, many of us do not own any shares of stocks of those companies in trouble. Since so many of us nevertheless own some stocks these days, we all have to be deeply concerned about such headlines.

Many different kinds of companies or enterprises exist in the business world. But, those companies the media talks about are corporations with limited liabilities. Most companies around us. The owners of such companies are of course all the shareholders, typically hundreds and thousands of us. The liability of shareholders is limited to the value of their shares.

Any corporation naturally has a founder or a few founders. It is not uncommon to have some majority shareholders. A person or a close family may own more

than 50 percent of all the outstanding shares. There could also be controlling shareholders. While each shareholder owns a tiny portion of a company, a person or a close family may own, say, 10 percent of all the shares to be able to exert some power. Regardless, the owners of a company are all the shareholders.

When a newspaper says "the government has asked the owner of a company to invest more money," it does not mean all the shareholders. Instead, it typically means some majority shareholders or the founders. A particular person or a certain group of people should never be confused with "the owner" of a company.

Who are the owners of Korea? Even elementary school pupils know the answer: the people of Korea own the country. Likewise, a corporation is owned by the shareholders. Corporations are "run" by CEO, president, executives, and managers. The shareholders choose some other "agents" to run a company. It is not different from the fact that the people elect or ask some government officials to run a country. The owner of a country is its citizens and the owner of a company is its shareholders.

I am 100 percent certain that if we make a survey and ask the general public about the owner of the country, almost all respondents will correctly recognize that the answer is the people. I am not so sure, however, what

will happen if we ask about the owner of a company. Whose company is Samsung Electronics? Whose company was Daewoo Motor three years ago? The answer for both is again all the shareholders, but not the founder or the chairman of the board or the president.

Quite a few people would respond that the owner of a company is either the founder or the president of the company. In my view, this misconception or misperception is indeed a large problem in Korea now.

During the Choson Dynasty, the country was very well believed to be owned by the king. Even a few decades ago, many people might have believed that the country belonged to President Syngman Rhee or President Park Chung-hee. People in fact demonstrated to ask President Rhee to give up the country. People did not seem to know how to exercise their power. All they had to do was not to elect him. People fought hard to claim something that was their own!

The democratic society works to its full potential when people understand and exercise their power: the fact that they own the country. Corporate governance will work equally well, if the owners of a company realize and exercise their rights.

(Continued on Page 4)

(Continued on Page 4)

Kim Jong-il to Visit Russia in April

By Son Key-young
Staff Reporter

North Korea and Russia have agreed on National Defense Commission Chairman Kim Jong-il's visit to Moscow in April, informed diplomatic sources said yesterday.

The two countries recently agreed, through diplomatic channels, on Kim's visit to Moscow for a summit with Russian President Vladimir Putin, while setting Kim's itinerary in Russia later, sources well informed of Pyongyang-Moscow relations said.

Moscow informed Seoul of the agreement late last month, according to the sources.

The North Korean leader's visit to Moscow will center after the first meeting between South Korean President Kim Dae-jung and U.S. President George W. Bush slated for March in Washington. Kim Jong-il is also set to visit Seoul for his second meeting with

President Kim sometime this year.

They said Kim Jong-il's Moscow visit, the first of its kind for the communist country in 15 years after his father's visit in 1986, reflects Pyongyang's efforts to study Russia's market economy and strengthen ties with the former ally in the process of opening its economy.

In his summit meeting with Russian President Putin, Kim is expected to discuss his planned meeting with South Korean President Kim in Seoul and

North Korean-Russian cooperation in economic and diplomatic areas, especially in coping with the new U.S. policies towards this region, the sources said.

In December, North Korea's Vice Foreign Minister Ri In-gyu visited Moscow and discussed with his Russian counterpart Alexandr Losyukov the time frame of Kim Jong-il's visit but failed to agree when the visit should take place.

skyquick@koreatimes.co.kr

Joint Survey on NK Power Shortage Due in Feb.

By Seo Soo-min
Staff Reporter

South and North Korea have agreed to conduct a joint survey on the North's electricity supplies this month to explore ways to alleviate serious power shortages facing the isolated country, a government official said Saturday.

The two Koreas will launch another study on anti-flood measures for the Imjin river, which flows across their border, next month.

The North's shortage of electricity has recently emerged as one of the biggest concerns to South Korea. At the fourth inter-Korean ministerial meeting held in Dec.12-16, North Korea brought up the matter, asking for a supply

duced an agreement on details on the formation of the vice-minister-al level economic cooperative body.

The two Koreas will form a working-level subcommittee under the economic cooperative body, consisting of five to seven negotiators from each side, to negotiate the provision of electricity to North Korea.

The subcommittee will hold its first official talks Feb. 7-10 in Pyongyang. Afterwards, a team formed jointly by the two Koreas will conduct on-site surveys.

The North's shortage of electricity has recently emerged as one of the biggest concerns to South Korea. At the fourth inter-Korean ministerial meeting held in Dec. 12-16, North Korea brought up the matter, asking for a supply

of electricity amounting to as much as 500,000 kilowatts.

After conducting heated debates, both sides agreed to further discuss the matter in the economic cooperative body meeting.

The economic cooperative body meeting held later in the month, however, yielded little results due to the sensitivity of the matter. South Korea's own power reserve hardly suffices and public opinion is divided on the provision of electricity to North Korea amid growing economic unrest.

Regarding the anti-flood measures for the Imjin River, the two sides will hold their first meeting Feb. 21-24 in Pyongyang, followed by on-site surveys next month.

They also plan to hold working-level negotiations within next month to fine-tune ongoing inter-

Korean projects, including the re-connection of the Seoul-Shinuiju line and an adjacent highway as well as the construction of the Kaesong industrial complex.

The railway project connecting South and North Korea, which kicked off on Sept. 18 last year, is set to be completed by this September. Currently, Hyundai Asan Corp. and the government invested Korea Land Corp. are jointly pushing the industrial park scheme spanning some 8 million pyong, hoping to start construction in the earlier half of the year. One pyong is 3.3 square meters.

The next inter-Korean economic cooperative body meeting will be held this month, with the exact dates to be fixed through further contacts.

ssm@koreatimes.co.kr

Investigations Focus on Kim's Funds

By Park Yoon-bae
Staff Reporter

The prosecution is intensifying its probes into the financial scandal involving former Daewoo Group chairman Kim Woo-choong who allegedly embezzled company money to raise almost 10 trillion won in slush funds.

The investigations gained momentum last week when law-enforcement authorities arrested several former top executives of five affiliates of the collapsed business conglomerate on charges of colluding with Kim in stashing the secret funds.

The arrested are accused of manipulating their firms' financial statements to secure illegal bank loans worth more than 13 trillion won, which was then funneled to

secret funds Kim formed overseas.

The prosecution was reported to have secured evidence showing that Daewoo Corp., the group's trading arm, ran $20 billion (25 trillion won) through its subsidiary British Finance Center (BFC) in London for three years starting from 1997.

The prosecution raised strong suspicions that the $20 billion was illegally transferred to BFC from the Korean headquarters of the conglomerate's affiliates.

The transfer was allegedly made through illegal methods such as set-ting falsified imports or hiding export payments at BFC's accounts without bringing them into Korea.

According to the prosecution's interim results, Kim was found to have funneled $2.6 billion won raised with forged documents on imports and $1.5 billion secured by

auto exports of Daewoo Motor Co.

The prosecution claimed that the disgraced business tycoon embezzled $4.1 billion won via some 30 secret accounts of BFC for the three-year period and borrowed $15.7 billion in overseas financing through the London-based subsidiary.

Thus, investigators are expected to concentrate on tracing the flow of the money and discovering how it was used. They seemed to believe part of the BFC's funds was illegally transferred to Kim's slush funds.

Prosecutors reportedly questioned Lee Dong-won, former BFC chief, to confirm allegations that the London-based financial operation was used to finance Kim's illegal funding scheme.

The prosecution appeared to believe Lee could provide crucial clues that would bring light to the case.

Lee, who has permanent resident status in Great Britain, returned to Korea voluntarily in late 2000 to testify before the financial regulator and the prosecutor's office regarding the manipulation of Daewoo's financial statements and illegal transfer of funds abroad.

Lee, a former bank official, worked for BFC for more than 10 years and managed Daewoo Group's overseas funds. He was one of Kim's close confidants who are suspected of helping the tycoon operate secret funds.

The prosecution also extensively interrogated the arrested seven former executives of Daewoo firms, including Lee Sang-hoon, ex-managing director of Daewoo Corp., and Kang Byung-ho, former president of Daewoo Motor.

(Continued on Page 3)

(Continued on Page 3)

Villagers in Desalpur line up for flour, grain and kerosene on Saturday. More than a week after a massive earthquake rocked western India, some villages are only now receiving aid.
AP-Yonhap

Rumsfeld Tells Allies That US Missile Defense Poses No Threat

MUNICH (AP) — U.S. Defense Secretary Donald H. Rumsfeld assured American allies on Saturday that President George W. Bush's plan for a national missile defense will be a "threat to no one" except aggressors. He did not provide a timetable for building a missile defense but left little doubt Bush will proceed.

On his first overseas trip since taking office Jan. 20, Rumsfeld also expressed concern in plans for a European military force that would appeal to crises when the U.S.-led NATO alliance chooses not to. Rumsfeld, a former ambassador to NATO, said he feared this could destabilize the alliance.

"I'm a little worried," he said.

In remarks to a European security conference at a Munich hotel, Rumsfeld spoke forthrightly about missile defense and other sensitive subjects while admitting he had much to learn after just two weeks on the job. "I'm brand spanking new," he said.

Rumsfeld, 68, also was defense secretary during the Ford adminis-

tration from 1975-77.

Judging by his trip schedule, Rumsfeld is energized by his return to the Pentagon. He flew overnight Friday from Washington, went directly into a dashing series of meetings Saturday and planned a brief stop at Spang-dahlem Air Base, also in Germany, to have dinner with troops before returning to Washington in early Sunday.

The topic expected to dominate the Munich conference — Bush's plan for a national missile defense system — was raised frequently but not with the hard-edged criticism heard in recent months.

German Chancellor Gerhard Schroeder, also speaking at the conference, cautioned against allowing European concerns over the missile defense plans to define trans-Atlantic relations with the new administration.

"Within NATO and within the alliance we must discuss what impact the feasible implementation of this system would have on the one hand, on relations with China and on the other hand relations with

Russia," he said.

Richard Burt, a State Department arms control official during the Reagan administration, noted that while the Europeans were "politely complaining" about missile defense, the Americans in Munich were doing the same on the subject of Europe's plan to create a military force as a subset of NATO.

Henry Kissinger, secretary of state when Rumsfeld was President Ford's defense secretary, told the conference that discussion of missile defense was being approached "like a visit to the dentist." Speakers touched lightly on the topic, as if eager to move on to something more pleasant.

Missile defense is divisive because many European leaders fear it would leave their countries unprotected, thus creating a trans-Atlantic division. They also oppose it on grounds that it would violate the 1972 Anti-Ballistic Missile treaty with the former Soviet Union, a pact Rumsfeld has called "ancient history."

Contractors Negotiating for Iranian Deals Worth $5.5 Bil.

By Nho Joon-hu
Staff Reporter

Korean contractors are currently negotiating an estimated $5.5 billion worth of plant projects in Iran, a country which is hoped to act as Korea's springboard into the business boom in the Middle East.

Following meetings with senior Iranian officials, including President Mohamed Hatami in Tehran, Commerce, Industry and Energy Minister Shin Kook-hwan said the Iranian government has expressed its eagerness to expand business partnerships with Korean companies in numerous sectors.

He said meetings with senior officials have shown that there

are strong prospects for Korean companies in Iran's 3rd economic development plan which begins in 2004.

"The Iranian government is eager to utilize the foreign currency that it has earned through the sales of its oil when prices were high and Korean companies can look to participating in the supply of plants for machinery, automobiles, electronics and shipbuilding.

"Already, Korean companies are negotiating a combined $5.5 billion worth of projects with the Iranian government and their partners in Iran," Shin said on the final day of his trip to Iran.

He went on to say that the infra-structure in countries like Iran is efficient and previous economic

cooperation has set the tone for further collaboration.

Sure enough, more than 300 Iranian businessmen and representatives from government and industry crowded the road show session held in Tehran yesterday.

"Based on such strength in bi-lateral relations, Korean companies can look to Iran as a spring-board for expanding its presence in the Middle East where economic development projects are actively underway," he said.

Shin is currently leading a business delegation on a two-leg tour of Middle East countries, including the United Arab Emirates, to explore new business opportunity in the prosperous region.

Among the major projects that

Korean companies are negotiating is the construction of a natural gas refining facility in South Pars estimated to cost around $1.2 billion.

Another prospective business is the development of a massive natural gas reserve in South Pars by LG Engineering and Construction and the building of a combined power plant by Han-jung (Korea Heavy Industries and Construction).

During his meetings with the senior Iranian officials, he also discussed the establishment of a bilateral industrial cooperation committee as well as the conclusion of agreements on trade and the avoidance of double taxation.

jokerho@koreatimes.co.kr

Indonesian Gov't Meets in Show of Unity Amid Wahid Crisis

JAKARTA (AP) — In a show of unity two days after parliament censured President Abdurrahman Wahid, Indonesia's government vowed on Saturday to stick together and crack down on corruption.

After the two-hour meeting attended by Wahid, Vice President Megawati Sukarnoputri, ministers and top military commanders, a spokesman sought to allay rumors

that some members of the administration were wavering in their support for the head of state.

"It's totally a fully functioning Cabinet team," Wimar Witoelar said. "If you compare it to past governments, this is the only time which issues are discussed with candor and openness."

Wahid has been under intense political pressure since Thursday,

when an overwhelming majority of legislators endorsed a report by a parliamentary inquiry that found he had misled investigators about his involvement in the two corruption cases.

Since then, there have been daily street demonstrations for and against Wahid's administration. On Saturday, pro-Wahid rallies blocked roads in central Java, me-

dia reports said.

The parliamentary report claimed Wahid knew about the illegal transfer of $4 million from the coffers of the state food agency, Bulog, by a former business associate. It also slammed him for failing to declare a $2 million donation from Sultan Hassanal Bolkiah, the ruler of neighboring oil-rich Brunei.

SUBSCRIBER SERVICE: (02) 724-2359, 734-0075 or FAX: (02) 732-4125, 739-5090   NEWSSTAND PRICE 500 WON

Figure 10   Courtesy of KT

✔ 제안 6: 현재형

헤드라인은 통상 전날 또는 당일 발생한 과거사건을 보도할 때 현재형으로 쓴다. 본문은 과거형으로 쓴다.

현재형은 사건의 즉시성(Immediacy), 생동감(Vividness)을 더해준다. 과거형은 오래된 사건으로 보이기 쉽다.

The present tense makes the event more dramatized. It has a sense of immediacy and is close to the life of the newspaper reader. The difference of one letter — "s" in place of "d" — activates the story.

다음의 현재형과 과거형을 비교해 보라.

과거형은 꽤 오래된 인질사건의 종결을 알리는 기사같이 진부하게 느껴진다. 사건의 신선도가 떨어진다.

Note

헤드라인에서 현재형 동사와 함께 "Yesterday" 또는 "Last Night" 같은 과거를 나타내는 단어를 함께 쓰지 마라.

The combination would be ungrammatical.

현재형

Muslims Free 2 Filipino Hostages

과거형

Muslims Freed 2 Filipino Hostages

그러나 상당 기간 지난 사건을 기술할 때는 과거형으로 한다. 예를 들어 역사적사건이나, 오래된 납치사건, 몇 년이 지난 경제지표를 기술할 경우 과거형으로 한다.

ex   Nazis Killed 6 Mil. Jews During WW II

현재형은 Figure 11에, 과거형의 예는 Figure 12에서 보여 주고 있다.

Stock Prices Slide Below 600

By Heo Yun-seon
Staff Reporter

Share prices on the Korea Stock Exchange plunged yesterday on a slew of foreign selling with the Korea Composite Stock Price In-

600-point level.

The broad-based index dropped 13.25 points from the previous day to close at 597.66.

Foreign investors posted net sales of 107.6 billion won, while individual and institutional investors bought 26.1 billion won

won more tha-

the falling gap of the KOSPI.

Trade volume stood at 360.31 million shares on a turnover of 1.8 trillion won ($1.3 billion).

Decliners led gainers 577 to 233, with 47 others unchanged.

Stock

co

Scientists Manufacture Human Eggs for Fertility Treatment

LAUSANNE (AP) — Scientists appear to have found a way that someday could allow women to become mothers after they no longer can produce viable eggs, a potential advance in breaking the last great barrier to fertility treatments.

Theoretically, the method could create an unlimited supply

is still in the preliminary stages, and it could be years before the technique produces a healthy baby, if ever. When they fertilized the manufactured egg with sperm, it divided once, then collapsed.

Dr. Gianpiero Palermo, a pro-

embryology at the Ce

ective M

Japan Tightens Immigration Controls

TOKYO (AFP) — Japan's government decided Friday to pour more resources into combating illegal immigration following the deportation fiasco last month involving a man believed to be the son of North Korean leader Kim Jong-il.

The cabinet approved a plan by the immigration bureau to boost the immigra-

May following a three-day detention here for entering using a false passport.

Press reports said the forged Dominican Republic passport used by Kim showed signs that he had entered Japan at least twice in the past, sparking criticism of the nation's immigration controls.

The pr

Tariffs, Customs, Labor Trouble Foreign Firms

By Seo Jee-yeon
Staff Reporter

Foreign firms complained in a recent survey that customs clearance procedures, tariffs, and labor affairs are the biggest hurdles to doing business here, according to the Office of Investment Ombudsman, a unit of the Korea Trade Investment Promotion (KOTRA).

problem. Following were 21 cases concerning legal issues, 20 cases surround financial issues and foreign exchange; 17 cases over construction difficulties; 15 cases about taxes, and 12 cases concerning real estate problems.

The companies in question were from all of South Korea's major partners. U.S. companies top with 63 com-

ly followed

Figure 11

GHOSTS OF VIETNAM

They Killed on Behalf of All Americans

By Murray Fromson

LOS ANGELES

As millions of Americans turned on their TV sets and stared into the eyes of Bob Kerrey and Gerhard Klann the other night, they saw, perhaps for the first time, the confusion, pain, guilt and moral ambiguity caused by a shameful war that wasted lives and distorted our values.

Kerrey and Klann are good men—sailors—which means not draftees

NK Leader's Son May Have Gambled on Cheju: Weekly

TOKYO (Yonhap) — Kim Jong-nam, the eldest son of North Korean leader Kim Jong-il, might have visited South Korea's Cheju Island a few years ago and gambled, a vernacular weekly here reported in its June 28 issue.

A man, who was widely believed to be the 29-year-old heir apparent to the reⁿ Korean lead⌐

Figure 12

제안 7: 능동형, 긍정문

헤드라인은 능동형 사용을 원칙으로 한다. 그러나 특정 사항을 강조할 경우 수동형이 더욱 편리할 수도 있다.

능동형은 행동의 주체를 앞에 나오게 함으로써 서술을 더욱 순차적으로 명료하게 하는 효과를 높일 수 있다.

능동형

Andean Quake Kills 47 Persons

수동형

47 Persons Killed in Andean Quake

47명의 사망자를 강조하려면 수동형이 더욱 효과적이다.

Figure 13은 코리아타임스 2001년 7월 5일자 초판 1면에서 하단부(수동형, 145 Killed…)와 같이 썼다가 2판에서 사진과 함께 4단으로 늘어나면서 여백을 고려하여 상단부(능동형, Russian Plane Crash Kills 145…)와 같이 처리되는 융통성을 보여준다.

Russian Plane Crash Kills 145 in Siberia

MOSCOW (AFP) — All 145 passengers and crew were killed when a Russian plane crashed, for reasons as yet unknown, in southern Siberia overnight, the interior ministry said Wednesday.

The three-engined jet, owned by regional airline Vladivostokavia, flying from Yekaterin-... mountains to the ...

were killed, the ministry said.

Reports said that the aircraft came down in an area studded with summer holiday homes, or dachas, causing a blaze. They added that there were no casualties on the ground. The ... of the crash was not ...

Picking ...

the T...

145 Killed in Siberian Plane Crash

MOSCOW (AFP) — All 145 passengers and crew were killed when a Russian plane crashed, for reasons as yet unknown, in southern Siberia overnight, the interior ministry said Wednesday.

The three-engined jet, owned by regional airline Vladivostokavia, had been flying from Yekaterin-... the Ural mountains to ...

All passengers on board flight 352 and the nine crew members were killed, the ministry said.

Reports said that the aircraft came down in an area studded with summer holiday homes, or dachas, causing a blaze. They add... ... casual-...

Emergencies Minister Sergei Shoigu, left Lensk in Siberia late Tuesday to coordinate operations as an enquiry was launched into the tragedy.

Rescue workers put out the fire from the plane and the scene was declared a disaster zone, Into...

President Vladimir ... his Prime Mi...

Figure 13

Point :

부정문 헤드라인을 사용하지 마라.

The business of the newspaper is to tell what happened, not what didn't happen. Avoid negative heads. Change negative heads into positive heads. It is easy to turn a negative head into a positive one.
(*cf :* Copy Reading and News Editing)

> Negative Head, Improper
> **Plane Crashes With 10 Aboard; No One Hurt**

> Positive Head, Proper
> **Plane Crashes With 10 Aboard; All Safe**

> Improper
> **Mayor Decides Not to Quit Council Race**

> Proper
> **Mayor Decides to Keep Hat in Council Race**

Point :

May 사용을 삼가하라.
동사 May의 사용은 문장을 애매모호하고 약하게 한다.

> Awkward
>
> ## Mayor May Quit Presidential Race
>
> Better
>
> ## Mayor Mulls Quitting Presidential Race

제안 8: Be 동사 생략

헤드라인에서 Be 동사는 생략된다.

Be 동사가 생략 되더라도 의미를 전달하는데 문제가 없기 때문이다.

Be 동사와 연계되어 의미를 전달하는 형용사, 숙어, 동사의 과거분사 만으로 뜻을 전달하는데 충분하다.

Be 동사의 생략은 간결성, 명료성을 더한다.

> ### Family Reunions [Are] Set for November 30
>
> ### Hwang Jang-yop [Is] Invited to US on Testimony
>
> ### Bush [Is] 'Thrilled' at Cheney's Return
>
> ### Foreign Firms [Are] Active in Recruiting Workers
>
> ### Voters [Are] Indifferent to Local Elections
>
> ### Government [Is] at Odds With Opposition Party
>
> ### Seoul [Is] Ready to Reopen Dialogue With Pyongyang

Note

A headline is stronger if the compound forms of "Is" and "Are" are omitted.

✔ 제안 9: 약어, 전문용어 사용은 삼가한다.

헤드라인은 가급적 제한된 공간에서 단어배열을 해야 하기 때문에 약어나 전문용어를 쓰는 예가 많다.

그러나 원칙적으로 약어나 전문용어는 가독성을 줄인다. 심한 경우 어려운 헤드라인의 사용은 독자들을 당황하게 하며, 독자의 기사접근을 방해한다.

약어사용은 각 신문사, 통신사, 잡지사들이 보유하고 있는 Stylebook에 의해 통일하는 것이 좋다. Space 때문에 임시방편이며 편의위주로 사용하는 것은 바람직하지 않다.

약어 가운데 YMCA, GOP(Grand Old Party, 미국공화당), ROK(Republic of Korea), U.S.(United States), U.N.(United Nations), CIA(Central Intelligence Agency), FBI(Federal Bureau of Investigation)같은 약어는 국제적으로 상용되는 약어로, 일반단어같이 부담없이 사용될 수 있다.

국내에서 발행되는 영어신문의 경우 정당의 이름이나 기관의 이름은 약어로 쓴다.

ex **MDP(Millennium Democratic Party, 새천년민주당)**
    GNP(Grand National Party, 한나라당)

| Note |

Do not use abbreviations or acronyms which the reader would not quickly recognize. Avoid alphabet soup.
최근 정보통신, 생명공학, 환경분야 등에서 홍수같이 쏟아지는 전문용어의 남용은 독자의 접근을 어렵게 한다.
가급적 일반용어로 쉽게 풀어 써 주는 것이 독자에 대한 서비스다.

■ 통용되는 약어

① Courtesy Titles Before A Name: Mr., Mrs., Ms.

② Professional Titles Before A Name: Dr./Doctor, Gov./Governor, Prof./Professor, Rep./Representative, Sen./Senator.

③ Military Titles Before A Name: Gen./General, Col./Colonel, Maj./Major, Capt./Captain, 2nd Lt./Second Lieutenant, Sgt./Sergeant.

④ Academic Degrees: B.A., M.A., Ph.D.

⑤ Months(When used with a specific date): Jan., Feb., Aug., Sept., Dec. 등.

⑥ Days of the Week(when used in a tabular format): Sun., Mon., Fri., Sat.

⑦ Others: mi.(miles), hr.(hour), mph(miles per hour), in.(inch), pct.(percent), Mt.(mountain), St.(saint), A.D., B.C., a.m., p.m., No.(number).

> **Note**
>
> 원칙적으로 달과 요일은 약어로 쓰는 것을 금한다. 그러나 달의 경우 "Sept. 5" 같이 날짜와 같이 함께 쓸 때 약어가 통용된다. 요일은 도표 같은 곳에 사용할 때 "Sun" 같이 3자 범위에서 줄여 사용한다.

Government(정부)를 Gov't로, President(대통령)을 Pres.로, Deputy Prime Minister(부총리)를 DPM 등의 약어로 쓰는 것은 바람직하지 않다.

제안 10: Infinitive Form

헤드라인에서 미래형을 나타낼 때 "To 부정사"를 사용한다.

이는 "Be + To Infinitive"용법에서 Be동사가 생략된 형태다. 예를 들어 "President Kim to Visit Japan"의 헤드라인은 "President Kim Is to

Visit Japan"에서 Be동사가 생략된 것이다. (Figure 14 참조)

이는 간략하게 To를 사용함으로써 공간을 줄일 수 있고 미래형의 Will을 사용하는 것보다 강한 의지를 전달할 수 있다.

부정사는 원칙적으로 미래를 표시하나, 아주 가까운 장래(예를 들어 오늘 또는 내일)에 있을 즉시성을 나타낼 때는 To를 생략하기도 한다.

ex   Seminar on Education Opens Today. Trade Fair Opens Tomorrow.

3 Ailing Daewoo Firms to Normalize by Year-End

By Park Yoon-bae
Staff Reporter

Deputy Prime Minister Jin Nyum yesterday predicted that three affiliates of the troubled woo Group will normalize ations within this year. hree are Daewoo tion Dae-

he said in an interview with KBS Radio yesterday.

He praised the management of the Daewoo units for their efforts to transform the once unprofitable firms into moneymakers through drastic restructuring.

However, he did not mention th fate of Daewoo Mc undergoing t tween i

financial restructuring was a kind of downsizing imposed by the government, he called on firms and financial institutions to reform themselves on their own.

In the meantime, Vice Finance-Economy Minister Kim Jin-pyo said in radio program on SBS that mment would do its best mer price hikes un-

He pledged to maintain the unemployment rate at the 3 percent level, saying that construction and service industries have recently picked up steam and provided more job opportunities.

The governm day announced tions f yea

BAI Director to Visit Austria, Russia, China

Lee Jong-nam, director of the Board of Audit and Inspection (BAI), will kick off an 11-day trip to Austria, Russia and China today.

During the trip, Lee will seek cooperation from the countries for the success of the of the

He will also discuss ways of promoting the exchange of auditors with those nations.

Established in 1953, INTOSAI is the organization of supreme audit institutions in countries that long to the United N

SAI supports its members by providing opportunities to share information and experiences about the auditing and evaluation challenges facing them in government ts and financial manag

USFK to Return Land to Tongduchon

The U.S. Forces Korea informed the city of Tongduchon on Monday that it would return part of the land that it expropriated during and after the Korean War (1950-53).

In a joint Korea-U.S. land management plan it handed to the city, the USFK work of selecting able for return locations

return all or part of the four closed bases, including Camp Mobile.

The city has six USFK bases covering a total area of 32.31 square kilometers, 33.8 percent of its total area of 95.67 square kilometers.

Late last month, South Korea and t tes agreed in a m inisters, held ss a joi

Jimmy Carter to Visit Seoul

Ex-U.S. President Jimmy Carter will visit South Korera Aug. 4 to start an international campaign to build houses for the homeless, a Korean branch of Habitat for Humanity International said yesterday.

Habitat said that from Aug. er and over 9,000 d foreign volunt the proi

Figure 14

✔ Punctuation Headlines

① Comma(,): And의 대용으로 사용.

10 Dead, 5 Injured in Car Collision

② Semicolon(;): 2개의 독립된 의미를 전할 때 사용한다.

Allies Back US Strikes; Media Question Their Timing

③ Dash(−), Colon(:), Quotation(' '), Question(?), or Exclamation Mark(!) Headlines: Dash는 동격, Colon은 Say의 의미, Quotation은 인용, 강조, 신조어의 사용에, Question Mark는 확실성의 결여, 감탄 부호는 독자의 시선을 끌기 위한 의도로 사용된다. (Figure 15 참조)

Perry: Bush to Pursue Continuity in NK Policy

Dow Ends Up 131; Nasdaq Rises 51

SK-Shinsegi — Leader of Next Generation CDMA

What Causes Inefficiency in the Public Sector?

'Public Support Essential for Engagement Policy'

Figure 15

Headline Vocabulary

제한된 공간에서 헤드라인을 쓰는 것은 쉬운 일이 아니다.

여기서 지혜가 요구된다. 문장의 주어와 목적어는 대부분 본문에 의존하게 된다. 문제는 동사다.

기사작성자는 헤드라인을 염두에 두지 않고 기사를 쓴다.

따라서 편집자에게는 본문의 의미를 짧은 동사를 사용하여 명료하고 간결하게 전달하는 기술이 요구된다.

이를 위해 편집자는 짧은 단어들을 암기할 필요가 있다.

다음에 제시한 것들은 Headline에 자주 등장하는 동사와 명사들의 모음이다. 한마디로 "Headline용 단골용어 모음"이라고 할 수 있다. 철자가 4자 이하의 짧은 단어들을 기억해 놓는 것이 편리하다.

Accord:	for Agreement
Bar:	for prevent or refuse
Bare:	for expose, reveal, or unfold
Balk:	for impede, prevent, or thwart
Bid:	for ask, invite, or request
Bilk:	for cheat
Blast:	for criticize
Board:	for commission
Body:	for committee
Cite:	for accuse, charge, or enumerate
Cow:	for capture, disarm, or frighten
Curb:	for strain or limit
Dip:	for decline
ex:	for former
Fell:	for defeat, knock down, repulse

Flay:	for criticize
Foil:	for thwart or reject
G.I:	for American soldier
Halt:	for impede
Hike:	for increase
Hop:	for flight
Job:	for appointment or position
Kill:	for murder
Lop:	for diminish, reduce, or trim
Love Theft:	for alienation of affection
Meet:	for convene or gather
Mum:	for silent
Nail:	for arrest or expose
OK:	for accept, adopt, or approve
Pact:	for agreement
Pit:	for oppose
Post:	for appointment or position
Probe:	for investigate
Quit:	for leave or resign
Quiz:	for investigate or question
Raze:	for destroy or wreck
Rift:	for disagreement
Row:	for wrangle
Rule:	for decision
Russ:	for Russians
Scan:	for examine or investigate
Score:	for criticize
Seize:	for arrest
Set:	for arrange or schedule
Shift:	for transfer
Sift:	for investigate
Slate:	for nominate or schedule
Slay:	for murder
Spark:	for encourage

Tell	for inform or reveal
Tiff	for argument or quarrel
Try	for attempt
Tryst	for clandestine meeting
TV:	for television
Urge:	for advocate or propose
Up:	for increase or rise
Vet:	for veteran
Vie:	for compete
Void:	for nullify
Vow:	for pledge or promise
Yanks:	for Americans, or American soldiers

(see p.153, Copy Reading and News Editing)

Headline에 자주 나오는 동사

✔Accent: 강조하다

Head Kim Accents Transparency of Political Funds
(김대통령 정치자금의 투명성 강조)

Text President Kim Dae-jung accented transparency of political funds.

✔Adopt: 채택하다

Head Prosecution Adopts 'Ethics' Charter for Political Neutrality
(검찰 정치적 중립을 위한 '윤리' 헌장 채택)

Text The prosecution adopted an 'ethics' charter for political neutrality.

Agree: 동의하다

Head	ROK, US Agree to Foster NK Openness (한미 양국 북한의 개방 촉진시키기로 합의)
Text	Korea and the United States agreed to foster North Korean openness.

Approve: 승인하다

Head	Hyundai's Mt. Kumgang Project Approved (현대의 금강산개발사업 승인)
Text	Hyundai's Mt. Kumgang project was approved.

Arrest: 체포하다

Head	Woman Arrested for Killing Student (학생 살인혐의로 여인 체포)
Text	A woman was arrested for killing a student.

Assign: 할당하다

Head	Students Assigned to Teachers of Their Choice (학생들, 자신들이 원하는 선생님 반에 배치)
Text	Students were assigned to teachers of their choice.

Attack: 공격하다

Head	Opposition Attacks Ruling Camp Over Economic Failure (야당, 여당의 경제 실패 비난)
Text	The opposition party attacked the ruling camp over the economic failure.

Ban: 금지하다

Head Eight Banned From Leaving Country in Draft Scandal
(병무비리 관련자 8명 출국금지)

Text Eight people were banned from leaving the country in draft scandal.

Be at odds with: …와 사이가 좋지 않다

Head Subway Operator at Odds With PCS Businesses
(서울 지하철 PCS업체와 불화)

Text The Seoul subway operator is at odds with PCS businesses.

Be charged with : …의 혐의를 받다

Head Prof. Park Charged With Accepting Bribes
(박교수, 뇌물 수수 혐의)

Text Prof. Park was charged with accepting bribes.

Be exempt from: 면제되다

Head Public Corporations Not Exempt From Tax Audit
(공기업체도 세무감사 안전지대 아니다)

Text The public corporations are not exempt from tax audit.

Be likely to: …할 것 같다

Head Assembly Hearing on Economy Likely to Open This Month
(국회경제청문회, 이번 달에 열릴 가능성)

Text A parliamentary hearing on the economic failure is likely to open this month.

Blame: …의 탓으로 돌리다, 책망하다

Head	N. Korea Blames US for Nuclear Problems (북한, 미국에 핵 문제 비난)
Text	North Korea blamed the United States for the nuclear problems.

Block: 방해하다

Head	'Screen Quota System' Blocks ROK-US Investment Accord (스크린 쿼터제, 한미투자협정 방해)
Text	The 'screen quota system' blocked an ROK-U.S. investment accord.

Clash(With): 충돌하다

Head	S. Korean Workers Clash With Police (한국 근로자들, 경찰과 충돌)
Text	South Korean workers clashed with police.

Collide(With): 충돌하다

Head	S. Korean Boat Collides With US Sub (한국어선, 미 잠수함과 충돌)
Text	A South Korean boat collided with a U.S. submarine.

Commit suicide: 자살하다

Head	Doctor Commits Suicide Due to Financial Problems (금전문제로 의사 자살)
Text	A doctor committed suicide due to financial problems.

Conduct: 행하다

Head	Daewoo Conducts World Cup Event (대우, 월드컵 이벤트 실시)
Text	Daewoo Group conducted a World Cup event.

Crack down: 단속하다

Head	Gov't to Crack Down on Pseudo Media (정부, 사이비언론 단속)
Text	The government will crack down on pseudo media.

Discover: 발견하다

Head	Body of Suspected NK Spy Discovered (북한 간첩으로 보이는 시체 발견)
Text	The body of a suspected North Korean spy was discovered.

Ease: 완화하다

Head	Pak's Success Eases Nation's Pain (박세리 우승, 국가적 위안)
Text	Golfer Pak Se-ri's success eased the nation's pain.

Elect: 선출하다

Head	Goh Elected Seoul Mayor (고건 서울시장에 선출)
Text	Goh Kun was elected the mayor of Seoul city.

Expand: 확대하다

Head   Probe Into Ice Hockey Coaches Expanded
          (아이스하키 코치 수사확대)

Text   The probe into ice hockey coaches was expanded.

Expel: 추방하다

Head   Russian Diplomat Expelled
          (러시아 외교관 추방)

Text   A Russian diplomat was expelled.

Extend: 연장하다

Head   Biz Hours in Itaewon to Be Extended
          (이태원 영업시간 연장)

Text   The business hours will be extended in Itaewon.

Eye: 눈여겨보다, 주목하다, 검토하다

Head   China Eyes Large Conglomerates
          (중국, 대기업에 주목)

Text   China is watching carefully large conglomerates.

Face: 직면하다

Head   More Russian Agents Face Expulsion
          (더 많은 러시아 정보요원들 추방에 직면)

Text   More Russian agents faced expulsion.

Flock: 떼지어 모여들다

Head   Japanese Tourists Flock to Korea
(일본인 관광객들, 한국으로 쇄도)

Text   Japanese tourists flocked to Korea last week.

Foster: 육성하다

Head   Seoul to Foster 'Model' Restaurants for Foreigners
(서울시, 외국인전용 모범식당 육성계획)

Text   Seoul City will foster 'model' restaurants for foreigners.

Freeze: 동결하다

Head   Most Companies Freeze or Cut Wages
(대부분 기업체, 올해 임금동결 또는 삭감)

Text   Most companies froze or cut wages for workers this year.

Halt: 멈추다, 중단하다

Head   Tokyo Halts Aid to Pyongyang
(일본, 북한원조 중단)

Text   The Japanese government halted aid to North Korea.

Hike: 인상하다

Head   Russian Central Bank Hikes Interest Rates
(러시아 중앙은행, 금리인상)

Text   Russia's central bank hiked interest rates.

Hint(at): 암시하다, 시사하다

Head	Opposition Party Hints at Attending House Session (야당, 국회참석 시사)
Text	The opposition party hinted at attending the House session.

Hit: (특정수치에) 이르다

Head	Jobless Rate Hits 30-Year High (실업률, 30년 만에 최고치 기록)
Text	The jobless hit the highest rate in 30 years.

Hold: 열다, 개최하다

Head	Diplomats' Wives to Hold Charity Bazaar (외교관 부인들, 자선바자회 개최)
Text	Diplomats' wives will hold a charity bazaar.

Inaugurate: 개관하다, 시작하다

Head	Opposition lawmakers Inaugurate Reform Group (야당의원, 개혁그룹 발족)
Text	The opposition lawmakers inaugurated a reform group.

Injure: 상처를 입히다

Head	Hansol Executive Injures Self During Questioning (한솔 간부, 심문도중 자해)
Text	An executive of the Hansol Group injured himself while being questioned.

Introduce: 도입하다

Head   Cyber Hospital Internet Homepage Introduced
(가상병원, 인터넷 홈페이지 도입)

Text   A cyber hospital Internet Homepage was introduced.

Launch: 시작하다, 착수하다

Head   Government Launches Reform Projects
(정부, 개혁 착수)

Text   The government launched reform projects.

Lay off: 해고하다

Head   50,000 Workers to Be Laid Off
(근로자 5만명 정리해고 예정)

Text   About 50,000 workers will be laid off.

Lift: 해제하다

Head   US Lifts Anti-Dumping Rules on TVs
(미국, 한국산 color TV에 대한 반덤핑 규제 철폐)

Text   The United States lifted the anti-dumping rules on Korean-made color television sets.

Lower: 낮추다, 내리다

Head   SK Telecom Lowers Call Charges
(SK Telecom, 전화요금 인하)

Text   SK Telecom lowered call charges.

Mount: 늘어나다

Head Financial Pressure Mounts in Korea
    (한국, 재정난 가중)

Text Financial pressure mounted in Korea.

Mull: 숙고하다

Head Prosecution Mulls Summoning Rep. Kim
    (검찰, 김의원 소환 고려)

Text The prosecution is considering summoning Rep. Kim.

Name: 임명하다

Head Kim Mo-im Named Health-Welfare Minister
    (새 보건복지부 장관에 김모임씨 임명)

Text Kim Mo-im was named health-welfare minister.

Oust: 내쫓다, 몰아내다

Head 30,000 Local Government Officials to Be Ousted
    (지방공무원 3만명 감원예정)

Text Some 30,000 local government officials will be ousted.

OK, Okay: 승인하다

Head South Korea Oks Fertilizer Aid for N. Korea
    (남한, 북한에 비료원조 승인)

Text The South Korean government has decided to provide
    North Korea with fertilizer.

Plunge: 급락하다

Head	Number of Pager Subscriptions Plunges for Successive Three Months (호출기 가입자수, 3개월 연속감소)
Text	The number of pager subscriptions plunged for the successive three months.

Propose: 제안하다

Head	Seoul Proposes Panmunjom as S-N Talks Venue (한국, 남북회담 장소로 판문점 제의)
Text	South Korea proposed Panmunjom as the venue for the South-North Korean talks.

Protest: 항의하다

Head	Daewoo Workers Protest Layoffs (대우 노동자들, 정리해고에 항의)
Text	Daewoo Group workers protested layoffs.

Reaffirm: 재 다짐하다, 재 확인하다

Head	Kim Reaffirms Opening to Japanese Culture (김대통령, 일본문화 개방 재확인)
Text	President Kim reaffirmed the opening to Japanese culture.

Resign: 사임하다

Head	Foreign Minister Lee Resigns (이 외무장관 사임)
Text	Foreign Minister Lee resigned.

Resort(to): 의지하다

Head	Parties Resort to Malicious Propaganda (여야, 흑색선전 돌입)
Text	The rival parties resort to a malicious propaganda.

Restore: 복원하다

Head	Fountain Plaza Festival Restored (분수대 광장축제 부활)
Text	The fountain plaza festival was restored.

Resume: 재개하다

Head	Korea, US Resume Auto Talks (한미 자동차협상 재개)
Text	Korea and the United States resumed auto talks.

Reveal: 발표하다

Head	FKI to Reveal Restructuring Plan Today (전경련 오늘 구조조정계획 밝힐 예정)
Text	The Federation of Korean Industries will reveal the restructuring plan today.

Scrap: 버리다, 폐기하다

Head	Playboy Magazine's Plan to Publish in Korea Scrapped (플레이보이지, 한국출판계획 취소)
Text	Playboy Magazine's plan to publish in Korea was scrapped.

✔ Set up : 세우다, 설립하다

Head   Opposition Camp to Set Up Special Panel for Political Reforms
(야당 정치개혁특별위원회 설립)

Text   The opposition camp will set up a special panel for political reforms.

✔ Shelve: 보류하다

Head   Government to Shelve Project to Build Stadium
(정부, 경기장 건설계획 보류)

Text   The government will shelve the project to build a stadium.

✔ Shrink: 축소되다

Head   Economy Shrinks 5.3 Pct
(경제 5.3% 축소)

Text   The economy shrank 5.3 percent in the first half.

✔ Sign: 서명하다, 조인하다

Head   Korea, Taiwan Seek to Sign Aviation Accord
(한국과 대만 항공협정 추진)

Text   Korea and Taiwan seek to sign an aviation accord.

✔ Strike: 공격하다

Head   US Strikes Afghanistan
(미국, 아프가니스탄 공격)

Text   The United States struck Afghanistan.

✓ Summon: 소환하다

Head	Prosecution to Summon Daewoo Execs
	(검찰, 대우 임원들 소환 예정)
Text	The prosecution will summon Daewoo Group executives.

✓ Surge: 급증하다

Head	Unemployment Rate Surges to 7.6 Percent
	(실업률 7.6%로 급증)
Text	The unemployment rate surged to 7.6 percent.

✓ Support: 지지하다

Head	US to Support Inter-Korean Talks
	(미국, 남북회담 지지)
Text	The U.S. will support the Seoul-Pyongyang Talks.

✓ Swear: 맹세하다, 선서하다

Head	KCLU Swears Strike on February 13
	(민주노총, 2월 13일 파업선언)
Text	The Korean Confederation of Labor Unions swore a strike on February 13.

✓ Take action: 조치를 취하다

Head	Seoul to Take Strong Action Against Tokyo
	(정부, 일본에 강경조치 취할 방침)
Text	The government will take strong actions against Japan.

Take over: 인계 받다

Head   Kim Woo-choong Takes Over FKI Chairmanship
             (김우중씨, 전경련 회장직 인계 받아)

Text   Kim Woo-Choong took over the chairmanship of the
             Federation of Korean Industries.

Threaten: 위협하다

Head   Election Defeat Threatens Ruling Party Leadership
             (선거패배로 위기에 처한 여당지도부)

Text   An election defeat threatened the ruling party leadership.

Undergo: (시련 등을) 겪다, 경험하다

Head   First Lady Undergoes Minor Surgery for Thighbone Fractures
             (영부인, 대퇴골 골절수술)

Text   First Lady underwent a minor surgery for thighbone
             fractures.

Unveil: 발표하다, 공개하다

Head   Government Unveils Economic Stimulus Package
             (정부, 경기부양책 발표)

Text   The government unveiled an economic stimulus package.

Urge: 촉구하다, 역설하다

Head   Kim Urges Inter-Korean dialogue
             (김 대통령, 남북대화 역설)

Text   President Kim urged dialogue between South and North
             Korea.

Vie: 경쟁하다

Head   Big 3 Department Stores Vie in Sales
(백화점 3사, 판매경쟁)

Text   Big 3 department stores vied in sales.

Vow: 서약하다, 맹세하다

Head   Gov't Vows to Punish Anyone Provoking Regionalism
(정부, 지역감정 조장자 엄벌천명)

Text   The government vowed to punish anyone provoking regionalism.

Warn(of): 경고하다

Head   Minister Jin Warns of Economic Hardship
(진장관, 경제난 경고)

Text   Minister Jin warned of a possible economic hardship.

진부한 단어(Threadbare Words)

헤드라인에서 짧은 단어만을 추구하다 보면 자칫 진부한 단어 (Threadbare Words) 사용에 유혹을 받기 쉽다.

이러한 단어들은 어떤 편집국에서는 사용을 금지하고 어떤 편집국에서는 사용제한을 하지 않는다.

Collection of Threadbare Words:

- confab for conference or meeting
- cops for police
- eyed for examined or studied
- feud for dispute
- grill for question
- gut for destroy the interior of(a building)
- kin for family
- meet for meeting
- nab for arrest or capture
- parley for meeting
- seen for expected
- solons for senators
- stir for incite

편집(Make-up) 4

편집의 정의 및 중요성

Make-up is the editorial design by which a newspaper displays its contents — texts, photos, charts, tables, diagrams, graphics, and illustrations.

편집은 신문, 서적에서 일정한 계획을 가지고 글과 시각물로 지면을 시각적으로 균형 있게 구성하는 행위를 말하며 "Layout" 또는 "Design"이라고 불리기도 하는데 본란에서는 "디자인"으로 표기한다.

기사나 시각물(Visuals, Arts)을 단순히 배열하는 차원을 넘어 "상업적인 예술형식"으로 지면을 꾸며 독자들의 시선을 끌어야 한다는 의미에서 "design"이라고 표기하는 것이 적합하다.

지금 우리는 전자영상매체의 발달로 인한 시각적 혁명시대에 살고 있다.

최근 미국을 비롯한 서구에서 발행되는 신문에서는 WED의 개념이 제작의 기본원칙으로 자리 잡고 있는데 이는 Writing, Editing, Design의 중요성이 강조되고 있음을 의미한다.

디자인의 절대적 원칙은 없다. 시대의 변천, 독자의 미적기준과 가치에 따라 변해왔고, 변하고 있고, 또 변할 것이다.

실제로 신문산업이 발달한 서구의 경우 Functionalism, Modernism, Post-modernism에 기초한 미학의 변천과 유행의 변화에 따라 Visual Journalism or Visual Communication이 많은 변화를 겪어 왔다.

1996년 미국의 Poynter Institute의 Mario Garcia는 자신이 참여했던 성공적인 신문디자인개혁(Redesign Project)의 결과물을 엮은 "Newspaper Evolution"을 출간했다.

다년간 300개가 넘는 신문사의 디자인을 연구작업해 온 Garcia는 종

래의 보수적 디자인 이론을 뒤집는 새로운 주장을 내놓았다.

예컨대 헤드라인 충돌(Butting Headlines), 컬러사용, 이탤릭체 사용 등에 대한 기존의 보수적 이론에 대해 개방적이고, 유연한 입장을 견지하면서 융통성 있는 사용을 주장한다.

본란에서는 논란의 대상이 되고 있는 쟁점부분에 대한 설명은 생략하고, 과거에서 현재까지 비교적 보편적으로 사용되는 편집관행만 제시하기로 한다.

과거의 이론이 절대적일 수 없듯이 Garcia의 이론도 영구불변 일 수는 없다. 시간이 흐름에 따라 독자의 미적 감각이 변하고 이와 더불어 건축, 예술부문 등의 미적가치가 달라지므로 신문디자인도 영향을 받게 된다.

게스탈트(Gestalt)는 "사람들은 사물을 볼 때, 부분적인 이미지보다는 전체를 보고 인지하는 경향이 있으며 독자들은 기사 하나 하나에 관심을 갖기 이전에 신문 한 페이지를 전체로 먼저 받아들인다. 따라서 전체를 조화롭고 질서있게 배열하는 것이 중요하다"고 말한다.

독자들이 신문 한 페이지에 대한 이미지에 대해 어떤 느낌을 갖느냐 하는 것은 전적으로 전체디자인에 달려 있다고 주장한다.

에머스(Ames, 1989)가 신문디자인요소(The Elements of Newspaper Design)에서 주장한 TPC(Total Page Concept) 개념은 디자인의 일차적 목적을 정보내용의 효율적 전달에 두고 있다.

TPC는 독자가 정보의 중요성을 쉽게 인식할 수 있도록 한 페이지 상의 모든 편집요소(사진, 헤드라인, 기사, 박스)를 통합적으로 관련짓는 것이다. 또한 각각의 페이지를 하나의 통합된 단위로 디자인하되, 각 페이지나 이슈마다 비슷한 스타일로 디자인하는 것을 말한다.

TPC 디자인 전략은 디자인의 일관성과 창조성을 통하여 독자들에게 뉴스의 상대적 중요성을 인식시키고 뉴스내용에 관심을 갖게 하는 편집을 말한다.

니론과 반허스트(Nerone & Barnhurst, 1995)는 신문디자인은 사회에 대한 시각적 지도라고 정의했는데 그들은 디자인이란 독자로 하여금 사회적사건들을 시각물을 통해 파악할 수 있도록 안내해 주는 것이라고 주장한다.

신문디자인이란 전문가인 저널리스트들이 문화적 권위를 가지고 정보를 조직화하고 뉴스의 중요성에 따라 위계질서를 부여하는 행위라는 이론이다.

신문디자인 개혁에서 가장 명심해야 할 점은 디자인만으로는 신문내용이나 전체 기사 편집을 향상시킬 수 없다고 말한다.

1980년대와 1990년대 디자인개혁을 실시한 많은 신문사들이 실패했다. 그 가장 큰 원인은 알맹이 없이 스타일만 바꾼 개혁이었기 때문이다. 디자인개혁으로 신문이 더 좋은 외양을 갖는 것은 분명한 사실이지만 단정하고 말끔한 외양에 내용의 참신함이 따라주지 않으면 오히려 역효과가 날 수도 있다.

디자인개혁을 성공한 다른 신문사를 모방하여 단지 외양만을 성형수술 하는 것은 잘못이다.

시각 커뮤니케이션

온라인, 오프라인 관계없이 신문, 잡지 등에서의 디자인은 그 자체가 목적이 아니고 신문의 기본기능인 정보전달의 효과를 극대화하는 데 있다.

신문디자인은 예술적 기능에 앞서 시각커뮤니케이션(Visual Communication)의 중요한 한 영역으로 자리를 잡아가고 있다.

문자를 통한 커뮤니케이션이 이성적이고 추상적이라면 디자인을 통한 시각 커뮤니케이션은 감성적이고 구체적이며, 즉각적인 특성을 가지고 있다.

시각 커뮤니케이션은 독이성, 정보성, 조직성을 우선적으로 고려해야 한다.

독이성

독자들이 볼 때 '신문이 얼마나 읽기 쉬운가?' 하는 "Easy-to-Read"의 개념이다. 독이성은 가독성(Readability)과 가시성(Legibility)의 함축된 의미로 볼 수 있다.

가독성, 가시성 모두 "읽기 쉬움"이라는 뜻을 가지고 있지만, 가독성은 보다 내용적인 측면을 강조하는 개념으로 "읽고 이해하기 쉬움"이라는 뜻을 내포하고 있으며, 가시성은 "글자가 보기 쉽고 명료하다"는 물리적인 측면을 강조하는 개념이다. 따라서 가시성이 Typography(인쇄체형)에 관련된 개념이라고 한다면, 가독성은 Typography 뿐만 아니라 전체 지면의 Layout과 상관된 개념이라고 할 수 있다.

가독성은 문장의 명확도, 길이, 헤드라인, 사진, 도표, 그래픽 등이 중요한 요소로 작용하고, 가시성은 활자의 모양, 크기, 활자의 배열, 여백 등이 독해율에 영향을 주는 요소로 볼 수 있다. 가독성과 가시성이 조화 있게 잘 어우러져 배열이 될 때 독이성이 높아진다.

정보성

지면의 시각화를 통해 정보량이 효율적으로 늘어났는가 하는 문제다. 컬러와 흑백사진의 선택, 차트, 그래픽, 삽화 등이 정보량을 증대 시키고 있는 것인가 하는 문제를 고려해야 한다.

일반적으로 컬러의 사용과 시각물의 효율적 사용이 독자의 시선을 끌어 들이고 정보전달을 확대시키는 데 크게 기여한다는 조사결과가 나오고 있다.

조직성

지면이 전체적으로 질서있게 구성되어야 한다.

디자인은 매일 변화하는 뉴스를 담는 일정한 틀로서 무질서해 보이는 단어들, 사진, 그래픽, 광고 등을 조합하여 시각적으로 연속성과 통일성을 제공해야 한다.

위에서 언급한 시각 커뮤니케이션의 3가지 특성을 살려 성공한 신문이 미국의 USA Today이다.

디자인의 최종 목표는 미(美)의 극대화다.

미를 구성한다는 것은 모든 부분요소를 통일시키고 상호조화 시키면서 아름다움을 창조하는 것이다. 고대이집트와 그리스시대 이래 많은 미적 형식원리가 제시되었으며 근대의 미학자들에 의해 정리되었다.

본래 미학상의 개념이지만 오늘날에는 많은 예술분야에서도 사용되는 원리로서 조화-통일(Harmony-Unity), 균형(Balance), 율동(Rhythm)의 개념이 중시되고 있다.

조화-통일(Harmony-Unity)개념은 두개 이상의 요소가 상호관계에 있어 서로 분리되어 배척하지 않고, 통일된 전체로서 미적효과를 높일 수 있어야 한다는 이론이다.

좋은 조화는 요소상호 간에 공통성과 동시에 차별성이 있을 때 얻어진다. 즉 적절한 통일과 변화가 이루어질 때 조화를 이룬다.

균형(Balance)의 미는 대칭, 비대칭, 비례의 요소에 의해 형성된다.

① 대칭(Symmetry): 인간신체의 대칭적 구조를 예술적으로 처리하는 원리.
② 비대칭(Asymmetry): 비슷하지 않은 사물들의 균형에 기초를 두고 있다. 명암, 대조 등.
③ 비례(Proportion): 모든 사물의 상대적인 크기의 관계에서 미를 추구하는 것이다.

율동(Rhythm)의 미는 각 요소와 부분사이에 강한 힘과 약한 힘이 규칙적으로 연속될 때에 생기는 것이다.

위에 언급한 미적 원리들은 1930년대에 레이아웃을 철학적 관점, 특히 그리스미학에서 접근한 Eugene De Lopatecki에 의해 체계화되었다. 그의 다섯 가지 원칙—대조, 균형, 비례, 리듬, 통일—은 타이포그래퍼, 그래픽디자인 교육자들을 통해 저널리즘에 도입되었고 결국에는 디자인 편집 핸드북과 교과서의 주내용이 되었으며 현재까지 통용되고 있다.

편집이론

Cybil Burt 이론

독자들은 개개 글자가 아니라 전체형태를 통해 문맥을 이해하며, 한 순간 볼 수 있는 범위는 가로 세로 1인치 즉 12포인트 활자 6자 폭이다.

Edmund Arnold 이론

가독성이 가장 좋은 글줄은 5.3cm이며 최소 길이를 3.7cm, 최대 길이를 8.6cm라고 본다.

이러한 연구결과에 의해 최적포맷(Optimum Format)이 구미신문에 도입되었다.

또한 독서의 방향 축(Axis of Orientation)과 구텐베르그 도표에 의한 독서중력(Reading Gravity) 및 중력역행(Against Gravity)도 독이성 논의에 과학적 근거를 제공하고 있다.

독서의 방향 축이란 좌측에서 우측으로 읽어가는 눈의 자연스러운 운동을 가리키는 것으로, 이러한 눈의 움직임은 독서중력과 중력역행원리에 의해서도 뒷받침된다.

독서중력의 원리는 눈의 움직임이 좌측상단 코너인 주시지역(Primary Optical Area: POA)에서 시작하여 우측하단 코너인 종점지역(Terminal Area: TA)에서 끝나게 된다는 것이다. POA에서 TA까지의 독서대각선을 독서중력이라고 하며 독자는 이러한 독서중력 이외의 지역에는 눈을 덜 돌리게 된다.

그러나 눈이 그 대각선만을 따라가는 것은 아니며 그 지역 밖으로도 갈 수 있다. 따라서 지면 곳곳에 독자의 눈을 끌어들이기 위한 읽을거리를 배치해야 하며, 특히 가로편집 신문이라면 우측상단과 좌측하단 코너는 읽을거리가 필요한 지역이다.

독자는 지구중력의 방향을 역행하여 움직이고 싶어 하지 않듯이 눈의 움직임에 있어서도 독서중력을 거슬러 올라가기 싫어하는데 이러한 현상을 중력역행원리라고 한다.

✔ Poynter Institute의 이론-반론

최근 미국의 포인터연구소(Poynter Institute)에서 독자들의 신문읽기 패턴연구를 위해 실시한 안구이동연구(EYE-TRAC)에 의하면 독자들은 페이지를 처음 대할 때 어느 부분에 먼저 주목 하는가?에는 정해진 법칙이 없다고 말한다.

독자들은 대개 사진이나 그래픽, 또는 커다란 헤드라인 등 강력한 시각적요소가 있는 곳을 가장 먼저 주목한다.

독자들은 그 출발점에서 시작하여 페이지에 있는 나머지 정보들을 보고 읽기 시작하는 것이다. 따라서 리드스토리의 위치가 페이지의 우측 또는 좌측 상단이 좋다는 증거는 없다. 독자들은 미리 정해진 법칙을 갖고 지면을 대하지는 않는다.

✔ 월터 옹(Walter Ong)

월터 옹(Walter Ong)은 인쇄에 있어서 여백은 쉼표이며 침묵이라고 말한다.

1960년대 이후 신문디자인의 가장 두드러진 특징의 하나는 신문크기가 커지고 신문에 흰 여백이 많아졌다는 것이다.

넓고 여유로운 레이아웃으로의 변화는 기술적발달이나 독이성에 관한 고려, 신문 증면 등의 영향을 주면서 현재 넓은 여백이 광범위하게 선택되고 있다.

공간학(proxemics)에 의하면 넓은 공간은 여유와 평등의 사회적 관계를 반영한다. 빽빽하게 채워진 신문은 답답하게 느껴진다. 넓은 신문의 넓은 여백과 간략한 활자를 사용한 NY Herald Tribune의 디자인은 여

유 있고 부드럽게 보인다.

1980년대의 포스트모던 스타일은 예술과 건축분야로부터 그래픽디자인 분야로 확산되었다.

포스트모더니즘은 근본적으로 서로 다른 스타일(가장 현대적인 것과 노스탤직한 것)을 혼합시켰다. 엘리트주의를 거부하는 대중주의(populism)와 가장 최신유행이 동시에 반영되는 것이 포스트모던 시대 신문디자인의 특색이라고 할 수 있다.

USA Today의 시각적 외양은 적어도 다른 엘리트 신문들보다는 권위적이며 훨씬 대중적이고 서민적이라고 볼 수 있다.

최근 나타난 몇몇의 대안적 신문들은 독특한 자신의 문화적 스타일을 존중하는 방향으로, 지나치게 정교하며 기계화하므로 매끈해진 디자인을 거부하고 오히려 조금은 엉성한 수공업적 분위기를 풍기는 방향으로 나아가기도 한다.

John E. Alen

제1차 세계대전(1914~1918)을 전후하여 근대적 신문디자인의 개념이 나타나기 시작했다. 그 후 문화, 예술적인 변화의 소용돌이 속에 1930~1940년대에 기능주의적 신문디자인이 모습을 보이기 시작했다.

신문에 현대적 디자인의 체계적 적용은 타이포그래퍼인 벤 셔보(Ben Sherbow)가 1916년 뉴욕 트리뷴(New York Tribune)지를 새로이 디자인하면서 확산되었다.

그 이후 1930년대에 "라이노타이프 뉴스"(Linotype News)의 편집인인 존 알렌(John E. Alen)이 시도한 단순한 기능주의적 신문디자인이 확산되고 다채롭고 장식적인 빅토리안 스타일은 퇴조하고 있다.

알렌은 헤드라인을 간결하게 할 것을 주장했다.

간결성법칙이란 왼쪽 끝 맞추기(Flush-Left) 기법으로 간결한 헤드라인이 지면을 절약하며 독자들의 가독성도 높인다는 점을 고려한 것이다.

왼쪽 끝 맞추기 헤드라인기법은 Cleveland News에서 처음 도입되었다.

1936년 Los Angeles Times가 간결성의 법칙과 왼쪽 끝 맞추기 헤드라인방식을 도입하여 1937년 최고 신문 편집상을 수상한 이후 이 기법은 확산되었다.

헤드라인의 변화와 더불어 본문활자의 크기와 사진의 크기가 커졌으며 여백의 사용도 증가했다

디자인의 고려사항

지금까지 디자인의 정의, 기능, 그에 따른 이론에 대해 알아보았다. 그러면 실제적으로 어떻게 디자인할 것인가?

현장에서 종사하는 편집책임자와 디자인책임자 들을 위한 실무적 차원에서 다루어 보기로 한다. 먼저 무엇을 디자인 할 것인가?

독자들은 무엇을 원하는가?

팀 해로우어(Tim Harrower, 1995)는 디자인혁신을 추구하는 편집관리자 들을 위해 다음과 같은 권고사항을 제시했는데 그 중 실제로 통용되는 주요부분을 재구성해 본다.

Harrower의 제언

① 제호(Flag): 독특하고 독창적이어야 한다. (회사 Logo 같이)
② 헤드라인: 간결하고, 우아하며 대담하고 힘차야 한다.
③ 부제목: Straight News와 Feature물에 다른 형태의 부제목 사용.
④ 고정기호(Standing Heads): 모든 지면의 로고와 사인 등을 하나의 글자체로 통일.
⑤ 본문: 읽기에 편안해야 한다. Readability와 Legibility 고려.
⑥ 특별기사: Graphics, Sidebar(관련기사), Packaging(꾸러미 기사)에 대한 글자체 선택.

⑦ 페이지 그리드(Grid): 칼럼 폭과 패키징 포맷의 선택과 광고지면과의 조화여부.

⑧ 페이지 헤더(Headers): 헤더위치의 선택, 그래픽요소들의 첨가여부.

⑨ 뉴스 요약란: Brief News를 위한 단신기사 모음란을 고정란으로 할 것인지의 여부.

⑩ 특별 피처: 여론조사, 통계, 달력 등을 고정 포맷으로 할 것인지의 여부.

⑪ 패선과 박스: 이상적인 선굵기, 박스스타일, 스크린농도 등의 결정.

⑫ 기사안내(Promos)와 색인: 아트(사진, 그래픽 등의 시각물)와 함께 눈에 띄게 처리.

⑬ 광고: 광고를 모듈라 형식에 맞추어 조화.

⑭ 섹션화: 각 섹션을 혁신적인 내용과 형식으로 재구성.

⑮ 연속성: 모든 지면을 연계시키는 흥미와 영향력 있는 주제의 선정.

⑯ 대안적 기사형태: 전통적인 뉴스 포맷에 대한 새로운 형태의 선택.

⑰ 상호 교류성: 독자의 참여를 높이는 공간도입 여부.

편집의 패턴

앞서 언급했듯이 편집에 절대적인 원칙은 없다.

그러나 각 언론사는 묵시적으로, 제작, 인쇄규칙에 관한 책(Stylebook) 유무에 관계없이 그들 사이에 통용되어온 관행이 있다.

이들 편집관행을 기초로 하여 언론학자들은 편집의 형태를 분류 연구하는 작업을 계속해 왔다.

학자들 사이에 이론이 다를 수 있고, 용어도 다를 수 있다.

그러나 신문디자인은 대체로 모듈라 편집, 균형식 편집, 대조-균형식 편집, 집중형 편집, 파격형 편집의 다섯 가지 정도로 요약된다.

그 중 균형식 편집, 대조-균형식 편집, 집중형 편집, 파격형 편집의 네 가지 패턴은 오늘날 이론에 그칠 뿐 거의 사용되지 않아 큰 의미를 갖지 못한다.

다만 모듈라형 편집만이 구미신문에서 가장 보편적인 디자인형태로 통용되고 있다.

모듈라형 편집(Modular or Quadrant Make-up)

가장 현대화된 디자인형식으로 꼽히는 것이 모듈라 디자인이다. 오늘날 구미의 많은 신문들이 이 디자인을 채택하고 있다.

국내의 국영문신문, 잡지, 온라인 News 편집 등에서도 많이 채택되는 기법으로 모듈라 디자인은 지면을 6개 내지 9개의 직사각형 조립부품 (모듈)으로 분할하여 한 개의 모듈 속에 본문, 사진, 도표, 제목을 집어넣어 부분과 전체가 모두 직사각형 형태로 보이는 편집기법을 말한다. 이는 가로와 세로의 여러 개 직사각형을 교차시키기 때문에 수직적 구성 (make-up)과 수평적 구성의 편집기법을 효과적으로 조화시키게 된다.

모듈라 디자인은 몬드리안과 독일의 바우하우스의 디자인철학을 응용한 형식으로 이는 전체지면을 수평적, 수직적 형태로 나눈 다음 황금 분할의 법칙 등 비례의 자연 철학적 원리를 신문디자인에 가장 과학적으로 적용하고 있는 신문디자인 형식으로 평가된다.

이 편집에서는 모든 기사를 사각형모양으로 만들어 한 지면에 엮어놓게 되며 조형미와 가독성을 높인다.

또한 지면에 기사를 맞추므로 기사가 규격을 벗어나면 다른 페이지로 점프 시키거나 잘라 버린다.

균형식 편집(Balanced Make-up)

균형식 편집은 인간의 신체가 대칭(Symmetry)이란 점에 착안하여 미적가치에 기초를 둔 예술적 노력의 산물이다.

균형식 편집은 중앙부를 기점으로 하여 상하 좌우로 대칭이 이루어지

도록 배치하여 균형을 잡는 형태로 신문디자인 초기에는 대칭성을 확립하려는 시도가 있었으나, Modern Communication에서는 시각적 대칭(Visual Symmetry)은 중요하게 간주되지 않는다.

전문 디자이너들은 완벽한 대칭성을 피하는 반면 아마추어들은 대칭성에 가치를 두는 경향이 있다.

근래 들어 이러한 대칭성이 쇠퇴함에 따라 편집에 위계질서(Hierarchy)개념이 발전하게 되었다.

Note

Balance기법을 전체로 확대할 것이냐, 부분적으로 적용할 것이냐에 따라 "Perfect Balance", "Balance Throughout the Page", "Balance at Top and at Bottom of the Page", "Balance at Top of the Page" 등이 있으나 지금은 잘 쓰지 않는 기법이다.

대조-균형식 편집(Contrast and Balanced Make-up)

대조-균형식 편집은 편집요소 들이 대각선으로 대칭을 이루므로 안정감과 균형감을 주면서 디스플레이 되는 형태이다.

A tree is beautiful not because of perfect symmetry, with each branch balancing another branch and each leaf balancing another leaf. It is beautiful, rather, because symmetry is preserved within a framework of contrast. Misshapen lopsidedness offends, but so does perfection if it appears artificial. (See pp. 203~204, Copy Reading and News Editing, Howard Taylor/Jacob Scher)

집중형 편집(Brace or Focused Make-up)

집중형 편집은 독자들의 눈을 그 페이지의 톱기사에 집중시키기 위해 사용되는 편집 형태로, 주요기사는 지면상의 다른 요소에 의해서 강조된다.

즉 톱기사 이외의 요소들은 톱기사보다 훨씬 더 작게 배치한다.

이 형태는 편집의 기동성과 신축성에서는 유리하지만 한 부분을 너무

강조하기 때문에 다른 부분들이 약화되어 버리는 단점이 있다

또한 주요기사가 없을 경우 문제가 발생한다.

Focus make-up achieves its typographic effect from the concentration of a mass in a focal point. A focal point is a zone of attention or interest. When the focal point is exploited by a stopper ─either typographic or pictorial─the adjacent areas receive subordinate attention.

파격형 편집(Broken Page Make-up/Circus Make-up)

여러 기사들이 거의 비슷한 비중을 차지할 때 사용되는 편집형태로 제목과 기사가 제호 위에 위치하는 경우도 있다.

디자인의 "20 계명"

지금까지 디자인의 정의, 기능 ,중요성, 변천하는 과정 등에 대해 알아보았다.

어떤 학자가 강한 이론을 제시한다 해도 반론은 끝이 없다.

그러나 국제적으로 수용되는 관행이 있다. 실무 차원에서 통용되는 관행을 근거로 하여 묵시적인 "원칙"을 제시한다.

절대적 원칙이 없음에도 불구하고 구미 각국의 신문사들은 디자인에 대한 Stylebook을 가지고 직원들을 교육시키거나 경험자 들이 구전으로 전수하기도 한다. 그들이 권장하는 디자인 실무지침 중 공통적으로 권장하는 사항을 20개로 요약해 "계율"로 제시코자 한다.

통상 신문은 대판(Broadsheet)과 타블로이드(Tabloid) 두 가지 크기로 발행되는 데 Broadsheet의 경우 56~61 × 36cm에 6~8Column Grid

사용이 보통이고, Tabloid의 경우 36~46×28~31cm에 4~5Column이 보통이다. 다음에 열거한 "20 계명"은 Broadsheet에 기준을 둔 것이다.

디자인의 20계명

계율1: 기사는 직사각형(Modular, Quadrant)모양으로 편집한다.

계율2: 헤드라인 충돌을 피한다. Avoid butting headlines.

계율3: 헤드라인의 단어는 5~10개의 범위 내에서 가급적 한 줄로 처리한다.

계율4: 본문(Text)의 칼럼 최적길이(Leg)는 5~25cm의 범위를 목표로 한다.

계율5: 한 칼럼의 기사의 폭이 8.5cm 보다 길거나, 4cm 보다 좁게 하는 것을 피한다.

계율6: Art(Picture, Graphics, Illustrations)는 전체 지면의 1/3 정도로 유지한다.

계율7: 컬러는 제한을 두고 사용하되 지면중심부에 사용한다.

계율8: 단신성 요약기사, 일정표 등은 한 곳에 모아 Packaging(꾸러미)로 처리한다.

계율9: 1면에 게재되는 기사 수는 4~7개 정도로 줄인다.

계율10: 불규칙/변형칼럼(Bastard Measures)을 적극적으로 활용한다.

계율11: 헤드라인에 대문자를 최소한(Downstyle)으로 사용한다.

계율12: 기사본문 수직단(Leg) 중간 또는 하단에 아트배열을 삼가한다.

계율13: 헤드라인 충돌방지를 위해 Box 사용을 삼가 한다.

계율14: 8 Point 이하의 글자체는 읽기 어려우므로 사용을 삼가한다.

계율15: 이탤릭과 볼드체는 특별한 효과를 위해 작은 양을 처리할 때 사용한다.

계율16: 기사점프 회수를 최소화하라. 한 기사에 한번만 점프한다.

계율17: 점프가 필요할 경우, 점프 전후기사는 각각 최소한 10.2cm, 15cm를 유지한다.

계율18: 사진은 반드시 Cropping하여 사용한다.

계율19: 광고 바로 위에 사진사용을 금한다.

계율20: 헤드라인에 컬러사용을 삼가한다.

실전응용

계율 1: 사각형 편집 ; Avoid snake designs. Keep a rectangular make-up.

모든 기사가 사각형 모양으로 단정하게 쌓여지도록 편집한다.

직사각형으로 만드는 과정에서 긴 기사는 자르거나 다른 면으로 Jump하고 짧은 기사는 Writer에게 기사를 늘려 줄 것을 요청해서라도 직사각형을 유지한다.

관련된 사진이나 Graphics 등 지원 시각물이 있을 경우 함께 조합해서 사각형이 되도록 한다.

편의 위주로 기사를 짜맞추어 꾸불꾸불한 모양의 "Snake Design"은 피하라.

신문이 조잡하고 힘이 없어 보인다.

직사각형의 편집은 Figure 1부터 Figure 5의 실제지면에서 보는 바와 같이 1면인 경우 4~7개 정도의 Module로 구성되어야 가지런하게 보인다.

반면 Figure 6~8에서 보는 바와 같이 일부지면에서 기사를 먹선으로 표시된 바와 같이 꾸불꾸불하게 배열하면 편집작업이 쉽게 끝날 수는 있으나 볼품없게 보인다.

Figure 1~5에서 보는 바와 같이 한국에서 발행되는 영어신문 The Korea Times, The Korea Herald, 미국의 전국지인 USA Today, 영국의 Financial Times, 일본의 The Daily Yomiuri, 대만의 Taipei Times 등을 포함한 여러 신문 들이 현재 Modular Design을 선호하고 있다.

Modular Designs(Proper)

Figure 1

Stalking Tiger

Challengers search for the secret to beating Tiger Woods at the U.S. Open
■ Cover story, 1B

David Duval heads field of Open rivals.

USA TODAY
AVAILABLE AROUND THE WORLD

Arbitrary justice

Workers say they are losing out in push to settle disputes without going to court
■ Cover story, 9A

Tuesday, June 12, 2001

Newsline
■ News ■ Money ■ Sports ■ Life

U.S. stocks fall on profit concerns

Japan's Nikkei index slides 203.74 points to 13,226.48. Hong Kong's Hang Seng dives 133.40 to 13,675.49. London's FTSE falls 80.30 to 5860.50. Frankfurt's DAX drops 10.30 to 6176.91. 9A.
► Dow Jones industrial unofficially closes down 54.91 to 10,922.09; Nasdaq is down 44.30 to 2170.80.

Bush begins European tour today

Amid criticism overseas on his environmental policies, President Bush arrives in Madrid, Spain, today after announcing new initiatives to study global warming. He has the support of many Americans, a new USA TODAY/CNN/Gallup Poll shows. 2A.

Death of 'Precious Doe' remains mystery

Recent discovery of an unknown black girl's body has had a unifying effect on many in Kansas City, Mo. But not much is known about her, including her name. Police call her "Precious Doe." 4A.

Philippines rebels take more hostages

Muslim rebels in southern region call off their threat to behead three American captives, but take 15 others at a hospital, including doctors and soldiers.

Weather: Sunshine in Madrid

European cities: London, cloudy; Paris, cloudy; Stockholm, showers; Berlin, rain; Madrid, sunny; Asian/Pacific cities: Tokyo, partly cloudy; Hong Kong, thunderstorms. U.S. cities: New York, cloudy; Los Angeles, partly cloudy. 12A.

■ Today's debate: McVeigh execution

In USA TODAY's opinion: "Life without parole would have been more punishing." 7A.
► "To impose a lesser sentence . . . is to denigrate and diminish the life of the victim," Oklahoma Gov. Frank Keating says. 7A.

■ Money: Travelers maximizing mileage

Business travelers might be taking fewer trips because of belt tightening, but they're taking longer trips and trying to squeeze more work in. 9A.

■ Sports: Lakers lead NBA finals

Los Angeles wins in Philadelphia to take a 2-1 series lead over the 76ers. 1, 4B.
► Wimbledon, next stop on Grand Slam tennis tour, is changing controversial way it seeds players. 1B.

■ Life: Disney dumping music videos

Pulling the plug on the TV launch pad for young pop stars sparks many in music industry. 9B.

By John O. Buckley

Get breaking news updated 24 hours a day, 7 days a week. Visit us on the web at .com www.usatoday.com

---

USA TODAY Snapshots®

Net spurs trademark rush

The number of applications for trademark registration increased nearly 213% from 1990 to 2000. Much of the jump was because of the sharp rise in the popularity of the Internet and efforts to register domain names and Web sites. Trademark applications in the USA:

1990 — 120,000
1995 — 175,000
2000 — 375,000

COPYRIGHT 2001 USA TODAY, a division of Gannett Co., Inc.

McVeigh execution

The Memorial: Tourists Joel and Carin Key of Marlow, Okla., look at photographs of the victims of the bombing at the Oklahoma City National Memorial Center.

Bomber dies by injection

Bush says McVeigh 'met the fate he chose for himself 6 years ago'

"I am the master of my fate,
I am the captain of my soul."
— Timothy McVeigh, quoting an 1875 poem

Survivors, relatives of victims saw his glare from a distance

"I think I did see the face of evil today."
— Kathy Wilburn, whose grandsons Chase Smith, 3, and brother Colton, 2, died in the bombing.

By Kevin Johnson
USA TODAY

TERRE HAUTE, Ind. — Timothy McVeigh, defiant to the end, was executed by lethal injection Monday for the 1995 bombing of the Alfred P. Murrah federal building in Oklahoma City that killed 168 people.

Strapped to a gurney and wearing a white tee-shirt, khaki pants and slip-on sneakers, McVeigh was officially pronounced dead at 7:14 a.m. local time (8:14 a.m. ET), four minutes after he was injected with the first of three lethal drugs.

Displaying no emotion, McVeigh, the worst mass murderer in U.S. history, stared straight at the ceiling as his eyes rolled back slightly and his breathing stopped.

The 33-year-old Gulf War veteran was the first federal inmate executed in 38 years.

In Washington, President Bush declared that McVeigh had "met the fate he chose for himself six years ago." He added: "For the survivors of the crime, and for the families of the dead, the pain goes on." Final punishment of the crime cannot diminish the enormity of the nocence of those who died.

Described by officials here at the U.S. Penitentiary as calm and cooperative in his last hours, McVeigh declined to make a final oral statement or to speak to any of the witnesses. Instead, he issued a written statement that consisted entirely of the 1875 poem Invictus, that includes the phrase "My head is bloody, but unbowed." The 16-line poem, written by William Ernest Henley, ends with the words: "I am the master of my fate; I am the captain of my soul."

The statement, handwritten and signed on a single sheet, reflected the importance of maintaining the defiance he has displayed since his arrest within hours of blowing up the Oklahoma City federal building on April 19, 1995. Nineteen of the 168 people killed were children.

By Kelly Kurt
The Associated Press

OKLAHOMA CITY — Bombing survivors and relatives who watched the closed-circuit telecast of Timothy McVeigh's execution said he stared into the camera as if he was glaring at them.

The telecast was shown to 232 survivors and family members at the Federal Transfer Center, where a wide-screen television and smaller sets were set up.

In the death chamber at the federal prison in Terre Haute, Ind., the camera was installed overhead, and before his death McVeigh stared straight up, seeming to concentrate on it.

Karen Jones, whose 46-year-old husband, Larry, was killed in the bombing, said McVeigh "just gave us that same glare that makes me think he got what he wanted. I was thinking he was really scared and he was really evil." Jones said she heard a few people clap after he was over and a few cried. "I just took a deep breath," Jones said. "It seemed like forever."

At the site of the bombing, now a memorial, no official announcement of McVeigh's death was made. People heard it from radio or gathered around a small battery-powered television.

Janice Smith, whose brother Lanny Scroggins died, prayed with her children and said, "It's over. We don't have to continue with him anymore."

Renee Findley, whose friend 41-year-old Teresa Lauderdale was killed, stood at the memorial with Lauderdale's parents, John and Chris Taylor. "There's some relief, but it really doesn't change anything," Findley said. "It still hurts."

At an exhibit at the memorial's museum, a new plaque was installed that read: "McVeigh is executed by lethal injection on June 11, 2001, at the federal Penitentiary in Terre Haute, Ind."

Earlier, a silent vigil began without fanfare — 168 minutes, one minute for each victim. Lynne Gist, whose 32-year-old sister, Karen Gist Carr, died, broke into sobs as she knelt at the memorial.

Attorney General John Ashcroft, who authorized the closed-circuit telecast, was in Oklahoma City when McVeigh was put to death but did not watch the telecast. Kathy Dutton, who lost a nephew in the bombing, said Ashcroft spoke for five minutes and apologized for the delay in the execution. Ashcroft postponed the execution date of May 16 after the FBI discovered 4,000 pages of documents it had failed to give McVeigh's lawyers.

Cover story

The writer was one of 10 news media representatives who witnessed Timothy McVeigh's execution.

Please see COVER STORY next page ►

Court opens schools to religious groups

Ruling provides use after hours

By Joan Biskupic
USA TODAY

WASHINGTON — Public school districts cannot refuse to let Bible groups use classrooms to teach children after hours because of fears of mixing church and state, the Supreme Court ruled Monday. The 6-3 decision could broadly open school facilities to religious organizations nationwide.

Thomas: Wrote opinion

With Justice Clarence Thomas and the conservative justices taking the lead, the court said the Milford, N.Y., school district violated the free speech rights of the Good News Club when it excluded it from groups that could meet in school premises.

The Club, which is an evangelical group with chapters across the USA, has been involved in numerous lawsuits over access to school grounds. "The Good News Club seeks nothing more than to be treated neutrally and given access to speak about the same topics as are other groups," Justice Clarence Thomas wrote for the court. He emphasized teachings on morality and ministry any chance the children, ages 6 to 12, could be "coerced into participating. He said the club focused on moral and character development and its religious nature was essentially inconsequential.

Dissenting justices insisted school districts should be able to exclude groups that proselytize religion or offer — as Justice David Souter called it — "an evangelical service of worship calling children to commit themselves in an act of Christian conversion." Justices John Paul Stevens and Ruth Bader Ginsburg also dissented.

"I think this will have a tremendous impact . . . ," says Thomas Marcelle, who represented the Good News Club. "There are courts that have said schools don't have to allow in groups that pray. But Justice Thomas's opinion pasted with a very broad brush. You can't discriminate against religious speakers."

Benjamin Ferrara, who represents the Milford school district in upstate New York, said officials were looking at how the ruling would affect not only school-use bans on religious groups but also political ones. "The fear that most of our superintendents have is, 'Do you have to allow the Nazi Club or the Ku Klux Klan?'" he said.

► Heat-sensing searches, 4A

Job market so ugly, many grads just give up

By Stephanie Armour
USA TODAY

Graduating college students are experiencing firsthand just how dramatically the job market has soured.

Employment offers are being rescinded, job hunts are taking months — even for graduates with advanced degrees — and competition is so fierce some students are dropping their searches. Instead they're enrolling in graduate school, traveling or trying second-choice jobs or non-profit work.

"I'd tried to find work in the U.S., and I couldn't," says Kate Hallman, 21, who graduated from Wesleyan University in Middleton, Conn.

Signs of the shift abound. About 65% of students who expect to work after graduation already have positions by graduation day, according to a May study by career site CollegeGrad.com. That means many are still are looking or setting other goals — in fact, 18% plan to attend grad school full time. About 9% say companies have postponed or withdrawn job offers that were made to students, according to a poll by The Empower Group, a New York-based provider of talent acquisition consulting.

How students are coping:
► Considering alternative jobs. Career counselors say more students who can't get the positions they want are taking part-time jobs, turning to agency work or accepting internships.

► Delaying career decisions. Travel is in style. Just 7% of freshmen in 1997 planned to take time off to travel or relax, according to a study by Milwaukee-based insurance firm Northwestern Mutual. Polled again as seniors, that number jumped to 14% this year.

► Staying in school. The number of students registering to take the Graduate Management Admission Test, which is required of business school applicants, has been increasing since the start of this year.

"The last couple of years, kids have been coasting. It's like 'You're breathing, you're hired,'" says Michael Sciola, director of the career resource center at Wesleyan University. "Now the class of 2001 and 2002 is getting a wake-up call."

Platinum, Gold, Silver or Standard, they're all calling cards.
See our ad on the back page of the Sports Section for details.

AT&T BOUNDLESS

Figure 2

Figure 3

THE DAILY YOMIURI

No. 18191   日刊 THE DAILY YOMIURI (2001)   **FRIDAY, APRIL 6, 2001**   PRICE ¥120 (¥2,650 a month)—tax included   (D)

Through Asian Eyes

Blind girl top grad
Plus Thais debate euthanasia, and more, Pages 10,11

World
4 Journalists at NTV resisting takeover bid

Sports
21 Arsenal, Leeds earn 1st-leg wins

Dow surges on Dell report

NEW YORK (AP)—U.S. stock prices shot up in early trading Thursday after Dell Computer and Alcoa gave Wall Street its first really good earnings news in months. The Dow Jones industrials surged more than 300 points.

In the first hour of trading on Wall Street, the Dow rose as much as 304 points before falling back slightly. It was up 260.59 at 9,775.61.

The Nasdaq composite index rose 88.67 to 1,727.47, while the Standard & Poor's 500 climbed 28.86 to 1,132.11.

After months of battering from a series of gloomy quarterly earnings reports, Wall Street found cheer in news from Dell and Alcoa.

Dell, considered one of the bellwethers of the high-tech sector, rose $2.56 to $24.75. The nation's top producer of desktop and laptop computers said it will not lower its targets for its fiscal first-quarter, which ends May 4. It still expects to earn about $8 billion, or 17 cents a share.

On Wednesday, Wall Street struggled to recover from its latest earnings-driven sell-off, but investors' nerves and a lack of conviction stifled several attempts at a rally.

Technology selling sent the Nasdaq composite index down 34.20 to 1,638.80, a 2 percent loss, keeping it at levels not seen since October 1998. The Standard & Poor's 500 index fell 3.21 to 1,103.25.

The Dow Jones industrial average closed up 29.71, or 0.3 percent, at 9,515.42.

■ Related story   Page 14

Doctor No
Boston Red Sox pitcher Hideo Nomo, center, celebrates his no-hitter against the Baltimore Orioles with teammates Brian Daubach, left, and catcher Jason Varitek on Wednesday at Baltimore's Camden Yards. Nomo, who struck out 11 and walked three, became the fourth major league pitcher to toss a "no-no" in each league. (Story on Page 24)

[handwritten: Module 2]

45 local chapters of LDP mulling preliminary poll

Outcome likely to affect result of final vote

Yomiuri Shimbun

Forty-five out of 47 Liberal Democratic Party prefectural chapters have decided on or are at least considering the staging of preliminary elections for the party presidential election, a Yomiuri Shimbun survey revealed Thursday.

The outcome of the preliminary elections at the LDP local chapters will be cited, confirmed and cast. Any vote before the presidential election slated for April 24. It is highly likely that the results in the preliminary elections will influence the voting behavior of LDP lawmakers in the presidential election, political analysts said. Therefore, LDP factions fielding their own candidates will need to channel their efforts into winning the preliminary elections, they said.

A candidate who loses in the preliminaries will not have the mandate of the party members to become president, said a senior member of the LDP faction led by Prime Minister Yoshiro Mori.

On Thursday, Kazuo Tanikawa, head of an LDP presidential election administration office said that the panel had decided to hold the party presidential election on April 24.

According to the Yomiuri Shimbun sur-

[handwritten: Module]

vey, 32 LDP prefectural chapters, including Tokyo and Kanagawa Prefecture, said they had decided to carry out preliminary elections. Thirteen local chapters, including Akita and Ibaraki prefectures said they are considering the holding of preliminary elections.

The LDP's Okayama and Hiroshima prefectural chapters said they will not conduct preliminary elections.

Asked how votes cast in the preliminary elections should be reflected in votes for the presidential election on April 24, 18 LDP local chapters said they will cast all their votes allocated to each local chapter according to the winner of their preliminary election. Nine chapters said they have decided to use the proportional representation system to reflect the results of the preliminary elections.

The LDP is currently considering revising its party regulations on the presidential election to increase the number of votes for each local chapter from one to three, bringing the total number of local chapter votes to 141.

A total of 346 LDP lawmakers will participate in the presidential election, along with representatives of the party's 47 prefectural chapters.

On the instructions of Mori, the LDP plans to hold the presidential election in an open manner. Kanagawa prefectural chapter decided in mid-March to conduct a preliminary election. The move was quickly followed by other chapters this month.

Many LDP members said the outcome

of the elections will affect the actual presidential election.

"If a candidate (for the presidential election) is declared winner in the preliminary elections, it's possible that other candidates may bow out of the April 24 election," said a senior member of the Mori faction, which is backing faction leader Junichiro Koizumi, former health and welfare minister, in the party presidential election.

In the preliminary elections, Koizumi will definitely garner the support of a large number of LDP members," another senior member of the Mori faction said.

"We can expect many of those who don't have clear voting intentions to vote for our candidate," a junior LDP member said.

It is very unusual for the LDP to hold preliminary elections. In fact, they have only taken place twice in the past.

In November 1978, former Prime Minister Masayoshi Ohira defeated former Prime Minister Takeo Fukuda in the preliminary election to become the LDP president.

In a preliminary election in November 1982, former Prime Minister Yasuhiro Nakasone beat former International Trade and Industry Minister Toshio Komoto.

In both cases, the outcome of the preliminary election greatly affected the result of the presidential election as the runner-up and the other candidates in the preliminary elections withdrew from running in the actual race.

■ *Far from unified*   Page 3

Chinese gangsters said using new hallucinogen

'Shaking-head' drug behind serious crimes, investigators say

Yomiuri Shimbun

Tokyo-based Chinese crime syndicates are increasingly abusing and trafficking in a new synthetic hallucinogen called yaotou (shaking head) in Chinese, according to the Metropolitan Police Department.

Police said they have already uncovered several cases of yaotou possession and abuse among syndicate members, most of whom reportedly are illegal residents, police said.

Early this year, the MPD raided a Chinese restaurant in the Kabukicho entertainment district of Shinjuku, Tokyo, in July last year, a Chinese man, later found to be a syndicate member, was found shot and seriously injured on a street in northern Tokyo, the apparent victim of a mental aberration induced by yaotou, police said.

The MPD is said to be taking stringent precautions to prevent problems attributable to drug-addled gangsters from spilling over to involve the general public.

"The drug is likely to induce excessive excitement in users, allowing even seemingly trivial quarrels to evolve into serious crimes," an MPD official said. "As many of the syndicate members are armed with handguns or knives, there is a possibility that the general public could fall victim to Chinese gang-related conflicts."

On the morning of July 22 last year, a man was found, covered with blood, lying on a street in Kita Ward, Tokyo. He apparently had suffered multiple gunshot wounds in the chest and other areas.

Police later identified the man as a 29-year-old crime syndicate member from Fujian Province, China.

In the early hours of the day, he reportedly took part in a yaotou party at a bar in Edogawa Ward, Tokyo, run by an individual originally from Taiwan.

While he was singing karaoke he increasingly felt under the influence of the

drug and got involved in a quarrel with another Chinese, who eventually shot him.

The man was reportedly dumped near a hospital.

On Jan. 11 this year, the MPD's special international organized crime squad raided the Yora Shanghai, a Chinese restaurant in the Kabukicho district of Shinjuku on suspicion that it was violating laws including the Immigration Control Refugee Recognition Law.

The squad found 66 yaotou tablets in the restaurant and arrested the manager and six others, police said.

The pink pills were seven millimeters in diameter and five millimeters thick. Analysis also detected in the pills traces of the synthetic narcotic commonly known as ecstasy, which is consider a strong hallucinogen, the said.

According to the MPD, several years ago, Chinese illegal residents started making yaotou tablets fashionable at privately reserved places and bars after midnight in such Tokyo entertainment areas as Kabukicho.

Groups of Chinese, apparently under the influence of yaotou, have been witnessed dancing, while violently shaking their heads, to loud music with a heavy beat in darkened discos. Some such parties were said to be in an added state of consciousness.

MPD investigators on a stakeout also reportedly witnessed Yora Shanghai staff members distributing yaotou at the party venues and Chinese men entering the restaurant to purchase the drug, leading the MPD to suspect that the restaurant was a yaotou trafficking center.

Further investigations led to the February arrest of a 36-year-old Malaysian man of Chinese descent working at another restaurant in Shinjuku Ward, who was found in possession of 500 yaotou pills, according to the MPD.

Police did not accept the man's explanation that an acquaintance had asked him to receive mail from Malaysia. Instead they suspect him to be a member of a Chinese drug-smuggling ring.

Last year alone, a total of 12,631 yaotou and ecstasy tablets were confiscated in a 9,000-pill increase from the previous year, marking a record high, police said.

[handwritten: Module 3]

U.S. offers chorus of regrets but no apologies to China

WASHINGTON (AP)—The administration of U.S. President George W. Bush offered Beijing a chorus of regrets but no apology for the collision between a U.S. spy plane and a Chinese policy team debated whether he needed to make a personal statement similar to Powell's, but there were no plans for one as of Wednesday afternoon.

Despite the signs of progress, both sides held publicly to contradictory positions: China called itself the "injured party" and blamed the United States for the crash while the White House called it an accident and Pentagone jet fighter. China, still detaining 24 U.S. crew members, said it was a stop in the right direction, and signs that both sides wanted a face-saving resolution.

Bush, who spoke briefly about the collision during a ceremony in the Rose Garden.

"We regret the loss of life of that Chinese pilot but now we need to move on," Secretary of State Colin Powell said. "We need to bring this to a resolution, and we're using every avenue available to us to talk to the Chinese side to exchange explanations and move on."

White House press secretary Ari Fleischer echoed Powell's remarks, saying, "We have expressed our concern and our regrets about that incident," but he declared China's demand for an apology. In China, a similar regrets-but-no-apology formulation was offered to the nation's foreign minister by the U.S. ambassador.

"The United States doesn't understand the reason for an apology," Fleischer said. "Our airplanes are operating in international airspace, and the United States did nothing wrong."

An apology would imply wrongdoing by the United States, officials said, something Bush has not been willing to concede.

A senior State Department official said Powell sent a letter to Chinese Deputy Prime Minister Qian Qichen stressing the importance the United States attaches to the release of the 24 U.S. citizens.

Powell handed the letter to Chinese Ambassador Yang Jiechi for transmittal to Qian Powell told Yang the United States would fall access to the crew and also emphasized the need to resolve the issue, the official said, asking not to be identified. Delivering the message was Deputy Secretary of State Richard Armitage.

Powell is a little-noticed comment, had said Tuesday that the crash was "fatal for the pilot of the Chinese plane and I regret that."

But the remarks Wednesday were the administration's most emphatic expressions of sympathy, designed to cut the course for a middle ground that could lead to Beijing's release and allow both sides to escape dangerous diplomatic territory.

Since the first day of the standoff, the president has steadily increased the rhetorical pressure on the Chinese while leaving room for a diplomatic settlement. Bush and his foreign officials said the Chinese

This satellite image shows the Linghui military airfield on Hainan Island on Wednesday where the U.S. spy plane was forced to land.

pilots buzzed the lumbering spy plane.

The Washington Post reported from Beijing Thursday that the crash occurred after a Chinese F-8 interceptor started to fly directly below the surveillance plane and the U.S. aircraft executed a banking maneuver off to the left.

■ Related stories   Page 5, 6, 15

[handwritten: Module 4]

Ruling partners to seek pact with new LDP leader

Yomiuri Shimbun

New Komeito and Hoshuto (New Conservative Party)—the Liberal Democratic Party's ruling coalition partners—plan to seek a new policy agreement with the LDP's new leader, who is to be selected in the upcoming party presidential election, party officials said Thursday.

The two parties are considering the inclusion in such a new policy agreement of such objectives as administrative reform and employment measures, based on the policy agreement reached by the LDP, Jiyuto (Liberal Party) and New Komeito in October 1999 under the cabinet led by former Prime Minister Keizo Obuchi, the officials said.

A new policy agreement is expected to create a framework for the coalition's election scheduled for the summer.

The policy proposals being considered by New Komeito and Hoshuto may also have an impact on LDP candidates running in the presidential election, scheduled for April 24, when they formulate their proposed policies for a new cabinet.

At New Komeito's standing committee meeting on Thursday, Tetsuzo Fuyushiba, secretary general of the party, referred to the policy agreement being sought with a new LDP president. "We have to reach a policy agreement with the LDP president selected in the forthcoming election before the new party president is appointed prime minister," he said.

[handwritten: Module 5]

[handwritten: Module 6]

Exchange Rates
Thurs. 5 p.m.   Wed. 5 p.m.
S=¥124.17-20   S=¥125.01-04
C=¥112.20-25   C=¥112.66-70
TOPIX Close:
1,317.83 +13.46

Weather
Tokyo — Fair, later cloudy
Osaka — Fair, later cloudy

Daily Yomiuri home page: http://www.yomiuri.co.jp/daily   e-mail: dy@yominet.ne.jp   Customer Service: delivery@yominet.ne.jp

editorial, commentary **6,7**   *stocks* **16,17**   *magazines* **18,19**   *TV & radio* **20**

Figure 4

A MEMBER OF THE LIBERTY TIMES GROUP

TAIPEI 台北 TIMES

INSIDE

GETTING A BUZZ
Taiwanese are gradually realizing the high social and medical risks of chewing betel nut.
Features, p11

SAD FAREWELL
The revered author and publisher of Taiwan's 38-year-old 'Biographical Literature' magazine eulogized yesterday in Taipei.
Taiwan, p2

INTERNET EXCITEMENT
Hong Kongers stood for hours in pouring rain for a chance to get their hands on shares in new Web start-up TOM.COM.
Business, p21

Weather

US lawmakers shred Clinton policy

CHINA THREAT: Beijing's statement in a white paper that it will pursue reunification by force if Taiwan procrastinates over negotiations reveals the folly of hopes of 'strategic engagement,' US lawmakers say

Foreign ministry says it agrees with US position

US TIES: Washington's response to the white paper — that it wants a peaceful resolution of the cross-strait issue — is what Taiwan wants too, the government says

Module 1 *Module 2*

> **The White House is using strong words to pre-empt any possible military actions from China. If [the white paper] reminds Washington of 1996.**
> — Joseph Wu, analyst of Chengchi University

At a meeting of the KMT's central standing committee yesterday, President Lee Teng-hui tells reporters not to speculate on the recent police raid on former Legislative Yuan speaker Liu Sung-fan's house. He also gave an explicit "no comment" on China's white paper.

Taipei Times wins one of world's top design awards

Module 3 *Module 4*

Air spat flares up again

Figure 5

Snake Designs(Improper)

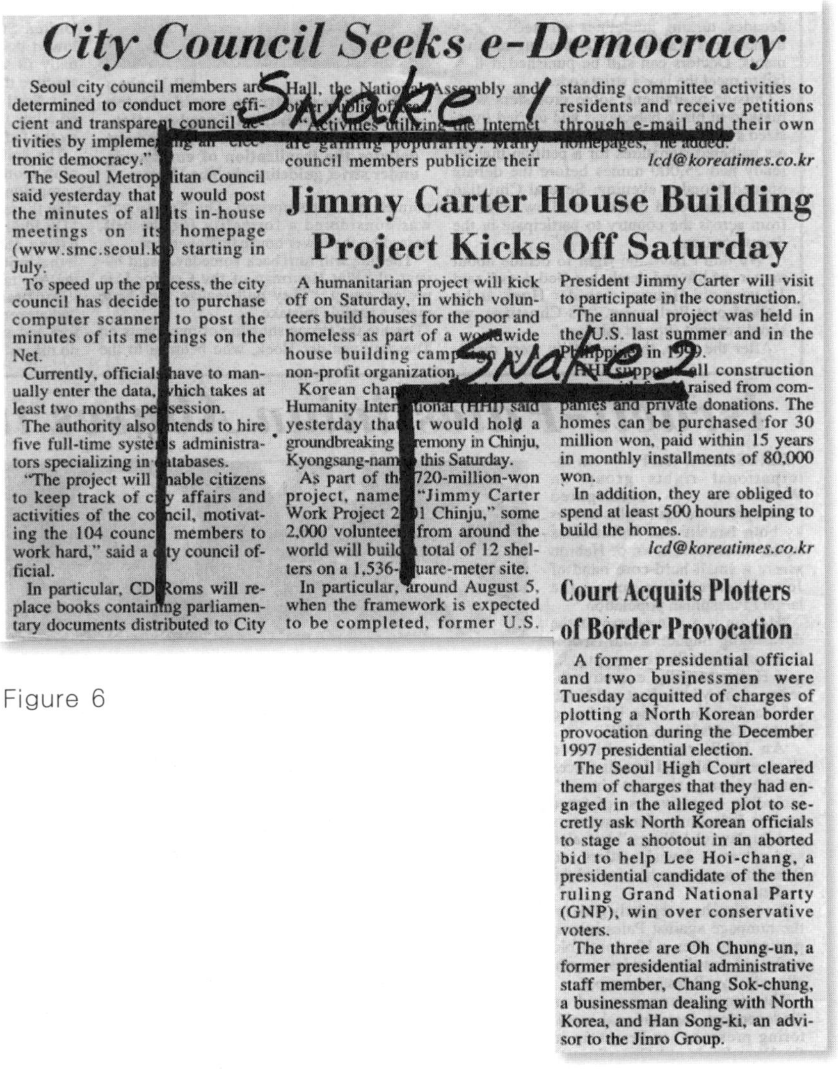

City Council Seeks e-Democracy

Seoul city council members are determined to conduct more efficient and transparent council activities by implementing an electronic democracy."

The Seoul Metropolitan Council said yesterday that it would post the minutes of all its in-house meetings on its homepage (www.smc.seoul.k) starting in July.

To speed up the process, the city council has decided to purchase computer scanner to post the minutes of its meetings on the Net.

Currently, officials have to manually enter the data, which takes at least two months per session.

The authority also intends to hire five full-time systems administrators specializing in databases.

"The project will enable citizens to keep track of city affairs and activities of the council, motivating the 104 council members to work hard," said a city council official.

In particular, CD Roms will replace books containing parliamentary documents distributed to City

Hall, the National Assembly and other public offices.

"Activities utilizing the Internet are gaining popularity. Many council members publicize their

standing committee activities to residents and receive petitions through e-mail and their own homepages, he added.

lcd@koreatimes.co.kr

Jimmy Carter House Building Project Kicks Off Saturday

A humanitarian project will kick off on Saturday, in which volunteers build houses for the poor and homeless as part of a worldwide house building campaign by a non-profit organization.

Korean chapter of Humanity International (HHI) said yesterday that it would hold a groundbreaking ceremony in Chinju, Kyongsang-namdo this Saturday.

As part of the 720-million-won project, named "Jimmy Carter Work Project 2 1 Chinju," some 2,000 volunteers from around the world will build a total of 12 shelters on a 1,536-square-meter site.

In particular, around August 5, when the framework is expected to be completed, former U.S.

President Jimmy Carter will visit to participate in the construction.

The annual project was held in the U.S. last summer and in the Philippines in 1999.

HHI supports all construction costs raised from companies and private donations. The homes can be purchased for 30 million won, paid within 15 years in monthly installments of 80,000 won.

In addition, they are obliged to spend at least 500 hours helping to build the homes.

lcd@koreatimes.co.kr

Court Acquits Plotters of Border Provocation

A former presidential official and two businessmen were Tuesday acquitted of charges of plotting a North Korean border provocation during the December 1997 presidential election.

The Seoul High Court cleared them of charges that they had engaged in the alleged plot to secretly ask North Korean officials to stage a shootout in an aborted bid to help Lee Hoi-chang, a presidential candidate of the then ruling Grand National Party (GNP), win over conservative voters.

The three are Oh Chung-un, a former presidential administrative staff member, Chang Sok-chung, a businessman dealing with North Korea, and Han Song-ki, an advisor to the Jinro Group.

Figure 6

Anti-Money Laundering Law to Regulate Political Fund

The rival parties yesterday agreed to submit two anti-money laundering bills to the National Assembly, the paving the way to regulate, among others, illegal political fund

The ruling Millennium Democratic Party (MDP) and the main opposition Grand National Party (GNP) reached a last-minute agreement on the new bills on the last day of the extraordinary session of the National Assembly.

However, they decided not to pass the bill at yeserday's Assembly session because they felt it is necessary to put the finishing touches to the agreed-upon law bills.

So far, the two parties faced mounting public criticism for excluding political funds from the anti-money laundry bills.

If the laws are passed proba-bly late this month, Korean people make found guilty of laundering political funds will face up to five years in prison or a fine of up to 30 million won.

The two rival parties also agreed to punish income and value added tax evaders under the new laws.

With the passage of the bills at the assembly, the new laws will take effect in three months.

ssj@koreatimes.co.kr

NK Stresses Independent Resolution

North Korea said yesterday that Korean reunification must be achieved through inter-Korean co-operation before "alliances with outer forces," a commentary indirectly referring to the South Korea-U.S. summit.

"South Korea will become unreliable if it continues to cooperate with foreign forces, the prime mover of the Korean division and confrontation, while speaking words of reconciliation and reunification," Radio Pyongyang said.

Although Pyongyang has issued no official comment on the summit in Washington between President Kim Dae-jung and U.S. President George Bush, the phrase, "alliances with outer forces," coming while Kim is still meeting U.S. officials, seems a clear reference to the United States.

"Inter-Korean cooperation and the alliance with foreign forces are incompatible," Pyongyang Radio said, adding that, "challenging 'the foreign forces' is the only way to promote reconciliation and reunification."

Figure 7

Charity Fundraising Falls Amid Economic Slump

The recent economic recession has forced companies to tighten their purse strings this year, resulting in a major for the needy.

As of Tuesday, companies contributed a total of 11 billion won during a fundraising event held from Dec. 31, said the Community Chest of Korea (CCK), a social welfare organization, yesterday. A with the Ministry of Health and Welfare, CCK con-Dec. 31 to Jan. 31. every year.

Only five companies have contributed amounts of more than 100 million won, a CCK official said. Samsung donated the most money with 10 billion won, Lotte next with 500 million, and Korea Yogurt and Nongshim each with 100 million won.

The figure is significantly lower last year's, when 23 companies donated a total of 15.6 billion won, the official said. Among the contributions, Samsung again donated 10 billion won, while Hyundai gave 5.5 billion, H&CB 1 billion, and LG and SK each donated 500 million won.

Donation by ARS (Tel: 700-1212) also decreased to 1.04 billion won, compared to 2.17 billion won a year earlier.

When adding individual contributions, the total amount of money collected so far is reported at 28.3 billion won, up one percent from the figure raised over the same period last year. But donations are cited to fall well short of the 42.7 billion won the ministry is aiming to collect during the campaign, when considering the economic slump as well as the lunar New Year's holidays that are included in the fundraising period.

"Our overall figures have been disappointing due to the sharp decrease of long-time contributions from major companies," said a Health-Welfare ministry official.

But he added that individual contributions in the Seoul area have increased, to 780 million won from 350 million won of last year.

jysoh@koreatimes.co.kr

Descriptions of 285 Korean Dishes Available in 6 Different Languages

Foreigners will be able to order food in local restaurants more easily from now on, as Seoul City has completed a database program that provides descriptions of various dishes in foreign languages.

The program will offer descriptions of 285 different kinds of Korean and other dishes in six languages; Korean, English, Japanese, Chinese, French and Spanish.

"We planned the program to offer better service to the increasing number of foreigners who will visit Korea for the 'Visit Korea Year 2001' as well as the 2002 World Cup games," said a Seoul City official. It was developed by a university-based team, led by Professor Chang Nam-soo of the Department of Foods and Nutrition at Ewha Womans University.

The main ingredients, characteristics, origin, amount of calories as well as photos of the dishes are included in the database, and will be distributed to restaurants and related government ministries in form of CD-ROMs. Citizens can also view the material by visiting .

Seoul city is also planning to make booklets containing information on 30 to 40 Korean traditional dishes that are popular with foreigners and distribute them to various traditional restaurants.

"Owners of small restaurants were reluctant to make separate menus for foreigners, as they had to pay additional fees. But thanks to this new program, the tedious task of manufacturing menus in foreign languages will become much easier," said a Seoul City official.

Figure 8

Courtesy of The Korea Times, Financial Times, Taipei Times, The Daily Yomiuri, USA Today.

계율 2: 헤드라인 충돌 회피

같은 면에서 인접하는 2개의 기사를 편집할 때 헤드라인이 서로 맞붙는(Butting Headlines) 경우가 있는데 헤드라인이 맞부딪히는 것을 금지하는 것이 오랫동안 미국에서 지켜지고 있는 제1의 신문디자인 원칙이다.

Figure 9와 Figure 10에서 보는 바와 같이 헤드라인이 충돌할 경우 시각적으로 볼품이 없고 조잡스럽다.

특히 활자체의 크기와 모양이 비슷하면 독자들이 다른 기사임에도 불구하고 순간적으로 충돌하는 2개의 헤드라인을 한 개로 착각해 연속적으로 읽을 수가 있다.

Petition Calls for Refugee Status for N. Koreans Who Fled to China

UNITED NATIONS — South Korean activists have submitted to U.N. officials a petition signed by 11.8 million people calling for refugee status for North Koreans who have fled to China.

The Commission to Help North Korean Refugees launched the campaign in 1999 to pressure China to grant the status to the North Koreans, which would bring them closer to receiving U.N.-supplied food and shelter.

Gillian Sorenson, assistant secretary-general of U.N. external relations, and Nicolas Bwakira of the United Nations High Commissioner for Refugees accepted the petition Wednesday at the United Nations in New York.

Kim Sang-chul, the activist group's chief, has said all but 120,000 signatures the group collected are from South Koreans.

Bwakira said the flood of names sent a strong message on the issue. The UNHCR, which just opened an office in Seoul, the South Korean capital, would do all it could to help the North Koreans in China, he said.

A large number of North Koreans have fled their famine-stricken communist homeland in recent years to northern China. Estimates of their numbers range from several thousand to a few hundred thousand.

Beijing maintains that North Koreans in its territory are not refugees under the U.N. definition because they crossed the border for economic motives, not political reasons.

South Korean activists, however, believe the refugees should be classified as political refugees because they would be subject to political persecution if they were deported to the North.

China is required by treaty with Pyongyang to return all North Koreans who cross the border into its territory.

(AP)

Japan Activists Visit for Joint Strategy on US Bases

A 14-member civic group delegation from the Japanese prefecture of Kanagawa arrived in Seoul yesterday to learn how residents in Maehyang-ri are dealing with damage from a U.S. bombing range near their village, a Korean civic organization said.

The Japanese delegates, who are pushing to close U.S. military bases in their prefecture, toured Maehyang-ri, some 100km south of Seoul, and the nearby cities of Pyongtaek and Osan, which also house U.S. bases, the National Alliance for Democracy and Reunification of Korea (NADRK) said.

The delegation also met with Lee Suk-tae, the lawyer handling Maehyang-ri residents' suit against the Korean government and United States Forces Korea (USFK).

Today they will watch bombing drills by U.S. military planes at Koon-ni range in Maehyang-ri. They will also attend events in Kwangju to commemorate the May 18, 1980 Kwangju uprising and visit the cemetery for the victims of the democratization movement there Sunday.

The delegation includes a lawyer and plaintiffs in Atsuki who filed a lawsuit against the U.S. bases there, a NADRK official said.

The Japanese prefecture contains the headquarters of the U.S Fifth Fleet's submarine forces in Yokosuka and the U.N. Command in Zama.

Like Maehyang-ri residents, Atsuki citizens frequently complain about noise pollution caused by U.S. military aircraft conducting night exercises at the base near their homes.

Figure 9

Int'l Ranking of Korean Firms Falls

By Kim Sung-jin
Staff Reporter

The international status of Korean companies is sharply declining, according to the Financial Times.

According to FT 500 Global Ranking, only four Korean companies ranked within the top 500 corporations worldwide in terms of market capitalization, compared with five last year.

The four domestic companies were Samsung Electronics Co. (SEC), SK Telecom, Korea Telecom, and Korea Electric Power Corporation (KEPCO). POSCO (Pohang Iron and Steel Co.), which ranked 461 last year, failed to make the list.

General Electric topped the ranking as the world's most valuable company with $477.4 billion in capital. IT network supplier Cisco Systems chased right behind with $304.6 billion. It was found that the "old economy" conglomerates showed superiority and the technology sector went bearish.

All Korean companies saw rankings fall by enormous numbers.

SEC's total market price was evaluated at 23.4 billion dropping 79 places to 225th, from 146th one year ago. SK also stepped down 53 rankings to number 270.

Korea Telecom sagged enormously by 182 ranks to 297th. KEPCO also fell 133 places to rank 403rd.

Four Korean companies' total market capitalization snapshot, taken at Jan. 4, was $74.4 billion. Korea ranked 16th in the country ranking.

Moreover, Korean corporations made very poor showing in Asia regional corporate ranking. Japan excluded, only 7 Korean companies were included among top 100 companies.

The rankers included above four companies plus POSCO ranking 45th, Kookmin bank 71st, and Housing and Commercial bank ranking the foot.

In the ranking, 239 American companies occupied the seats with Japanese companies following behind seizing 64 places. Japan was the only Asian nation that was included among top 10 countries.

A total of 25 Asian companies were included in the ranking. Regarding the gravity that Asian companies have in the world market, Asian companies evaluations came out to be very poor.

It was found that investors worldwide are favoring "old economy" companies over technology-based companies. GE, which ranked second, defeated by Microsoft, last year, won the crown this year and Exxon Mobil ranked third, stepping up four places with the help of high crude oil prices.

On the other hand, IT companies showed a downward trend with Amazon.com and eBay falling off the list. Softbank was the most declined company falling to number 447 from 44th last year.

Pharmaceutical companies showed an upward tendency with Pfizer and Merck coming 4th and 13th relatively.

sjkim@koreatimes.co.kr

Lee Kun-hee Most Admired CEO

Samsung chairman Lee Kun-hee has been surveyed to be the most admired and respected among chief executive officers of top Korean conglomerates.

According to the survey conducted by P&P Research, Lee came in with a score of 93.93 points out of a possible 100, followed by SK chairman Sohn Kil-seung and Yoo Sang-boo, chairman of POSCO (Pohang Iron and Steel Co.).

Also popular among the Korean public was LG chairman Koo Bon-moo and Lotte chairman Shin Kyuk-ho, both of whom registered more than 90 points, P&P Research officials said.

The others rounding out the top 10 conglomerates in terms of assets were Hyundai Motor chairman Chung Mong-koo, Hanwha chairman Kim Seung-yeon, Hyundai chairman Chung Mong-hun, honorary Hanjin chairman Cho Choong-hoon and Kumho chairman Park Jeong-koo.

The survey was based on responses from 1,212 men and women aged above 20 on the morality, social contribution, role in economic development and corporate transparency of the CEOs of the top 10 Korean conglomerates.

Asked about what the most important credos of top CEOs are, 28.7 percent of the respondents picked corporate transparency, 27.6 percent reasonable mentality, 22.9 percent leadership and 11.6 percent effective risk management.

Figure 10

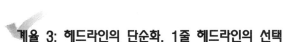

계율 3: 헤드라인의 단순화, 1줄 헤드라인의 선택

　　현대 신문디자인을 할 때 단순, 명료한 형태로 가고 있어 헤드라인에 들어가는 글자수가 적어지는 경향이다. 많은 신문들이 한 줄 헤드라인을 선호한다.

　　Figure 11에서 보는 바와 같이 한 줄 헤드라인은 독자들에게 명쾌한 느낌을 주며 신문의 가독성을 높여준다.

　　한 면에 한 줄 헤드라인이 많으면 독자들의 가독 속도를 빠르게 할 수 있다. 5～10자의 헤드라인 글자수가 가독성을 높이는데 이상적이다.

Figure 11

계율 4~5: 최적의 본문기사 길이, 최적의 칼럼 폭

신문의 크기와 레이아웃은 제2차 세계대전 기간 동안 많은 변화를 겪게 된다.

제2차 세계대전 당시의 신문들은 크기를 줄이면서 더 많은 광고와 기사를 넣기 시작했다.

전쟁 전에는 7개 칼럼이던 것이 8개로 늘어난 반면 크기는 줄어들었다.

전후에도 신문들은 8칼럼 형식을 오랫동안 유지해 왔다.

최근에는 다시 7개 칼럼을 유지하는 신문이 늘고 속지나 기획물 기사면에는 변칙 칼럼을 활용, 6~8 칼럼을 비교적 많이 쓰고 있다.

신문의 정규판(Broadsheet)인 경우 가로, 세로 56~61cm × 36cm가 한 면이라고 생각하고 편집한다면 기사의 길이와 폭이 얼마일 때 외견상 모양이 좋고 독자들에게 부담을 적게 주느냐 하는 문제가 연구자들의 관심사항]이었다.

일반적으로 본문의 최적길이는 5~25cm 이다. 30cm 이상의 긴 기사는 피해야 한다.

너무 짧은 것도 피해야 하며 2.5cm보다 짧아서는 안 된다.

변칙칼럼을 쓰더라도 한 칼럼에 들어가는 기사의 폭이 8.5cm 이상, 4cm보다 좁게 하는 것은 피하는 것이 좋다.

부득이 작은 분량의 기사라면 이탤릭체, 볼드체로 처리하여 일반본문과 차별화하는 편이 바람직하다.

계율 6: Art 사용의 확대(지면의 1/3)

현대 신문들의 특징 중 하나는 컬러 사진과 차트, 지도, 다이어그램 같은 정보그래픽을 많이 사용한다는 것이다.

이와 같은 시각물(Visuals) 등의 이용은 독자들의 시선을 집중시키고 정보를 쉽게 전달하기 위함이다.

1986년을 전후하여 많은 신문사들이 "읽는 신문"에서 "보는 신문"으

로의 시각적 개혁을 추진해 왔다. 특히 이들 시각물들을 컬러로 처리함으로써 장식적 기능과 기능적 기능을 확대해 왔다.

시각물들은 현실적으로 손이 많이 가는 작업이다. 그러나 시각물들이 없는 지면은 가라앉고 단조롭게 보인다. 전체 지면의 1/3정도는 시각물로 처리되는 것이 이상적이다.

특별히 예를 들지 않더라도 손쉽게 얻을 수 있는 신문, 잡지 등에서 확인할 수 있다.

계율 7: 지나친 컬러 사용의 삼가

신문의 컬러 사용에는 논란이 많았다. 오랫동안 보수적인 편집자들은 정규 뉴스지면은 흑백이어야 하고 컬러는 오락 같은 기사에만 맞는다고 주장해 왔다.

그러나 흑백 TV가 컬러 TV로 대체되고 모든 영상물이 컬러화 되면서 컬러의 중요성이 대두되었다.

특히 1982년에 미국의 전국지로 등장한 USA Today가 컬러 특집을 과감하게 도입하면서 컬러는 독자와 광고주 들을 유인하는 주요 디자인 기능을 하게 되었다.

그럼에도 지나친 컬러 사용은 오히려 특정 부문에 독자들의 시선을 끌어보려는 본래의 취지를 퇴색케 하고 제작비용만 높이는 결과를 초래한다.

검정과 흰색도 중요한 컬러라는 것을 잊지 말아야 한다.

컬러를 단지 그 자체만을 위해 사용하지 마라. 정보전달의 효과를 높이기 위해 의미있는 사진, 정보 그래픽 등에 사용하라.

지나친 컬러의 사용은 천박한 느낌을 주기 쉽다. 제한된 컬러를 사용하여 지면상의 균형을 잘 맞추어야 한다.

컬러의 사용은 일관성 있고 조화 있게 사용하라.

연구결과 컬러는 독자들의 시선을 면의 상단에서 하단으로 이끈다.

따라서 면의 중심부에 컬러를 사용하는 것이 독자들의 시선을 끄는데 효과가 크다.

계율 8: 요약기사, 일정표 등은 한 곳에 모아 꾸러미(Packaging)로 처리

기사의 꾸러미(Packaging)처리는 여러 가지 이점이 있다.

① 짧은 뉴스요약이나 일정표 등을 한 장소에 모아 놓으면 시각적으로 깨끗해 보인다. 만일 일일이 짧게 배열했다고 가정해 보라. 얼마나 산만하겠는가?
② 짧은 기사와 긴 기사, 주요기사와 비중이 적은 기사를 구별·처리함으로써 주요기사를 더욱 강조할 수 있다.
③ 오늘날과 같이 바쁜 시대에 살고 있는 독자들에게 호소력이 크다.

대부분의 독자들은 매일 같은 장소에서 같은 종류의 뉴스를 접하기를 원한다.

Figure 12~14에서 금융, 업계동향, 항공부문 뉴스의 기사를 꾸러미 처리함으로써 장식적이고 기능적 효과를 기대할 수 있다.

Financial Briefs

Good Morning to Launch PDA Service

Good Morning Securities today starts an online trading service "goodi mobile," accessible through personal digital assistants (PDA).
The PDA trading service will include information on securities and futures prices, security orders, account inquiries, chart analyses and money transfers.

KEB EZ Card Wins Master Card Award

The Korea Exchange Bank Credit Service announced yesterday that its EZ Card won the Best Program Award in the 2001 Master Card Asia-Pacific annual general meeting currently being held on the Gold Coast in Queensland, Australia.
A company official explained that Master Card gave high marks to the EZ Card's revolving settlement system.
The system enables members to use the card continuously just by paying back certain portions of the used money, and then automatically extends the maturity date of the remaining outstanding balance.
Korea Exchange Bank Credit Service was the first company to adopt a revolving settlement system in Korea in March 1999, and launched the EZ Card together with various benefits including discounts and free-of-charge insurance services in February this year.

Lycos-LG Card to Issue New Card in July

Lycos Korea yesterday announced it will form a business tie-up with LG Capital Service to launch the "Lycos-LG Card," which offers discount benefits to users of its online charged services, starting in July.
Lycos-LG card members will also be given various benefits to use all sorts of services from both companies, including Lycos' online entertainment content, according to an official at LG Capital.

Gov't to Select 1,000 New CPAs in 2001

The government will select 1,000 new certified public accountants (CPAs) this year, 250 more than previously announced, to meet the growing need for CPAs to secure transparency in corporate accounting practices, the Ministry of Finance and Economy said yesterday.
The measure will also help ease the manpower shortage after the recent introduction of the system in which companies are required to undergo inspections of financial statements by CPAs on a quarterly basis.

Figure 12

Business Briefs

New AGFA President

Mathias Eichhorn, 40, was appointed president and general manager of AGFA Korea yesterday.

He has worked for AGFA Industries Korea in Ansan, Kyonggi-do, as managing director and as factory manager since 1997.

A graduate of Johann Wolfgang Goethe-University in Frankfurt, he was awarded a Ph.D. in chemistry in 1990.

Mathias Eichhorn

AGFA Design Works

AGFA Korea will display from June 3-9 about 50 winners' work from the "AGFA Young Creative Contest", held in May, at the Korea Design Institute of Promotion center in Taehak-ro.

The annual, worldwide design competition was organized by the local branches of AGFA in each country. The contest aims at giving an opportunity for college students to exhibit their creative work.

AGFA Korea held the local design competition under the theme of "A Day At The Circus" and 50 works were selected as winners.

TV Decoder Chip

Conexant Systems Korea released its third-generation interactive TV decoder chip for a set-top box, the company announced yesterday.

Conexant's new decoder targets the rapidly growing personal video recorders (PVRs) market on digital pay TV networks.

According to a survey by Cahner's In-Stat Group, a market research firm, consumer interest in PVR technology is growing rapidly, with shipments of PVR-enabled set-top boxes expected to reach eight million units by 2003.

PVR allows consumers to store live television and rewind, fast-forward or pause it during playback.

According to the company, Conexant's decoder will enable users to record one TV show while watching another, or record two shows simultaneously.

Conexant Systems, a U.S.-based communications and applications company, launched its Korean arm in 1999.

CDMA Market in China

SK Telecom said yesterday it signed a $1 million contract with China Unicom to export its code division multiple access (CDMA) technological consulting services.

It said it will dispatch a technological task force to optimize China Unicom's pilot operations of the CDMA network ahead of a commercial launch scheduled at the end of this year across China.

By 2003, the second largest mobile phone operator in China has planned to deploy its CDMA network with some 50 million telephone lines.

Oil B2B Marketplace

As three big-name petrochemical companies announced business plans to launch an online oil trading service from August, fierce competition is expected among small- and medium-sized frontrunners and latecomers to take the lion's share in the business-to-business (B2B) oil e-marketplace, industry sources said yesterday.

According to the source, three major oil companies — SK Corp, LG-Caltex and Hyundai Oilbank — formed their oil B2B website, Oilchain.com, with six billion won of paid-in capital late last month.

The three oil refiners will aggressively promote computer literacy and e-commerce as keys to prosperity in the high-tech "New Economy," it said.

Figure 13

KAL Flights to Resume Normal Service Today

The flights of Korean Air will return to normal operation today as pilots ended a two-day strike Wednesday night, KAL officials said yesterday.

As of Friday, 84 percent of KAL's international flights were normalized, they said.

But Asiana Airlines, South Korea's second-largest airline, canceled a quarter of its flights on Friday after talks with union leaders failed to end a four-day-old strike.

The airline had cut back domestic flights since 2,300 employees walked off the job on Tuesday, in response to a nationwide strike by the powerful Korean Confederation of Trade Unions. Asiana's 4,500 non-union workers and 800 pilots are not taking part in the strike.

The collapse of negotiations late Thursday forced the airline to cancel 22 of its 79 scheduled international flights and 45 of its 168 domestic flights.

3 US Airlines to Offer Internet Connections

Check your e-mail. Change your hotel reservation because the plane is late. Download that last document for your presentation. Surf the Web.

Passengers of three major U.S. airlines should be able to do all that from the air beginning next year, as American, Delta and United start providing fast Internet access aboard their planes.

The three airlines announced Wednesday they are developing the system with Boeing. They eventually plan to install high-speed connections on 1,500 of their planes and sell the system to other airlines.

According to the plan, special antennas aboard the airplanes would provide connections to satellites for Internet access. Passengers would use their own computers on board and pay around $20 an hour for the hookup.

All passengers on a plane that is wired for the Internet would be able to log on, but the speed of sending and receiving would depend on the number of fellow passengers online at the same time.

The equipment will first be available to passengers on long-distance flights within the United States.

Cathay Pacific to Launch Internet Service

...thay Pacific said yesterday that it ...nication service in July.

...the Internet, includin...

Figure 14

계율 9: 1면의 기사 수는 4∼7개 정도로 구성

1면은 신문의 얼굴이다.

신문 판매대에서 시선을 끌 수 있도록 디자인 되어야 한다.

중요한 뉴스가 있는 날은 그 뉴스를 강조하고 큰 뉴스가 없는 날은 다양한 뉴스로 조화되게 제작한다.

Front Page는 독자들의 시선을 끌기 위해 보수적인 뉴스 전달요소와 마케팅요소로 조화를 이루어야 한다. 따라서 기사를 많이 넣는 것만이 좋은 것은 아니며 중요뉴스를 어떻게 효율적으로 나타내느냐가 중요하다.

분량과 다양성을 고려하여 정규 신문규격에서는 4∼7개 정도의 기사가, 타블로이드에서는 2∼4개 정도의 기사가 바람직하다.

Figure 15에서 보는 바와 같이 Financial Times는 꾸러미기사 2개를 포함하여 모두 5개의 기사 군으로 처리하고 나머지는 사진, 도표들로 채웠다. Figure 16에서 보는 바와 같이 The Korea Herald는 크고 작은 기사 6개로 처리했다.

Figure 15 Courtesy of Financial Times

The Korea Herald

www.koreaherald.com

LATE CITY EDITION ★★★

No. 14,813 THURSDAY, JUNE 14, 2001 500 won

ECONOMIC INDICATORS (June 13)

Stock index	3-year gov't bond	Dollar vs. won
+6.90	-0.03	+2.90
614.05	6.10	1,293.30

Farmers and volunteers plant rice near Seoul yesterday, as light rain in parts of the country helped to relieve a protracted drought.

More rainfall today to ease drought

By Yoo Soh-jung
Staff reporter

Many regions throughout the nation can expect rain today, but still not enough to relieve the worst drought in almost a century, meteorologists said.

Light rain will fall across the country, thanks to a trough of low atmospheric pressure, according to the Korea Meteorological Administration (KMA).

Jeju Island is expected to receive 10 to 50 mm of rain, KMA officials said.

South Jeolla and South Gyeongsang Provinces will likely have 10 to 20 mm of rain. North Jeolla, North Gyeongsang and Chungcheong regions can expect 5 to 10 mm.

Seoul, Gyeonggi and Gangwon regions will have brief light showers, KMA officials said.

Light and intermittent rain yesterday for most regions proved insufficient to relieve the drought.

Some areas in northern Gyeonggi Province and the mountainous Gangwon Province recorded no rain.

Jeolla Provinces received on the average 6 mm of rain, they said. They added that at least 200mm more rain is needed to resolve the drought.

Many regions have received less rain this year than in previous years.

According to the KMA, the central region has recorded its lowest amount of rain, which is 145.5 mm, since 1967.

About 118.5 mm of rain fell in Chuncheon this year, a 41.3 percent drop from the average 287.0 mm the city received during the past 30 years.

In Seoul, the rainfall recorded since March is 46.9 mm, which is the second lowest record since 1907.

For the last three months, the nation has received only 30 percent of the average rainfall it usually receives around this time of year, the KMA said.

(sohjung@koreaherald.co.kr)

AmCham head calls for easier layoff system

By Kim Mi-hui
Staff reporter

A more flexible labor environment will ensure greater competitiveness for Korean businesses and, in order to achieve it, the government will have to enforce tougher labor regulations, a leading foreign businessman said.

"Laws should be changed to permit restructuring, such as layoffs, before bad financial situations occur," Jeffrey Jones, president of the American Chamber of Commerce in Korea (AmCham), said in a phone interview with The Korea Herald.

"But, at the same time, there will have to be greater unemployment systems to back it up. The National Assembly can implement the social security net," he said.

According to Jones, Korea can finance healthier unemployment insurance by increasing social welfare tax on the public while cutting back on income tax, which is the system practiced by the United States.

"When there was the air traffic controller strike in the U.S. in 1985, the Reagan administration took control and changed the system so that they can handle strikes. But at the same time, he improved unemployment benefits," Jones said. "It's not just the U.S. model, it is the U.K. model and other countries as well."

Meanwhile, Jones expressed great concern that the current airline labor union demonstration will soon become a serious public interest issue, possibly bringing about a national economic disaster.

"There are no bad guy, good guy in such situations. I hope that the union and the management will work together to resolve their differences," he said.

Jones also pointed out that such frequent labor unrest could affect another aspect of the Korean economy — foreign investment.

"Though investors probably won't make their decisions based solely on the country's labor environment, it is one of the factors they look at closely, he said.

"Frequent labor unrest make people nervous about doing business in Korea and that may affect their decisions," he said.

On the other hand, Korea has been lucky to have a lower unemployment rate than many other countries, he said noting that Europe's rate is about 10 percent. Once a better social benefit system is established, the rate will be even lower, he said.

(mihui@koreaherald.co.kr)

Jeffrey Jones

Gov't likely to lower growth estimate

By Park Sang-soo
Staff reporter

Reflecting the continuing business downturn, the government is likely to lower the country's gross domestic product (GDP) growth estimate for this year to 4-5 percent down 1 percentage point from its original projection of 5-6 percent, officials of the Ministry of Finance and Economy said.

The ministry attributed the move to lowering interest rates surrounding the U.S. and Japanese economies, which hold sway over the performance of the country's exports and overall economy.

In its revised macroeconomic indicators to be announced late June, the ministry will also drastically reduce this year's export target, as
(Continued on Page 9)

Korean Air pilots end strike, clipping wings of labor protests

Fewer hospital workers than expected join walkout

By Kim Min-hee
Staff reporter

Unionized pilots at Korean Air ended their two-day strike after reaching a last-minute agreement with the management last night, raising hopes of an early resolution of the nation's worst aviation crisis to date.

The cancellation of the strike by Korean Air pilots increased hopes that the walkout by pilots from Asiana Airlines would also end.

It is also expected to take the heat out of a general strike being engineered by the Korean Confederation of Trade Unions (KCTU), a hard-line umbrella labor organization.

Korean Air officials said flight operations could be resumed as early as this afternoon.

The pilots' strike was called off as the union and management struck an agreement on a number of issues, including wages, reduction of foreign pilots and adding pilots on the commuter line. The management also gave its word that it would withdraw legal charges brought against striking pilots and minimize punishment on those who participated in the strike.

Earlier in the day, the government convened a meeting of labor-related ministers, who warned that those participating in illegal strikes would face legal punishment.

The prosecution has already obtained a court order to arrest 14 leaders of Korean Air's pilot union in connection with the walkout.

For the second consecutive day, Korean Air and Asiana Airlines cancelled more than half of their flights, leaving passengers and cargo stranded.

In the absence of about 1,400 pilots, Korean Air, the nation's largest airline, cancelled 272 of its 556 flights scheduled for yesterday, including 43 of its 92 international flights.

Asiana Airlines, who had about 1,100 flight crew and ground staff walk off their jobs with the second day, cancelled 130 of its 706 flights, including one of 66 international flights it originally had scheduled.

Meanwhile, unionized workers at six major university hospitals, including the Seoul National University Hospital, joined the general strike yesterday.

Unions at three hospitals, including Kyung Hee University Medical Center, however, called off their strikes after reaching a last-minute compromise with their respective management groups.

Unionized workers of Gongnam, Yeoido, and Ulleongbu St. Mary's hospitals initially joined the strike, but returned to work in the afternoon after their management agreed to a 7.2 percent wage rise.

The hospital strike did not cause major disruptions to the medical service as was initially feared, as doctors were not part of the striking unionists.

The KCTU said 42,000 people from 69 firms took part in yesterday's strike. However, the Labor Ministry put forward a much lower figure, stating that just 12,000 workers from 31 workplaces participated in the strike.

(mkhin@koreaherald.co.kr)

U.S., N.K. to resume dialogue this week

WASHINGTON (AFP) — The United States and North Korea are to resume their dialogue this week in New York after the Stalinist state accepted President George W. Bush's offer to restart the talks, the State Department said Tuesday.

"As a follow-up to the president's statement last week on North Korea policy, Jack Pritchard, special envoy for Korean Peace talks, will meet with North Korean (U.N. ambassador) Li Hyong-chol on June 13 in New York to make arrangements for bilateral talks," spokesman Philip Reeker said.

"It's a start," a senior department official added. "We said we would like to begin a dialogue and the North Koreans responded, they agreed to meet."

After spelling out a tough line towards North Korean leader Kim Jong-il early in his administration, Bush suspended talks with Pyongyang. He undertook a review of the engagement strategy followed by former president Bill Clinton.

But last week, Bush said in a statement that his team had been completed and he was now ready to re-launch the dialogue.

The new president enraged Pyongyang and supporters of the Clinton approach by saying in March that he did not trust Kim Jong-il and doubted whether he could be counted upon to keep agreements.

On Wednesday, though, he said he was prepared to focus on improved implementation of a 1994 deal which ended Pyongyang's nuclear program, "verifiable constraints" on its missile development, a ban on missile exports and "a less threatening" conventional military posture.

After meeting with South Korean Foreign Minister Han Seung-soo a day after Bush's announcement, Secretary of State Colin Powell said no preconditions had been imposed on the talks.

Powell's comments followed a warning from Pyongyang that it would refuse to come to the table if Washington made the dialogue conditional on any
(Continued on Page 4)

SPEECH CONTEST WINNERS — Winners of the 41st Korea Herald Annual English Speech Contest For Koreans pose with Kim Kyeong-cheol (left), president-publisher of The Korea Herald-Naeway Economic Daily, and Horace G. Underwood (right), head judge of the event. The winners are, from second left, Lee Ga-hyun of Sinsa Middle School, Hur A-ram of Daewon Foreign Language High School, Lee Jun-seop of Yeoido Elementary School and Lee Jung-woo of the adult division. (Story on Page 16)

Family reunions leave painful memories, millions hopeful of seeing separated kin

By Kim Ji-ho
Staff reporter

It seemed like a miracle to Lee Ho-deok, 77, when she met her daughter in Pyongyang in February and discovered that the child who was abducted from her 32 years ago had actually been living in comfort in North Korea ever since that fateful day.

Although the reunion took place four months ago and the two
Related story on Page 3

The summit one year on

Koreas have begun to lose momentum for rapprochement, the emotion from their brief meeting is still fresh.

Now, all Lee can do back in South Korea is to sob over the photos of her 55-year-old daughter, Seong Kyong-hee, who was a flight attendant on a Korean Air jet hijacked to North Korea in 1969.

"Until February, I thought I could even die now I only able to see my daughter once again," Lee said. "But now, it's much more painful to think about Kyong-hee, who broke down in tears saying she's sorry that she had to stay in the North."

The tearful meeting between Lee and Seong, people during the three-day inter-Korean reunions of separated families in North and South Korea, anxiously in front of Pyongyang.

The event was the third, and the first of its kind since the South and the North launched a reconciliation process following a historic summit between their leaders a year ago.

Through some additional reunions, more than 3,600 family members have met their separated kin for the first time since the Korean War (1950-53). A few hundred of those reunited exchanged letters later.

Pyongyang cut off all contact with Seoul in March, however, leaving millions of other aging Koreans unlikely of ever hearing from their lost relatives before they pass away.

Compared with those in despair, the reunited families may well feel they are lucky. But at the same time, their sorrow deepened following the reunions.

Choi Kyong-gil says that every morning during the past 10 months, he has feared that his wife might die from a serious case of Alzheimer's disease in North Korea.

"When I saw her, she was just skin and bones. She couldn't even recognize me due to her illness," said Choi, 80.

Choi met his 76-year-old wife, Song Ok-sun, in Pyongyang during last August's family reunions.

"It was really hurtful to hear that she, unlike me, didn't marry again in the North, bringing up our son on her own," Choi said.

According to Seoul officials, those who had temporary reunions with their loved ones often report having mental problems.

"Out of despair that they couldn't meet their family ever again and due to shock they received in the North, many people suffer from insomnia or other mental problems," said Park Seong-woon, an official at the Korea National Red
(Continued on Page 2)

계율 10: 불규칙/변형 칼럼(Bastard Measures) 활용

대부분의 신문들은 6~8단의 고정 컬럼을 사용한다.

그러나 기사성격에 따라 컬럼수를 줄이거나 늘려 변칙적으로 활용함으로써 시각적 효과를 증대시킬 수 있다.특히 사진, 그래픽, 삽화 등의 사용 시에 변칙 컬럼은 효과가 크다.

엄격한 지면 그리드로부터 벗어나게 하여 기사가 특별하다는 것을 보여 주는 효과적인 방법이다. 기사 폭은 기사별, 지면별로 융통성 있게 처리한다.

Figure 17은 The Korea Times가 고정 컬럼으로 쓰고 있는 7단의 형태를 벗어나 Book Review 기사의 편집에 5Column을 사용했다.

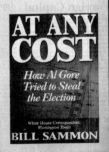

Figure 17

계율 11: Downstyle형의 헤드라인

과거, 많은 신문들이 헤드라인에 대문자를 사용했다. 그러나 오늘날 신문에서는 대자를 적게 쓰는 Downstyle 선호경향이 있지만 구미 여러 나라들은 신문특성에 따라 아직도 대자를 쓰는 신문들이 적지 않다. (상세한 것은 3장의 헤드라인 설명참조)

계율 12: 기사본문 수직단(Leg) 중간 또는 하단에 아트 배열 삼가

시각물로 인해 본문 기사의 흐름을 방해해서는 안 된다. 기사단(Leg) 의 중간에 사진 또는 도표 같은 시각물을 배열하면 독자들은 하나의 기사가 끝나고 시각물 다음부터 새로운 기사가 시작된다고 착각하기 쉽다.

Leg끝에 시각물을 배치하면 다른 기사 또는 인접하는 광고와 연계해서 생각하게 하여 오해를 불러일으킬 수 있다.

계율 13: 헤드라인 충돌 방지를 위한 Box사용을 삼가

편집자들이 Layout하다가 헤드라인이 충돌할 때 이를 피하기 위해 편의위주로 Box로 처리 하는 경우가 있는데 박스를 남용해서는 안 된다.

박스는 경성기사가 대부분을 차지하는 지면에서 연성기사를 특별히 구별하여 처리할 경우, 큰 기사 옆에 작은 기사를 처리해야 할 경우, 그리고 정기적인 Column(뉴스요약, 의견 란) 등을 처리할 때 사용한다.

기사를 박스처리 하는 것은 시각적으로 강조하는 것이며, 독자들에게 "이 기사는 다른 것과 특별히 구별되는 것이다"라고 알리는 것이다.

계율 14: 8 Point 이하의 작은 글자 사용의 삼가

오늘날 신문에서 Typography(활판술)은 Visual Communication 의 한 중요한 영역이다. 글자체, 글자의 크기, 글줄 사이, 글자 사이, 단어 사이 등이 가시성에 영향을 주는 중요한 요인으로 등장했다.

Cybil Burt는 독자들이 한 순간에 볼 수 있는 범위는 가로 세로 1인치,

즉 12포인트 활자 6자폭이라고 지적한 점에 유의해야 한다.

8포인트 글자체는 읽기 어렵다.

오늘날 글자체가 점점 커지는 추세다.

계율 15: 이태릭과 볼드체의 효율적 사용

본문에서 작은 분량의 기사를 특별히 강조할 때 Italic체나 Bold체(굵은 글자체)를 사용한다.

이텔릭체나 볼드체는 일시적으로 특별한 효과를 낼 수는 있으나 너무 길게 오래 쓰면 오히려 효과가 감소된다. 이 두 글자체는 독자들에게 "낯설기" 때문에 읽히는 속도가 느리다. 따라서 길게 사용하는 것은 비효율적이다.

계율 16~17: 점프기사의 최소화

기사가 길게 늘어지면 지루하고 불안정하게 보인다. 이때 편집자들은 기사를 다른 면으로 점프시키는 기법을 사용하게 되는데 가급적 피하는 것이 좋다.

독자들은 점프기사를 좋아하지 않는다. 점프기사는 독자, 편집자 모두의 시간을 빼앗고 읽기를 방해한다. 따라서 점프기사는 최소화할 필요가 있다.

부득이 편집상 점프를 해야 할 경우 점프 전에 10.2cm 이상의 기사를 게재하는 것이 바람직하고 점프 후 연결된 기사는 적어도 15cm 이상이어야 한다.

점프는 가능하면 같은 지점에서 한번만 하도록 해야 한다. 점프횟수를 늘리는 것은 독자들을 귀찮게 하는 일이다.

계율 18: 사진 Cropping

사진은 원래 모양에 관계없이 지면에 맞게 기사를 편집하듯 가지치기(Cropping)하여 사용한다.

Cropping 하기에 따라서는 이미지를 강하게 할 수도 있고 입체적으로 보이게 할 수도 있다.

Cropping 할 때는 불필요한 부분을 과감하게 잘라내어 필요한 부분이 상대적으로 부각 되게 한다.

명심해야 할 점을 정리해 본다.

① 불필요한 것을 제거하라: 하늘, 땅, 행동의 주역이 아닌 주변사람들.
② 부각 되어야 할 부분의 주변은 일정한 공간을 주어라.
③ 신체의 연결부분(손목, 발목 등)은 자르지 마라.
④ 예술작품의 Cropping은 조심하라.

계율 19: 광고 바로 위에 사진사용을 삼가

덜 중요하다고 생각되는 사진을 하단에 배열하여 광고와 맞붙게 하는 경우가 있다. 독자들은 광고와 관련된 사진으로 착각하기 쉽다.

계율 20: 헤드라인에 color 사용의 제한

컬러는 신문을 더 현대적으로 보이게 하며 젊은 독자층을 유인할 수 있으며, 컬러 사진이 흑백사진 보다 독자들의 시선을 더 끌 수 있다는 연구 보고는 많다.

그러나 헤드라인을 컬러로 하는 것이 흑백으로 하는 것 보다 주목을 더 받는다는 연구보고는 없다. 헤드라인에 어설픈 컬러 사용은 경성뉴스의 경우 오히려 권위와 품위를 떨어뜨린다.

편집의 유형

1면

1면(Front Page)은 전체지면의 문패요 창이며 신문의 전체를 대표하는 얼굴이다. 따라서 독자들을 끌어들이기 위해 전통적 리포팅 요소와 현대적 마케팅 요소들을 고려하여 편집 한다.

대부분의 신문들은 다음의 1면 디자인 유형을 고려하여 사용한다.

① **전통적 형태**: 단순히 그날의 톱뉴스를 1면에 싣는다.
타블로이드의 경우 2~4개 기사, 대판은 4~7개 기사를 싣는 것이 보통이다. 직사각형 형태를 유지하면서 기사, 사진, 헤드라인을 결합하여 편집한다.
② **잡지형태의 편집**: 기사의 양보다 시각적인 면을 강조, 커다란 아트(사진, 그래픽)와 역동적인 헤드라인으로 토픽을 강조한다.
③ **정보의 창**: 기사의 양과 다양성을 강조하면서 그래픽, 사진, 요약문 등을 혼합하여 그날의 주요기사 들을 안내한다. 역동성 있는 1면은 지면전체에 대한 창문 같은 역할을 한다.

Feature면과 섹션

피쳐(Feature)면이나 본면과 분리해 제작되는 섹션(Section)에는 역동성 있고 과감한 디자인을 사용한다.

기획물을 다루는 지면에서는 큰 활자를 쓰고, 특이한 사진, 컬러 등을 많이 사용한다.

대부분의 신문에서는 피쳐 면의 수가 적지만 몇몇 큰 신문은 매일 주

제별로 매거진 성격으로 제작한다.

예를 들면 월요일에는 금융, 화요일에는 건강, 수요일에는 요리 등 요일별로 주제를 변화시켜 다룬다.

최근 신문들이 많이 쓰는 주제들을 열거해 본다.

① 라이프스타일뉴스: 패션, 건강 등 독자들의 일상생활에 영향을 주는 Topics.
② 오락뉴스: 영화, 음악, 책, 예술 등에 대한 리뷰.
③ 음식: 영양정보, 새로운 주방 상품 등.
④ 기타: 만화, 칼럼, 낱말 맞추기.

스포츠면

스포츠 섹션은 극적인 사진, 생생한 기사, 동적인 헤드라인, 분석칼럼 등을 결합시켜 과감하고 공격적으로 편집한다.

스포츠면에 자주 쓰이는 편집 구성품들:
① 통계: 스코어, 운동선수의 기록, 팀의 역사 등.
② 경기일정: 경기일정의 시간과 장소.
③ 칼럼: 특색 있는 집필자의 분석기사.
④ 정보와 가십: 스코어, 투표결과, 예상, 분석과 선수의 프로필 등.

의견페이지와 사설

뉴스와 의견기사를 나란히 혼합 배열하는 것은 위험하다.

독자들은 어디에서 "사실"이 시작되고 어디에서 "의견"이 시작되는지 구별하기 어렵다. 따라서 거의 모든 신문들은 의견-사설란을 따로 두며 이는 서구 저널리즘의 일반적 관행이다.

의견-사설란은 다음의 기본요소로 이루어진다.

① 사설: 주요문제에 대한 신문의 입장을 대표하는 의견 란.
② 의견칼럼: 외부기고가의 글로 구성.

③ 시사만화(Cartoon): 공적 인물이나 정책을 풍자 하는 Illustrations.
④ 독자들의 편지: Letter to the Editor 란으로 독자들의 의견을 게재.
⑤ 발행처 표기란(Masthead): 신문의 편집인, 발행인 등의 사무실주소,
전화번호, Fax, Email 등을 표기한다.

편집에 사용되는 용어

- **Flag** * : 신문제호. Nameplate라고도 함.
- **Skybox** : Teasers, Promos라고도 함. 주목할 만한 기사들을 1면 상단에 배열한 기사 안내란.
- **Byline** : 기사작성자 이름이 들어가는 행.
- **Masthead** : 신문, 잡지 등에서 발행에 관한 정보를 다루는 란.
- **Deck** : 주 헤드라인 아래에 덧붙이는 작은 부제목.
- **Subhead** : 긴 기사를 처리할 때 기사를 조직화하고 지루한 본문을 개선하는데 문장 내에 사용되는 굵은 글자체의 소제목.
- **Standing Heads** : 특별한 항목(요약문, 칼럼, 그래픽, 티저스 등)을 하나로 모으는데 사용되는 라벨(표기).
- **Sidebar** : 주기사를 수반하는 관련기사로 종종 박스로 처리되는 란.
- **Modular Design** : 직사각형 편집. 앞서 기술한 설명참조.
- **Grid** : 원래의 뜻은 그물이며, 그래프지나 바둑판 모양을 말한다. 편집에서 그리드는 하나의 시각적 구성물을 연결시켜 주는 하부구조다. 시간을 절약시켜

---

* *ex* Financial Times, The Wall Street Journal, The New York Times, USA Today 등. 원래 신문 이름 앞에 정관사 "The"를 붙이는 것이 상례였으나, 최근 USA Today에서 보는 바와 같이 생략하는 추세임.

주고 제작을 원활히 하게 한다.

- **Logo** : 특별한 기사나, 연재물 등에 사용되는 작고 박스 처리 된 시각물. Sig, Bug라고도 함.
- **Bastard Measure** : 변칙칼럼 또는 변형활자.
- **Art** : 사진, 그래픽 등 지면에 사용되는 시각물.
- **Spot Color** : 원색인쇄 이외의 모든 컬러 인쇄.
- **Jump Line** : 어느 페이지에 기사가 계속되는지 말해 주는 행.
- **Jump Headline** : Jump된 기사의 헤드라인.
- **Mug Shot** : 얼굴사진.
- **Caption** : Cutline 이라고도 하며 사진설명을 말함.
- **Initial Cap** : 특별 기획기사의 시작 문단에 사용되는 큰 글자체. Drop Cap이라고도 함.
- **Photo Credit** : 사진의 출처.
- **Drop Head** : 부차적 헤드라인.
- **Gutter** : 기사간, 지면간의 여백.
- **Headline** : 기사제목.
- **Liftout Quote** : Pull Quote 또는 Breakout Quote라고도 함. 그래픽으로 강조된 인용문.

신문 디자인 우수작

지금까지 신문 디자인에 대해 이론과 실제를 다루어 보았다. 다음은 세계적으로 우수한 신문 디자인으로 수상 된 신문들의 예를 들어 보기로 한다.

신문디자인협회(The Society of Newspaper Design)는 전세계 약 2,400명의 디자이너, 편집자, 사진작가 등을 회원으로 하는 Visual Journalist들의 단체이다. 해마다 우수디자인을 선정하여 부문별로 시상

하고 있다.

이를 위해 매년 2월 뉴욕주 시라큐스의 커다란 강당에서 신문디자인 협회와 시라큐스 대학(S. I. Newhouse Public Communication)이 주관하는 SND 디자인상 심사와 전시회가 열린다.

1996년 24개국 250개 신문이 출품된 가운데 5개국 21명의 심사위원이 10,000여 편의 신문을 심사했다. 이중 7개국 22개 신문이 선정되었다.

다음은 우수한 디자인으로 수상한 22개 신문 중에서 발췌한 것이다.

(다음에 열거하는 것은 1996년 한국언론재단에서 발행한 책자 "신문디자인"에 게재된 것을 재인쇄한 것이다)

수상작 Figure 18~22의 공통점은 모두 Modular Design을 채택했다는 점이고 과감한 시각물과의 균형된 조합을 이루고 있어 시선을 끌고 있다.

Figure 18
Courtesy of The Daily Telegraph

Figure 19   Courtesy of The Detroit News

Figure 20   Courtesy of The Oregonian

Figure 21   Courtesy of The Sunday Star

Figure 22   Courtesy of Diario de Noticias, Spain

Photo & Caption 5

Photo

　모든 사진(Photo)은 기사다. 모든 사진은 정보다. 모든 사진은 Art다.
모든 사진은 가독성을 높이는 중요한 요인이다.

　모든 사진은 독특한 것이어야 하고 사진의 효과를 극대화하기 위해
크기와 위치를 전문적인 시각에서 고려해야 한다.

　편집자는 사진을 수평으로 쓸 것인가, 수직으로 쓸 것인가, 위치를 좌
측에 할 것인가, 우측에 할 것인가, 중앙에 할 것인가, 상단에 할 것인가,
하단에 할 것인가, Front Page에 쓸 것인가, Inside Page에 쓸 것 인가
등의 모든 요소를 기사의 중요도, 다른 시각물들과의 조화를 고려하여
결정해야 한다.

　사진설명(Caption, Cutline)은 어떻게 쓸 것인가, 사진 하단에 쓸 것인
지, 측면에 쓸 것인지, 어떤 요령으로 쓸 것인지에 대해 사려 깊게 분석해
야 한다.

　사진편집자는 지면 설계(Dummying), 페이지 설정(Pagination), 정보
그래픽 등 시각물 배열작업에 깊게 관여해야 한다.

사진 사용의 용례

✔ 수평사진

Figure 1에 보는 바와 같이 직사각형의 사진에서 가로가 세로보다 긴 형태를 말한다. 가장 많이 쓰이는 안정된 모양이다. 기사 본문, 사진, 헤드라인이 어울려 한조각의 직사각형이 되도록 편집(Modular Design)한다.

사진의 크기는 사진자체와 관련기사의 중요도에 따라 정한다. 크기가 정해지면 주어진 지면에 맞고 입체감이 나도록 가지치기(Cropping)한다.

동적인 사진에서는 움직이는 행동방향이 관련기사를 바라보게 편집한다. 반대방향으로 하면 독자들은 사진과 기사가 별개인 것으로 오해하기 쉽다.

Figure 1

Note

Figure 1은 가로 15.5cm 세로 9.5cm의 사진을 헤드라인 "President Kim Receives Nobel Peace Prize"과 본문을 직사각형이 되게 편집한 예이다. 한국인으로는 처음 받는 노벨평화상의 중요도에 따라 기사 5단에 사진 3단의 수평사진을 Modular Design으로 처리했다.

수직사진

Figure 2~3에서 보는 바와 같이 세로가 가로보다 긴 사진을 말한다. 수직사진은 극적인 효과는 있지만 디자인에 많은 제약이 있고 본문과 어울리게 하는데도 어려움이 많다.

일반적 수직사진의 Size는 폭은 2~3단, 길이는 13~38 cm로 한다. 본문과 연계해서 쓸 때 밑에 사진설명, 헤드라인과의 조화를 고려하는 일반적 관행을 지키도록 한다.

기사의 수직단(Leg)이 길게 늘어지는 것을 피하도록 하며 관련된 기사본문이 있는 경우는 사진을 지면의 상단에 배열하는 것이 좋다.

Korea's Lee Bong-ju kisses the winner's trophy after winning the 105th Boston Marathon in Boston, Monday. AP-Yonhap

143

Figure 2

Pak Wins 3rd Jamie Farr Title

SYLVANIA, Ohio (AP) — Pak Se-ri pulled away from Maria Hjorth with birdies on the last two holes Sunday to win the Jamie Farr Kroger Classic for the third time in four years.

Pak finished at 15-under 269, closing with a 3-under 68 after rounds of 70, 62 and 69. She earned $150,000.

In her 16 competitive rounds at Highland Meadows Golf Course — which for obvious reasons she calls her favorite layout in the world — Pak is 54-under par. In addition to winning in 1998 and 1999, she was third a year ago — a shot out of the playoff between eventual winner Annika Sorenstam and Rachel Teske.

It was the ninth time Pak has led or shared the lead heading into the final round in her four years on the LPGA tour. She has held on to win eight times.

The victory was Pak's third this year, but Hjorth might be the hottest player on the tour. She hasn't finished worse than a tie for third in six of her last seven starts.

Pak started the day with a four-stroke lead but strung together 11 pars before rolling in a 3-meter (10-foot) birdie putt at the 12th. Then she hit her approach to 90 centimeters (3 feet) at No. 13 and holed the birdie putt.

She bogeyed the par-4 15th to fall back into a tie with Hjorth — who birdied six holes in an eight-hole span — after hooking her drive next to a tree.

Hjorth, however, bogeyed seconds later.

On the 17th, rated the easiest hole on the course, the long-hitting Hjorth found the rough off the tee and came up well short of the green on the 467-meter (513-yard), par-5 hole with her second shot. Her sand wedge from 95 meters (104 yards) end-ed up short of the sand trap fronting the green. She was unable to get up and down from there, missing a 1.2-meter (4-foot) putt for par.

Trailing by a shot to Pak, Hjorth hit a wedge approach — her third shot on the par-5 18th — to 90 centimeters (3 feet). The ensuing birdie evened things once again.

Pak countered almost immediately. Also a long hitter, Pak's second shot came up just short of the green near a bunker at No. 17. She ran her chip to 60 centimeters (2 feet) and made the birdie putt to regain the lead.

The 25-year-old South Korean then closed it out on the final hole, hitting a big drive and a perfect fairway wood before knocking a wedge shot to 2.4 meters (8 feet). She then dropped the birdie putt in the middle of the cup.

AP-Yonhap

Pak Se-ri raises her trophy after winning the Jamie Farr LPGA tournament in Sylvania, Ohio, Sunday. Pak shot 15 under par to become the first three-time winner of the event.

Figure 3

Note

Figure 2에서 이봉주 선수의 105회 보스톤 마라톤대회 우승사진을 가로 2.5단, 세로 15cm로 처리했다.

Figure 3에서 박세리 선수의 골프대회 우승사진을 2단, 13cm로 본문, 헤드라인과 함께 직사각형으로 편집했다.

중심사진

온라인, 오프라인 어느 경우든지 각 면마다 여러 장의 사진이 쓰이게 된다. 이 경우 중심이 되는 한 장의 사진을 두드러지게 하여 독자들에게

강렬한 인상을 주어야 한다. 중심사진(Dominant Photo)을 부각시키는 것이다. 독자들은 무엇이 가장 중요한 사건이고, 어떤 사진이 가장 중요한 것인지 신문이 결정해 주길 기대한다.

　Dominant Photo는 다른 사진보다 크게 사용함으로서 중요성을 강조할 수 있다.

　중심사진은 기사 또는 지면에 안정감을 주지만 같은 크기 두 장의 사진이 나란히 편집되면 서로 경쟁적으로 충돌할 수 있다.

Figure 4

Note

Figure 4는 박지은 선수에 대한 Feature 기사를 처리하면서 쓴 2장의 사진이다. 왼쪽의 인물사진은 2.5단 넓이에 16cm의 길이로 과감하게 처리함으로서 독자의 시선을 끌기에 충분하다. 오른쪽 사진은 흔히 볼 수 있는 평범한 사진이다. 이 경우 과감한 인물사진이 중심사진이 된다.

A Japanese official officially announces the government decision on history textbooks in Tokyo, Monday.　　　Yonhap

Foreign Affairs-Trade Minister Han Seung-soo, right, looks serious as he shakes hands with Japanese Ambassador Terusuke Terada who visited the Foreign Ministry to notify Han of the results of his government's review of Korean demands for the revision of Japanese history textbooks, Monday.　　　Korea Times

Figure 5

| Note |

Figure 5는 일본정부의 역사교과서 왜곡과 관련한 두 개의 사진으로 왼쪽은 일본정부의 역사교과서 개정방침을 발표하는 사진이고, 오른쪽은 일본정부의 방침을 통고하기 위해 한국 외무부를 방문한 일본대사를 맞는 한승수 외무장관의 표정을 담은 사진이다. 왼쪽은 비중이 없는 사진이고 오른쪽은 장관과 대사의 표정에서 양국의 불편한 관계를 읽을 수 있는 의미 있는 사진이다. 따라서 오른쪽 사진이 Dominant Photo라고 할 수 있다.

✔ **얼굴사진(Mug Shot)**

기사의 얼굴사진 크기는 넓이는 한 칼럼의 폭과 같고, 길이는 8∼10 cm가 바람직하다. 얼굴사진은 프레임을 꽉 채우는 것이 좋지만 지나치게 칼럼을 채우면 답답하며 머리 윗부분은 어느 정도 공간을 남겨야 한다.

얼굴사진에는 설명이 필요하다. Caption은 종종 2행 형식을 취하는데 첫째 행은 사람이름, 둘째 행은 직함을 쓴다.

반 단 얼굴사진을 사용할 경우, 많은 공간을 차지하지 않고도 사진을 유용하게 쓸 수 있다. 반 단 사진의 경우 본문의 폭이 적어도 2.5cm는 되어야 한다. 지면하단에 사진사용은 금한다. (Figure 6 참고)

Figure 6

Caption 쓰기

Caption이란 사진설명을 말한다.

News 기사는 가독성을 극대화하기 위해, 사진, 그래픽 등을 쓰게 된다. 경우에 따라서는 한 장의 사진이 본문기사의 몇 배에 해당하는 효과를 낼 때가 있을 정도로 News 구성상 매우 중요하다.

사진을 사용할 때는 선택된 사진의 설명을 어떻게 쓸 것 인가가 매우 중요하다.

사진을 설명하는 데에는 몇 가지 원칙이 있다.

How to Write A Caption

원칙 1: 반드시 사진을 보고 써라. (Don't write a caption without seeing the picture.)

원칙 2: 5 W's and 1 H(Who, What, When, Where, Why and How)의 원칙에 입각하여 써라.

원칙 3: 현재형으로 하라. (Write in the present tense.)

원칙 4: 정확하고, 흥미를 유발하도록 써라.

원칙 5: 사람이름, 지명 등 고유명사를 명확하게 써라.

원칙 6: 주관적 의도가 가미된 형용사 사용을 삼가하라.

원칙 7: Spelling, Comma, Period, Colon, Semicolon, Dash, Hyphen, Quotation Marks(인용부호), Capitalization(대문자), Abbreviations(약어) 등을 정확하게 Check 하라.

Caption
ex **1** President Kim Dae-jung, right, shakes hands with North Korean leader Kim Jong-il in their first face-to-face meeting at Sunan Airport on the outskirts of Pyongyang, Tuesday. As a major step to end the longstanding animosity between the two rival states on the Korean peninsula which have been technically at war for 55 years, their tete-a-tete won the spotlight of the international media. Kim will stay in Pyongyang until Thursday.

Chong Wa Dae Press Corps

President Kim Dae-jung, right, shakes hands with North Korean leader Kim Jong-il in their first face-to-face meeting at Sunan Airport on the outskirts of Pyongyang, Tuesday. As a major step to end the longstanding animosity between the two rival states on the Korean peninsula which have been technically at war for 55 years, their tete-a-tete won the spotlight of the international media. Kim will stay in Pyongyang until Thursday.

Chong Wa Dae Press Corps

Figure 7

어 휘

- shakes hands: 악수하다
- face-to-face: 마주보는
- longstanding animosity: 오랜 반목
- technically at war: 기술적으로 전쟁상태 하에 있는
- tete-a-tete: 단독회담

원칙 1~7 해설

✔ Who are seen in this picture figure 7?

《President Kim Dae-jung, right, North Korean leader Kim Jong-il.》

서술하고자 하는 사람들의 위치(Right, Left, Center 등)를 표기함으로써 독자들로 하여금 등장인물들을 용이하게 식별하도록 돕는다.

✔ What do they do?

《shake hands》

Shakes or Shake Hands(악수하다)를 초심자들 중에는 현재진행형(Is Shaking Hands or Are Shaking Hands)을 쓰는 예가 많은데 Caption에서는 현재형이 최선의 표현이다.

Improper	President Kim Dae-jung and North Korean leader Kim Jong-il are shaking hands.
Proper	President Kim Dae-jung and North Korean leader Kim Jong-il shake hands.

oint :

The present tense imparts immediacy and vividness to the news.

When?

《Tuesday》

시기를 나타낼 때 요일 또는 날짜 중 하나를 선택해서 쓰면 된다. 사진설명은 사건이나 행사가 주로 일주일 전, 후의 행사를 서술하기 때문에 주로 요일을 쓴다.

이 경우 "last Tuesday"나 "next Tuesday"같은 표현은 어색하며 "last"나 "next"같이 시기를 나타내는 수식어사용은 불필요하다. 이미 동사가 지난사건인지 미래사건 일지를 서술하기 때문이다.

Where?

《at Sunan Airport on the outskirts of Pyongyang》

Why?

《to end the longstanding animosity between the two rival states》

How?

《in their first face-to-face meeting》

Caption **President Kim Dae-jung, center, flanked by First Lady Lee Hee-ho**
ex **2** **and The Korea Times-Hankook Ilbo newspaper group chairman Chang**
Jae-kook, raises his glass in a toast during a reception Wednesday
marking the 50th anniversary of The Korea Times' founding at the
Sejong Hall of the Sejong Center for the Performing Arts in downtown
Seoul. Also joining the session are, from left, Culture-Tourism
Minister Kim Han-gill, Colombian Amb. Miguel Duran Ordonez,
Board of Audit and Inspection(BAI) chairman Lee Jong-nam, Hankook
Ilbo president Chang Myong-sue, Foreign Affairs-Trade Minister Lee
Joung-binn and Seoul Mayor Goh Kun.

President Kim Dae-jung, center, flanked by First Lady Lee Hee-ho and The Korea Times-Hankook Ilbo newspaper group chairman Chang Jae-kook, raises his glass in a toast during a reception Wednesday marking the 50th anniversary of The Korea Times' founding at the Sejong Hall of the Sejong Center for the Performing Arts in downtown Seoul. Also join-ing the session are, from left, Culture-Tourism Minister Kim Han-gill, Colombian Amb. Miguel Duran Ordonez, Board of Audit and Inspection (BAI) chairman Lee Jong-nam, Hankook Ilbo president Chang Myong-sue, Foreign Affairs-Trade Minister Lee Joung-binn and Seoul Mayor Goh Kun. *Korea Times*

Figure 8

 어 휘

- Flanked by: …가 옆에 서있는
- Raise a glass: 건배를 위해 잔을 들다

해설 2

✔ **Who are seen in this picture figure 8?**

《President Kim Dae-jung, center, First Lady Lee Hee-ho, The Korea Times-Hankook Ilbo newspaper group chairman Chang Jae-kook, Culture-Tourism Minister Kim Han-gill, Colombian Amb. Miguel Duran Ordonez, Board of Audit and Inspection(BAI) chairman Lee Jong-nam, Hankook Ilbo president Chang Myong-sue, Foreign Affairs-Trade Minister Lee Joung-binn and Seoul Mayor Goh Kun.》

✔ **What do they do?**

《They raise glasses 》

✔ **When?**

《Wednesday》

✔ **Where?**

《at the Sejong Hall of the Sejong Center for the Performing Arts in downtown Seoul》

✔ **Why?**

《Marking the 50th anniversary of The Korea Times' founding》

 How?

《in a toast during a reception》

사진편집시 유의사항

주목 1:   사진 – 사진설명(Caption) – 헤드라인 – 본문의 순서로 편집하라.
주목 2:   사진사용 시 따라오는 본문은 조형미상 2.5cm 이상 유지토록 하라.
주목 3:   실제 행동을 담은 사진을 사용하라.
주목 4:   사진설명(Caption)이 밑에 올 경우, 사진 양쪽 끝에 설명문을 일치시켜라.
주목 5:   방향성 있는 사진은 인물이 본문을 향하도록 하라.
주목 6:   사진설명이 옆에 올 때, 측면 Caption은 적어도 2.5cm 너비를 유지하라.
주목 7:   사진설명(Caption)에 반드시 사진제공자(Credit)를 밝혀라.

U.S. President George W. Bush, right, Swedish Prime Minister Goeran Persson, center, and EU Commission President Romano Prodi, left, conduct a joint press conference at the conclusion of the EU-U.S. summit in Goteborg, Thursday. The United States and the European Union agreed to cooperate on climate change, despite their split over the Kyoto protocol.

AP-Yonhap

Bush Spars With European Leaders on Global Warming

GOTEBORG (AP) — U.S. President George W. Bush sparred Thursday with European leaders over climate change, unwavering in his opposition to a global warming treaty. Sweden's prime minister accused Bush of pursuing "wrong policies" that endanger the environment.

Emotions ran high in this quaint seacoast city as demonstrators hurled bottles and cobblestones to protest globalization, the European Union and Bush policies. Police arrested more than 200 as the president met with EU leaders at the mid-

mate change is a serious issue and we must work together," Bush said at a news conference with Prodi and Persson. It was the second day of U.S.-European discord after a breach among NATO allies Wednesday over Bush's plans for a missile defense system.

Bush put Prodi on the spot — encouraging a question about the failure of EU countries to ratify the same global warming treaty that Bush is criticized for rejecting. The president also hosted a private dinner

when the World Trade Organization meets in November. The two sides have a series of disputes pending, notably over EU fears that Washington is moving to block steel imports and over European restrictions on genetically modified food imports.

— Urged Israel and the Palestinians to keep their cease-fire.

— Renewed their commitment to peacekeeping missions in the Balkans.

After a stop Friday in Poland, Bush will conclude his trip Saturday

Figure 9

Slam Run Cold

When Capriati sent a forehand wide on match point, Henin tossed her racket skyward in tribute to her late mother, who died of cancer seven years ago.

"You can't imagine what it means for me to be in the final of a Grand Slam," she said. "That's not a dream — that's something I couldn't imagine."

On Saturday, the 5-foot-6 Henin will be the underdog, this to the 6-foot-1 Williams. won their only previous in May, but that was on and the grass-loving Williams carries a 13-match Wimbledon winning streak into the final.

"Once you win here, it's pretty addictive," Williams said.

In the second set against Davenport, Williams blew a 4-1 lead, failed to convert a match point at 5-4 and played a nervous tiebreaker, double-faulting twice. Then Williams took charge again, winning 12 of the first 15 points in the final set and breaking Davenport three times in a row.

Consistently hitting serves around 120 mph, Williams slammed nine aces and held on 13 of her 14 service games.

"It was hard to find any rhythm on her serve, serving that hard," Davenport said. "Women's tennis is just not used to it coming that fast."

slender her own rom the errage

raf, ith her ot both. She un-watting a nd the re-

ckhand in man or mbledon id.

Belgium's Justine Henin follows through on a serve during her semifinal match Thursday at Wimbledon against Jennifer Capriati of the United States. The 19-year-old Henin advanced with a 2-6, 6-4, 6-2 victory.

AP-Yonhap

Figure 10

Norwegian Crown Prince Haakon and his fiancee, Mette-Marit Tjessem Hoiby, sit on a park bench in Oslo, Norway, Oct. 16, 2000. Haakon plans to marry his live-in girlfriend Hoiby, an unwed mother, in August. Haakon's lifestyle has stirred a debate on the future of the monarchy in a Scandinavian nation looking for a down-to-earth royal family that isn't too normal.
AP-Yonhap

Figure 11

Former East German Prime Minister Lothar de Maiziere, right, shakes hands with Kim Chong-ryang, left, president of Hanyang University, after receiving an honorary doctorate in politics from the school in Seoul on Tuesday.
Korea Times

Figure 12

주목 1~7 해설

　Figure 9의 사진은 Photo - Caption - Headline-Text의 순서로 조화된 편집을 보여주고, 본문길이가 2.5 cm 이상 유지된 모습으로 안정감이 있다. 주목 1~4의 요건을 충족시키고 있다.

　Figure 10은 테니스선수의 행동하는 모습이 본문을 향해 있다. 독자들은 본문과 사진이 연계되어 있음을 쉽게 알 수 있다. 주목 5와 일치하고 있다.

　Figure 11은 측면 Caption인데 길이가 7 cm 정도로 위아래 여백과 알맞은 조화를 이루고 있으며 폭도 주목 6의 요건을 충족시키고 있다.

　Figure 12는 코리아타임스에서 찍은 사진이다. 따라서 주목 7에서 제시하는 바와 같이 "Korea Times"를 Credit로 표기하고 있다.

　코리아타임스가 찍은 사진이면 Korea Times, 외부에서 제공받은 사진이면 Yonhap, AP-Yonhap 등의 단독 또는 공동 Credit를 표기한다.

　사회단체, 기업체, 공공기관, 또는 독자 제공인 경우도 이름을 밝히는 것이 원칙이다. Credit은 Caption 상단 혹은 하단에 표기한다.

　Figure 12는 하단에 표기했다.

　다른 언론사 또는 방송사에서 빌려온 사진을 제공자 양해 하에 사용하는 경우 "Courtesy(of)"의 게재양해 문구를 삽입한다.

Note

Courtesy(of) The Hankook Ilbo, Courtesy The Dong-a Ilbo.
(…의 호의로 라는 뜻의 단어 "Courtesy"는 문장에서는 "Courtesy of"와 같이 "of"를 사용하고 사진 Caption인 경우 "of"를 생략하여 "Courtesy"만 표기할 수도 있다.)

Style Sheet **6**
in News Writing

영문작성에 있어 단어사용 못지않게 중요한 것이 있다.

숫자(Numerals), 구두점(Punctuation), 대문자(Capitalization), 약어
(Abbreviations)에 대한 규약이다.

다음에 열거하는 것들은 News Writing 또는 Editing에서 일반적으로
통용되는 규약이다.

규약 1: 숫자로 시작되는 문장에서 숫자는 Spell Out한다.

> Never begin a sentence with numerals.
> Spell out the number.

Wrong 65 persons were killed in a fire.

Right Sixty-five persons were killed in a fire.

규약 2: 1부터 9까지의 숫자는 Spell Out하고 10 이상은 숫자로 표기한다.

Wrong Police arrested 9 persons. A plane crash killed eighty-five passengers.

Right Police arrested nine persons. A plane crash killed 85 passengers.

서수표기의 예: First, Second, Ninth, 10th, 22d, 33d 등.

규약 3: 날짜, 온도, 시간 등은 숫자로 쓴다.

- 날짜(Jan. 5)
- 온도표시(20 degrees centigrade)
- 물건 가격(A pencil costs 10 won, yen, dollars)
- 퍼센트(20 percent)
- 전화번호(734 - 0075)
- 시간(3 p.m.)
- 경기시간(3: 08)
- 경도, 위도(8 degrees east longitude)
- 투표(ruling party, 1000; opposition, 2000)
- 내기비율(at odds of 7 to 3)
- 경기점수(ROK won Japan 2 to 1)
- 이름 다음의 나이(Kim, 7)
- 신장(5 feet 3 inch tall)
- 치수(3 feet by 4 feet)
- 큰 수(5 million citizens)
- 연도(2001)

규약 4: 여러 사람의 의견을 한목소리로 인용하는 직접화법의 표현은 불합리하다.

초심자들은 흔히 기사를 쓸 때 한 사람과 인터뷰해서 나온 의견을 여러 사람이 말한 것처럼 직접화법 기사로 부풀리는 경우가 있다. 매우 위험한 기사작성 이며 자주 사용할 경우 기사의 신뢰도가 떨어진다.

각 개인의 목소리가 일률적으로 같은지 일일이 확인되지 않는 한 간접화법으로 풀어 쓰는 것이 좋다.

Wrong	Unionists said, "The government step was a great help to workers".
Right	Unionists said that the government step was a great help to workers.

Wrong	Financial experts said, "The Korean economy was in an unhealthy state".
Right	Financial experts said that the Korean economy was in an unhealthy state.

규약 5: 1 주일 전, 후의 일은 요일로 표기한다.

현재시점에서 1 주일 전,후에 일어난 혹은 일어날 사건이나 행사는 Monday, Tuesday 같이 요일로 표기한다.

Avoid such redundancies as last Monday or next Monday.

독자들에게 요일로 표기하는 경우 과거라 해서 "last"를 쓰거나 미래라고 해서 "next"를 쓰는 중복적(redundant)인 표현은 좋지 않으며 과거 사건인지 미래사건인지는 동사를 보고 알 수 있다.

> **Note**
>
> 신문발행 당일에 있을 행사는 요일 대신 today, this morning, this afternoon, tonight 등으로 표기한다.

Wrong	Beijing was awarded the 2008 Olympics last Friday.
Right	Beijing was awarded the 2008 Olympics on Friday.

| Wrong | The IOC will elect a successor to IOC president Samaranch next Monday. |
| Right | The IOC will elect a successor to IOC president Samaranch on Monday. |

규약 6: 오전, 오후 표기는 a.m., p.m.으로 한다.

정오(noon)나 자정(midnight)을 제외한 시간은 a.m.(ante meridiem, 오전) 또는 p.m.(post meridiem, 오후)이라고 표기한다.

Avoid such redundancies as 11 a.m. this morning, 11 p.m. tonight or 11 p.m. Tuesday night.

위에서 a.m., p.m. 뒤의 morning, tonight, night 등은 불필요한 중복이다. 11 a.m. today, 11 p.m. today, 11 p.m. Tuesday로 해야 한다.

| Wrong | A press conference will be held at 9 a.m. this morning. |
| Right | A press conference will be held at 9 a.m. today. |

규약 7: 구두점(Punctuation) 사용을 정확히 한다.

구두점(Punctuation)은 문장에서 대단히 중요한 역할을 한다.

마침표(Period), 의문부호(Question Mark), 감탄부호(Exclamation Mark), Comma, Colon, Semicolon, Dash 등을 어떻게 쓰느냐에 따라 문장이 명료해지기도 하고 강조되기도 한다.

그러나 문장을 아무리 잘 써도 구두점을 잘못 쓰면 독자들이 전체문맥을 이해하기 어렵게 된다.

Period(.):

① 평서문(Declarative Sentence), 명령문(Imperative Sentence), 대답이 불필요한 주문형 의문문에 사용되어 문장의 종결을 나타낸다.

She said that she would help the poor.

Help the poor.

Madam, will you help the poor.

② 칭호, 직급, 기타 약어에 사용한다.

Mr. Kim, Ms. Lee, Mrs. Han, Lt. Park, Dr. Nam, a.m., etc., Ave., Ph.D.

③ 소수점에 사용

22.5percent, $155.7

Question Mark(?):

① 직접의문문에 사용한다.

What time do you get up every morning?

What time is it? He asked.

② 간접의문문에는 사용 안 한다.

I was asked what time I get up every morning.

He asked what time it was.

③ 대답이 불필요한 의문문에는 사용 안 한다.

Would you please be quiet.

④ 감탄형 의문문에는 사용 안 한다.

How dare you!

⑤ 평서문형의 의문문에 사용한다.

The bus was late: The bus was late?

Really: Really?

⑥ 확실하지 않은 사건들을 기술할 때 괄호 안에 사용한다.

The crowd numbered 500.(?)

Exclamation Mark(!):

① 평서문에 붙여 명령, 훈계, 강조 등을 나타낸다.

"Don't go away!" he ordered.

"Get out!" he screamed.

What a beautiful day!

② 감탄사(Interjection)로 연결되는 감탄문에 사용한다.

Whew! It was a close call.

Comma(,):

① 여러 항목을 열거할 때 사용.

Dogs, cats, and chickens play together.

② 짧은 인용문, 격언 등에 사용.

The teacher said, "It's a happy day".

The saying is, "Where there is a will, there is a way".

③ 년, 월, 일, 그리고 지명을 행정지역 순으로 표기할 때 사용.

She was born on Jan. 20, 1950.

Their office is located in Chunghak-dong, Chongno-ku, downtown Seoul.

④ 사람들의 이름과 직책을 열거할 때 사용.

The panel consists of Kim, CEO; Lee, vice president; Park, treasurer, and Han, secretary.

Note

이름, comma, semicolon의 순으로 하되 and 앞에서 semicolon 대신 comma 사용).

⑤ 숫자 표기에서 천, 백만, 그 이상의 위치를 끊어서 표기할 때 사용.
1,357,911 won; A total of 40,000 workers went on strike.
※ 연도(2001), 방 번호(1234), 거리번호(1235 St.), 전화번호(734-4989)는 예외.

⑥ 동격, 관계 대명사, 종속절 등과 함께 사용.
동격(Apposition): Han, foreign minister, is in office.
관계대명사(in non-restrictive use): He made good grades in English, which he likes.
종속절(접속사와 함께): Kim, though he is a cub reporter, knows a lot about journalism.

Colon(:):

① 주로 두 문장으로 된 긴글을 인용할 때 사용(짧은 문장은 Comma사용)
Walter Lippmann said: "For the newspaper is in all literalness the bible of democracy, the book out of which a people determines its conduct. It is the only serious book most people read. It is the only book they read every day".

② 강조하기 위해 사용
He has only one hobby: Reading

③ 도표형식, 나열형의 긴 문장
Fifteen people were killed in a train collision.
The dead were:
Thomas Kim, 30, of Chunghak-dong, Chongno-ku
John Lee, 20, Samsong-dong, Kangnam-ku

Charles Hong, 40, Ahyon-dong, Mapo-ku

④ 시, 분, 초를 나타내는 시간표시

2 : 41 : 08, 9 : 34 p.m., 7 : 49 a.m.

⑤ 질문-대답형 인터뷰기사에 사용

Question: Did you visit Pyongyang?

Answer: Yes, indeed.

Semicolon(;):

① Comma를 포함하는 여러 개의 글을 분리, 연결 시켜 주는 기능.

She leaves a son, Thomas Lee; two daughters, Linda Lee and Jane Lee.

② 문장의 절(Clause)과 절을 접속시키는 기능.

The package was due last week; It arrived home today.

oint :

- Commas always go inside quotation marks.
- Place semicolon outside quotation marks.
- Colons go outside quotation marks unless they are part of the quotation itself.

Dash(−):

① 변화를 주거나 강조 하는 기능

I will buy a computer next month − if I get a raise.

The government announced a plan − it was unprecedented − to raise revenues.

② Comma로 연결되는 여러 단어들의 의미를 함축하는 문구에서 사용

He listed the qualities — diligence, independence, intelligence — that he likes.

③ 저자와 저자의 인용문을 연결시킬 때 사용.

"The economic race does not go to the short-term sprinters. It requires a marathoner's ability to put together a century of 3 percent or better annual growth rates". — Lester Thurow.

④ "All", "These", "Such" 의미의 대용으로 사용.

Mt. Sorak, Mt. Paektu, Mt. Chiri — these are great mountains in Korea.

oint :

Do not use the en dash or hyphen to indicate inclusion when the words from or between precede the date.

Wrong   Vacation will be from June-September.
Right   Vacation will be from June to(or through) September.

Wrong   He was in the Army between 1999-2001.
Right   He was in the Army 1999-2001.

Hyphen(-):

① 단어의 의미를 보다 명확하게 전달할 때 사용.

Improper   He will meet small businessmen.
Proper   He will meet small-business men.

② 단어를 복합시켜 한 단어 같은 의미를 전달할 때 사용.
 • on-the-job training(현장연수)
 • on-the-scene newscast(현장뉴스보도)

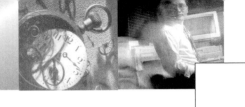

- on-the-record(뉴스보도를 전제로 한 발언)
- full-time job, first-quarter growth, socio-economic, korean-American, anti-globalism, cell-like 등

③ 전화번호, 여권번호, 통장번호, 주소 등을 나타낼 때 사용.

Quotation Marks(" "):

① 연설자나 저자의 말, 작품을 인용할 때 사용.

"The United States will close 15 major military installations in Korea", the Ministry of Defense said.

An official said, "I object to the closure of 15 U.S. military installations in Korea".

"I do not object", a scholar said, "to the closure of 15 U.S. military installations in Korea".

A speculator said the U.S. will close "at least 15" military installations in Korea.

> **Note**
>
> 제3자의 입을 통해 인용 보도할 때는 "quote someone as saying"의 형식을 취한다.
>
> The newspaper quoted him as saying "Korea's jobless rate fell to 3.3 percent last month".

② 특정사회, 특정시대에 생겨나는 신조어를 표기할 때 사용.

Police announced a list of those involved in "wonjo kyoje" scandal.

Point :

2개 이상의 Paragraph(단락)이 연속적으로 인용될 경우 각 단락이 시작될 때마다 Open-Quote Mark를 하고 Close-Quote Mark는 마지막 단락이 끝날 때만 표기한다.

"The government will not take pump-priming measures.

"It is not desirable to take such measures to kick-start the economy", he said.

Ellipsis(…):

① 마침표 3개의 연속점으로 표기하는 생략부호는 문장에서 덜 중요한 부분을 생략할 때 사용.

President Nixon said in his resignation announcement: "…However, I no longer have a strong enough political base in Congress".

② 망설이는 표현으로 사용

"Well…"

Asterisk(*):

Asterisk(별표)는 참고 자료로서 별도의 설명을 요할 때 각주 (Footnote)의 역할을 대신 하는 기능으로 사용된다.

Slash/Diagonal/Virgule(사선):

This is used to indicate that any of the terms so joined may be used in the sentence without altering the meaning. (2개 이상의 단어로 의미 를 변경없이 붙여서 나열할 경우 사용)

규약 8: Capitalization(대문자사용)

① Capitalize the first words of sentences.

ex) I was born in Seoul.

② Capitalize proper names, names of months, days of week.

ex) Seoul, Pusan, Panama Canal…, January, February…, Sunday, Monday.

③ Capitalize titles preceding names.

ex) Prof. Kim, Rep. Hong, Foreign Minister Han.

④ Capitalize names of races and nationalities.

ex) Korean, Japanese.

⑤ Capitalize names of organizations, schools, newspapers.

ex) OECD(Organization for Economic Cooperation and Development), Harvard University, The New York Times.

⑥ Capitalize names of religious denominations, holidays, festivals, wars, distinguishing words.

ex) the Bible, the New Testament, God, Catholic, Protestant, the Koran, Christmas Day, World War II, Korean National Red Cross.

✔ Do Not Capitalize.

① 이름 다음에 오는 칭호, 또는 독립적으로 쓰는 칭호: Han, foreign minister.

② 계절이름: spring, summer, autumn, winter.

③ 동·서·남·북을 나타내는 방향: east, west, south, north.

④ 학위: bachelor of science, master of arts, doctor of philosophy.
⑤ 오전·오후의 약어: a.m., p.m.

규약 9: Abbreviations(약어)

① 이름 앞에 사용되는 직함: Gen. Kim, Capt. Lee, Pvt. Han, lst Lt. Park, Dr. Kwon.
② 주요기구, 단체, 정당이름: WTO, ROTC, GOP.
③ 미국 주요 주 또는 영토이름: N.Y.(New York), D.C.(District of Columbia).

Do Not Abbreviate:

① President: Pres. Kim.
② Vice President: Vice Pres. Cheney
③ Days of Week: Sun. Mon.(except in tabular forms)

Common Errors 7

News Writer는 논리적 모순, 문법적 오류, 단어의 중복사용, 비슷한 단어들의 혼용 등으로 영문작성에 있어 많은 실수를 범하게 된다.

더욱 심각한 문제는 이러한 오류가 습관적이며 반복적으로 일어나고 있다는 것이다.

이러한 실수는 원어민 News Editor에 의해서도 수정되지 않고 그대로 인쇄되어 나가는 예가 적지 않다.

다음은 News Writer들이 잘못 사용하는 단어들을 오류빈도가 높은 순으로 모은 것이다.

✓ Task Force

Wrong	Special Task Force, or Special Task Force Team
Right	Task Force

Wrong   The Korean government has formed a special task force to tackle the Japanese government's approval of middle-school textbooks which distort historical facts to glorify its wartime atrocities.

"정부는 일본정부가 과거 전쟁의 잔악행위를 미화하기 위해 역사적 사실을 왜곡한 중학교 교과서의 검정 통과문제를 다루기 위해 특별대책반을 구성했다".라는 취지의 발표문을 기사로 작성한 것이다.

위 영문에서 "special"은 삭제되어야 한다.

Take out "Special".

"Task Force" means a "unit specially trained to execute a special mission"의 뜻으로 자체적으로 이미 "special"과 "team"의 의미를 함축

하고 있기 때문이다.

수 없이 발표되는 정부기관의 "특별대책반" 구성에 관한 기사를 쓸 때, 초임 writer들이 흔히 겪는 논리적 함정이다.

Riot Police

Improper	Riot Police Force
Proper	Riot Police

ex   The riot police force dispersed demonstrators.

Take out "force".

진압경찰(폭동, 데모 등을 진압하는)이라고 표현할 때 Force는 불필요하다.

Legislate, Enact

이들 두 단어가 "입법 즉 법률을 제정하다"(To make a law or laws)의 의미로 사용될 때 "Enact"는 목적어(Law or Laws같은)를 수반하나, "Legislate"는 목적어가 필요 없다.

Enact	North Korea has recently enacted a new law on processing trade with an eye to luring more foreign investment into the cash-strapped economy.
Legislate	North Korea has recently legislated on processing trade···.

ex   The new legislation will help the poor.

Note

"Legislation" means the making of a law or laws.

Book, Arrest, Indict

• Book: 입건하다

A 30-year-old worker has been criminally booked without physical detention on suspicion of having killed a student.

• Arrest: 구속하다

Police arrested a company worker on suspicion of having raped and killed a woman.

• Indict: 기소하다

Prosecution indicted him on charges of rape and murder.

Accident, Incident

일반적으로 사건, 사고를 나타내는 뜻으로 사용되는데 초심자들이 틀리기 쉬운 단어다.

• Accident: 자연재해나 화재, 폭발, 충돌, 추락 등의 예기치 못한 사고.
• Incident: 사람 사이의 불화에서 야기된 살인(Murder), 싸움(Fight) 같은 사고.

ex 1 A bus collided with a truck in downtown Seoul yesterday, killing five persons.
The accident(not incident) occurred in front of the Seoul Railroad Station at 5 a.m.

ex 2 A fire broke out at a hotel restaurant yesterday and police are investigating the cause of the accident. (not incident)

Note

Accident는 Unintentional(고의가 아닌)한 사고, Incident는 Intentional(고의성이 있는)한 사고를 뜻함.

ex **3** A housewife yesterday stabbed a child to death in Hwasong, Kyonggi-do. Police are now questioning three persons in connection with the incident. (not accident)

ex **4** The people of the former Soviet Union offered prayers yesterday for those killed by the explosion at Ukraine's Chernobyl nuclear power plant. More than 70,000 Ukrainians were disabled by the accident. About 7 million people are estimated to suffer physical or psychological effects of radiation related to the Chernobyl disaster. The Chernobyl atomic plant has been closed down but human calamities born by the catastrophe remain. (the Associated Press wire service story)

Biannual, Biennial, Biennale

"연 2회의", "2년에 한번", "격년행사"의 의미로 혼동하기 쉽다.

- Biannual: Occurring twice a year. Half-yearly. Semiannual.
- Biennial: Occurring every two years. Lasting or living for two years.
- Biennale: Event occurring every two years. Kwangju Biennale

AIDS, HIV

- AIDS: Acquired Immune Deficiency Syndrome의 약어로 "후천성 면역결핍증".

A disease that attacks the body's immune system, rendering it unable to fight disease.

- HIV: Human Immunodeficiency Virus의 약어로 면역결핍을 일으 키는 바이러스의 일종.

AIDS is caused by a microorganism called HIV, transmitted in body fluids through contact with infected blood, sexual intercourse, and the use of non sterile hypodermic needles.

AIDS는 병명, HIV는 바이러스의 일종.

> *ex*　　South Africa has the world's largest population of AIDS cases (or sufferers).
> 　　An estimated 4.7 million people are HIV positive(11 percent of the population. (AIDS cases: 후천성 면역결핍증 환자, HIV positive: 면역결핍을 일으키는 바이러스감염 양성 반응)

Percent, Percentage Point(s)

- Percent: 전체에 대한 비교치의 양을 100분율로 나타냄.
- Percentage Point(s): Percent를 나타내는 수치들 간의 차이.

> *ex*　　Korea's unemployment fell to 4.8 percent in March from 5 percent in February, 2001.
> 　　The jobless rate in March, 2001, represented a 0.1 percentage point increase over the same period a year ago.

Demand, Ask for, Call for

"요구하다", "청구하다"라는 의미로 쓰이나 함축하는 뜻이 다르다.
- Demand(To ask for authoritatively): (고압적으로) 요구하다.

> *ex*　　He demanded that I help him.

- Ask For, Call For: 일상적으로 요청할 때 쓰인다.

> *ex*　　American firms have asked for(or called for) the opening of Korean auto markets.

Note
미국인들은 자동차시장 개방협상에서 한국신문들이 "demand"라는 표현을 쓰는 데에 불만을 표시한다.

···Was Learned to Have Said, Reportedly

확인이 덜된 말을 인용하여 "···이라고 말한 것으로 알려졌다"라고 표현할 때 쓰이는 경우, Reportedly를 사용한다.

Awkward	Minister Kim was learned to have said so.
Better	Minister Kim has reportedly said so. (들리는 바에 의하면···)

Drastic, Sharp or Remarkable

The word "drastic" is overused or often misused.

"Drastic" implies "dire" or "dreadful". It would be awkward to say "drastic increase" of something good.

Awkward	Korea saw a drastic increase in production last month.
Better	Korea saw a sharp(remarkable) increase in production last month.

Second/ Third, Secondly/Thirdly

"둘째", "셋째"의 뜻으로 쓰인다.

"Secondly/Thirdly" is used in stuffy, archaic expressions. Modern language holds with "Second/Third".

Awkward	Secondly(Thirdly), he said···
Better	Second(Third), he said···

Repairs, Repairing Works

"보수작업"의 의미로 "Repairs"로 충분하다.

Works는 redundant(중복의)이다.

Awkward	The shop will be closed during repairing works.
Better	The shop will be closed during repairs.

Criticize Against, Discuss About

"비판하다", "토의하다"라는 의미에서 전치사사용에 현혹되기 쉽다.

Wrong	He criticized against Korean politics. They discussed about Korean politics.
Right	He criticized Korean politics. They discussed Korean politics.

Bare, Disclose, Reveal

"밝히다", "공표하다"라는 의미로 쓰인다.

"Bare"는 "(비밀 등을) 폭로하다"라는 의미로 사용.

Awkward	He bared the fact that he is a Korean-American.
Better	He disclosed or revealed···

Note

Use sparingly "Bare".

Aim to, ···Designed to, ···Meant to

"목표로 삼다"의 의미로 사용되는 단어들.

다양성을 위해 "···Designed to" or "···Meant to"로 대체 사용가능.

"Aim to" is overworked in news writing.

ex   The program aims(is designed) to develop the travel industry.

179

Noteworthy, Worthy of Note

"주목할 만한"이라는 의미로 사설 등에 많이 사용되는 단어.

These words are perfectly acceptable as synonyms. These are used for what catches, captures, or attracts the public attentions, to be emphasized, not to be overlooked, missed or ignored···

Dialogue, Dialogues

"Dialogue" means conversation between two parties or more, hence almost always in the singular. It is not a synonym for "talks" in this sense. (Dialogue, Dialog 병용)

Improper   The two parties plan to have dialogues soon.
Proper   The two parties to have dialogue soon. South-North Korean Dialogue.

Third Placer, Third

"3위 입상자"로 표현할 때의 다양한 표현.

Passable   Kim was the third placer.
Better   Kim was third, or ···came in third, ran third, took third place, placed third.

Equipment, Work , Real Estate, Furniture, Baggage/ Luggage

장비, 일, 부동산, 가구, 수화물의 의미로 쓰일 때 단수로 처리한다.
These are collective nouns. These must be always singular in form.

Wrong   Equipments, Works, Real Estates, Furnitures, Baggages, Luggages.

> **Note**
>
> "Work"가 "작품"의 뜻으로 사용될 때는 예외.
> The literary works of Thomas Hardy.

Missing, Disappearance

A person who has disappeared is "missing", but "missing" is not what has happened to him. Thus, someone's missing is wrong and someone's disappearance is right.

Wrong   Police are investigating his missing.
Right   Police are investigating his disappearance.

Inauguration, Wedding, Funeral

취임식, 결혼식, 장례식의 뜻으로 사용.

These words imply "ceremonies". It is usually redundant to say "⋯" ceremony because these words by themselves would suffice.

Improper   Inauguration Ceremony, Wedding Ceremony, Funeral Ceremony.
Proper   Inauguration(s), Wedding(s), Funeral(s).

Iron, Steel

These are not the same.

Steel is iron that has been treated in a special way to give it qualities which iron does not possess. Building materials such as girders are made of steel, not iron.

Prevent, Prevent in Advance

"Prevent" means to keep from happening, as by previous measures. Thus, using "in advance" with "prevent" is redundant.

Sports, Sports Games

Sports are by definition games, so the word "sports" alone are sufficient. Sports refer to outdoor or athletic games such as football, baseball, track, tennis, swimming etc.

This does not mean, however, that all sports are all games. A boxing bout is not a game but a fight and the participants are boxers or fighters, not players.

Improper	Students like sports games.
Proper	Students like sports.

Signed Between···, Signed By···

Wrong	The agreement was signed between two ministers.
Right	The agreement was signed by two ministers.

Within This Week/Month/Year

"금주 중", "이달 중", "금년 중"의 의미를 표기할 때 "Within"의 사용은 불필요하다.

Awkward	The project will be finished within this week/this month/ this year.
Preferable	The project will be finished this week/ this month/ this year.

To say "by the end of this week" or "before the end of this week" is acceptable.

During This Week/Month/Year

"During" can be omitted.

The play will be held (during) this week/month/year.

Occupation, Profession, Vocation, Job

- Occupation: 시간, 관심, 정력을 차지하는 총체적 직업을 나타냄.
- Profession: 학문적 소양이 필요한 직업. (의사, 변호사, 문필가, 언론인 등)
- Vocation: Avocation(부업)의 대어(對語)로 "본직"의 의미. 천직, 재능의 의미에 가깝다.
- Job: 임금을 받는 모든 일(아르바이트) 포함.

Gut, Destroy

화재 기사에서 많이 사용되는 용어.

"Gut"는 건물 내부만 탈 때 사용.

We may say a building is gutted by a fire when the inner parts of the building have been destroyed, leaving the outer walls standing.

A building that has burned to the ground has not been gutted. It has been destroyed.

Note

"Gut" is not a synonym for "Destroy".

Buildings Were Instructed···, Cars Were Told···?

"Buildings" or "Cars" are inanimate objects. "Buildings" or "Cars" and other inanimate objects cannot "hear" instructions. Thus, they cannot be "instructed" or "told".

Wrong	Taxis were told to fasten seat belts. Buildings were instructed to do···
Right	Taxi drivers were told to fasten seat belts. Owners of buildings were instructed to equip them with fire-fighting appliances.

Open

Once the meeting is opened, it continues(usually) but it does not go on opening. That happens only once. Thus, to say "The meeting was opened from···to ···" is nonsense.

Wrong	"The meeting was opened from Jan. 1 to Feb. 1".
Right	"The meeting opened on Jan.1 and continued until Feb.1".

Hold

"Hold" is often misused. It is nonsense to say the "committee was held···" because a committee is a group of people, not an occasion or a period of time.

Wrong	The steering committee was held.
Right	A meeting of the steering committee was held. The committee was convened.

Note

In some case, "hold" is unnecessary. If you write, "During the meeting held on···", "held" should be invariably taken out because it is redundant. If a group of people met on a certain day, then their meeting was "held" on that day.

Cyclone, Hurricane, Typhoon, Tornado

선풍(旋風), 태풍, 폭풍우의 뜻으로 발생지역에 따라 달리 불린다.

- Cyclone: 인도양 방면의 폭풍우.
- Hurricane: 멕시코만 방면의 폭풍우.
- Typhoon: 서태평양, 남 중국해 방면의 폭풍우.
- Tornado: 미국의 Mississippi 강 유역 및 서부 아프리카에서 일어
  나는 폭풍우.

···Hoped, ····Believed

회견 또는 인터뷰 내용을 인용할 때 주의를 요하는 표현이다.

Wrong   The minister hoped···, He believed···
Right   The minister said he hoped···, He said he believed···

Note

How do you know what the minister hoped or believed? All you know is what he said.

Exempt

Someone or something is always exempt from something. You cannot exempt a tax.

What would you exempt it from?

Wrong	The government has decided to exempt the residence tax.
Right	The government has decided to exempt the people from the residence tax.

In, At, During

"At" is sometimes overworked or misused in news writing. The preposition "at" almost always indicates either a place or a time. Meetings or organizations are neither places nor times. Thus, someone cannot make a speech "at" the National Assembly or "at" a meeting of the committee.

Improper	He spoke at the National Assembly. He revealed the plan at a session.
Proper	He spoke in the National Assembly. He revealed the plan during a session.

Early, Soon

- Early: 어떤 정해진 시간 보다 "일찍" 또는 어떤 시간의 "초기"란 뜻
- Soon: 현재 또는, 어떤 시점으로부터 "바로", "곧", "오래지 않아", "이윽고"란 뜻

I got up early in the morning. Soon learned, soon forgotten.

Relations, Relationship

"관계"란 의미로 쓰인다.

- Relations: (사람과의, 국제사회에서의)관계. 흔히 복수로 사용.
- Relationship: 친족관계, 연고. Connection by blood. Don't say "relationships".

In general, "relations" is to be preferred. Diplomatic Relations. (외교관계)

Other Related

There is always a main subject and there are related subjects. In this case, "other related matters" doesn't make sense. "Other" should not be used in discussing or dealing with matters.

> *ex*   They discussed the medical care system and(other) related matters.

Budget, Money

국문기사에 "예산부족으로…"라는 표현을 영역할 때 유의해야 한다.

A budget is a plan for the use of money. It is not itself money. Using "money" or "funds" is preferable in most cases of news writing.

Wrong   "Lack of budget". It has not been built due to lack of budget.

Right   "Lack of funds". It has not been built due to lack of funds.

This Time

This phrase is usually not necessary and often misleading. Some cub reporters often write awkwardly, "Foreign Minister Han's U.S. visit this time is …" as if he had made previous visits, which he has not. In this case, "this time" is unnecessary.

Incumbent, Present

"현직의" 의미를 표현할 때 초보자들이 잘못 쓰는 경우가 많다.

"Incumbent" refers to persons presently holding office. It does not refer either to institutions or to documents. It is used of individuals, not groups.

Wrong   Incumbent Constitution.
Right   Incumbent President or Prime Minister.

Jewels, Jewelry

- Jewels: Jewels are precious stones such as diamonds, rubies and so forth. They are not precious metals such as gold and silver.
- Jewelry: Jewelry refers collectively to ornaments made of precious stones or precious metals or both.

Have Willingness, Be Willing To

Awkward He has willingness to do it.
Better   He is willing to do it.

Education, Training

Education may include training, but most training is not education. Training is instruction in the performance of certain specific tasks. Education is the acquisition of a wide range of knowledge useful not only for practical life but also for intellectual development.

Improper He was educated to operate a machine. She was educated to repair a TV.
Proper   He was trained to operate a machine. She was trained to repair a TV.

Create, Create…new

"창조(창출)하다"라는 뜻으로 사용될 경우 "Create" 자체에 "new"의 개념이 있음을 유의해야 한다.

Improper   The government has worked out a plan to create 2 million new jobs.

Proper   The plan will create 2 million jobs. (or an additional 2 million jobs)

Obstruct Evidence, Destroy Evidence

"증거를 인멸하다"라는 뜻으로 쓰일 때 틀리기 쉽다.

Wrong   The prosecution arrested him for fear that he would obstruct evidence.

Right   The prosecution arrested him for fear that he would destroy evidence.
(검찰은 증거인멸을 우려해서 그를 구속했다.)

Killer, Killer Suspect, Culprit

살인 사건에 연루된 혐의자를 영문으로 쓸 때 국문기사에서 "범인" 또는 "살인자"라는 표현을 직역하면서 오류를 범하기 쉽다.

법원판결이 나기 전에는 '범인(Culprit)'이란 표현은 삼가 해야 한다.

또 직설적으로 '살인자(Killer)'란 표현도 판결이 나기 전에는 '살인혐의자(Killer Suspect)'라고 표기해야 한다.

Wrong   He killed a man. Police are investigating the "killer" or "culprit".

Right   Police are investigating the "killer suspect".

A certain Lee, "··· identified as Lee"

사건, 사고 기사에서 확정판결이 나기 전까지 비록 관련된 사람의 신원이 밝혀진다 해도 인권적 차원에서 이름을 완전히 밝히지 않는 것을 관례로 하고 있다. 성만 쓰는 경우 "···identified as+성" 보다 "A certain +성"으로 표기하는 것이 바람직하다.

Improper　　He killed a student. The man, identified as Lee, is investigated by police.

Proper　　The man, a certain Lee, is investigated by police.

Symptom, Syndrome

증후, 증후군의 의미로 일시적이냐 지속적이냐 여부에 따라 다르다.

• Symptom: An organic or functional condition indicating the presence of disease.
일시적으로 일어나는 징후, 조짐, 증후, 증상.

ex　　He has all the symptoms of malaria.

• Syndrome: The aggregate of symptoms and signs characteristic of a specific disease or condition.
지속적으로 일어나는 징후(증후)군, 일정한 행동양식.

ex　　Acquired Immuno-Deficiency Syndrome(AIDS).

Virus, Germ, Bacteria

• Virus: Any of a group of ultramicroscopic infective agents causing disease.
• Germ: Any microscopic organism, especially of the bacteria that causes disease.
• Bacteria: Typically one-celled microorganisms causing disease.
(단세포 미생물)

Avenge, Revenge

"복수하다", "앙갚음하다"라는 의미로 사용상의 차이가 있다.

- Avenge: This implies the infliction of deserved and just punishment for wrongs or oppressions. (정당한 앙갚음)
- Revenge: This implies the infliction of punishment as an act of retaliation, usually for an injury against oneself, and connotes personal malice, bitter resentment, as the moving force. (사적감정으로 야기된 보복)

Note

He avenged his sister upon her faithless lover. He revenged his brother's death.

Emigrate(Emigration, Emigrant), Immigrate(Immigration, Immigrant)

"이민(移民)"이 출국성이냐, 입국성이냐에 따라 구별하여 사용한다.

- Emigrate(Emigration, Emigrant): 출국성 이주하다. (이민, 이민자)
- Immigrate(Immigration, Immigrant): 입국성 이주하다. (이민, 이민자)

Note

They emigrated from Korea to Hawaii. Many immigrants came to the United States from Brazil.

Coalition, Alliance

"연합, 합동(union)"의 의미로서 임시적이냐 or 지속적이냐에 따라 사용상 구별이 요망된다.

- Coalition: A temporary alliance of factions, parties for some specific purposes, usually in times of national emergency. Coalition Cabinet(연립내각).
- Alliance : A close association for a common purpose, as of nations, political parties. The Holly Alliance(신성동맹).

Ally, Friendly Nation(Country)

"동맹국", "우방국"을 표현할 경우 군사동맹 등 조약에 의해 결속된 동맹적 관계에 있는 나라와 기타 일반적으로 우호적인 국가와 구별하여 표기한다.

- Ally: 동맹국(allied state). A country, group, leagued by (defense) treaty with others.
- Friendly Nation(Country): 우방국.

Wrong	Japan is Korea's ally.
Right	The U.S. is not only a friendly country to Korea but an ally to it. Japan is a friendly country to Korea.

Last, Latest

- Last: 연속되는 것의 "마지막"에 오는 것.
- Latest: 연속되는 것의 "최신의" 것.

Note

This is the last news.
This is the latest news.

Cry, Weep, Sob, Wail
- Cry: (소리치며) 울다. It is no crying over spilt milk.
- Weep: (시적인 표현으로)울다. She wept over her baby's death.
- Sob: (감상적으로 흐느끼며)울다. She sobbed out the whole sad story.
- Wail: (통곡하며)울다. He wailed over his misfortunes.

Stock, Share
주, 주식과 관련된 경제용어로 쓰일 경우 구별하여 쓸 필요가 있다.

- Stock: (집합적 의미의) 증권, 주식, 주.

Shares representing capital investment in a company.

- Share: (각각의) 주.

A vested interest in a company, as a share of stock.

> **ex**　The Seoul stock market extended its losing streak last week, as investors continued to unload their shares in tandem with the U.S. investors. Stock investors dumped tech shares.

Current Account, Trade Balance
- Current Account: 경상수지.

Current account implies a national balance of payments that include international trade in goods and services along with transfer payments and short-term credit.

- Trade Balance: 무역수지.

A balance of trade difference over a certain period of time between the value of a country's imports and exports.

Non-military Government, Authoritarian Government

"문민정부" "독재정권"의 바람직한 표현.

Avoidable   Civilian Government, Dictatorial Government.
Recommendable   Non-military Government, Authoritarian Government.

Former, ex-

These indicate the office(post) held previously.

Acceptable   ex-president, ex-foreign minister.
Better   former president, former foreign minister.

Armistice, Ceasefire, Truce

These words imply a temporary cessation of warfare by agreement.

Truce(Ceasefire, Armistice) Talks: 휴전(정전)회담.

Football, Soccer

축구를 표기할 때 미국, 영국식 표기에 따라 달리 사용.

- Football: 미국에서 주로 "미식축구" 영국에서는 "축구" "럭비"의 의미로 병용.
- Soccer: Football과 함께 축구의 뜻으로 병용되고 있다.

The Federation International de Football Association(FIFA, 국제축구연맹), The Korea Football Association(대한축구협회), 2002 FIFA World Cup Korea/Japan.

Asset, Capital

경제기사에서 "자산", "자본"의 용어사용 시 내용상의 차이가 있다.

- Asset(자산): Current cash and other items readily converted into cash, usually within a year.
- Capital(자본): Money, equipment or property in a business by a person or corporation.

Lay Off, Dismiss, Discharge, Fire, Sack

"해고하다"의 의미로 사용되는 단어들.
"Lay Off"는 원칙적으로 일시적 해고를 뜻함.

> **Note**
>
> They got laid off. (discharged, dismissed, fired, sacked)

Invade, Intrude

- Invade: To enter with hostile intent for conquering, usually a foreign country.
- Intrude: To thrust or force without leave or excuse, usually others' house.

Ambassador to…, Consul General in…

Ambassador(대사) 다음에는 전치사 "to", 이어 나라이름, Consul General(총영사) 다음에는 전치사 "in", 이어 도시이름이 온다.

> **Note**
>
> Korean ambassador to Japan, Korean consul general in Hawaii.

Ambassador, Minister, Envoy

외교 관련 기사에서 틀리기 쉬운 용어다. Ambassador는 "대사", Minister는 "공사", Envoy는 "외교사절"의 의미를 갖고 있다.

- Ambassador: 대사(大使)는 파견국의 원수가 접수국의 국가원수에게 파견하는 외교사절이며 공관의 최고 직급의 외교관이다.

An accredited diplomatic agent of the highest rank, appointed as the head of the diplomatic mission.

- Minister: 장관, 목사 등의 뜻도 있으나 외교관련 기사에서는 대사 다음 직급에 해당하는 공사(公使).

One commissioned to the diplomatic mission, ranking next below an ambassador.

- Envoy: 공관의 공식적인 직책은 아니고 일반적인 "외교사절" 또는 "특사"를 지칭할 때 사용됨. 원칙적으로 대사 아래의 공사 (one ranking next below an ambassador)를 지칭하나, 신문 기사에서는 간혹 대사급을 포함하여 정부가 상대국에 파견하는 포괄적 의미의 국가대표를 의미한다.

An official sent as a government representative on a diplomatic mission.

ex The Seoul government yesterday recalled Korean Ambassador to Japan Choi Sang-yong in a strong show of protest against the Tokyo government's approval of middle-school textbooks justifying wartime atrocities. The envoy will be in Seoul for a few days.

(한국정부는 일본정부의 전쟁 잔학상의 정당화를 언급한 중등교과서 인준에 대한 강력한 항의의 하나로 주일 한국대사를 소환했다. 그는 서울에 며칠간 체류할 예정이다.)

Charge d′Affaires, Acting Ambassador

외교용어로서 전문적인 단어다. 이 같은 전문용어를 본란에서 다루는 이유는 신문이나, 홈페이지, 또는 각종 기관홍보물 등에서 외교관의 직급을 잘못 표기해 정정보도를 하기도 한다.

대사가 없는 경우 차석에 해당하는 외교관이 대사직을 대행하는 사례가 많다. 이때 직역해서 "Acting"이란 단어를 쓸 때가 많은데 의미는 통하나 정확한 표현은 아니다.

대사업무를 대행하는 사람은 정식으로 Charge d'Affaires로 표기하며, Charge d'Affaires en pied 또는 Charge d'Affaires en titre로 표기하는 "대리대사"와 Charge d'Affaires ad interim로 표기하는 "대사대리"의 2종류가 있다.

- Charge d'Affaires en pied or en titre: 공관장이 부임하지 않은 상태에서 대사업무직을 수행하는 공관장으로 "대리대사"라 칭함.
- Charge d'Affaires ad interim: "대사대리"라고 부르는데 대사가 질병 또는 기타 사유로 업무를 수행하지 못할 때 임시로 대리직을 수행하는 자를 말함.

▌Note▐

Charge d'Affaires en pied or en titre는 공관장이고 Charge d'Affaires ad interim은 임시직이다.

- Acting Ambassador: 대사직을 대행하는 자들 모두를 호칭할 수는 있으나 올바른 표현이 아님.

Commission, Committee

Commission, Committee 모두 "위원회"란 뜻으로 쓰이는데 성격에 따라 차이가 있다.

- Commission: 일반적으로 상설 기구인 경우에 쓰이고 행정기관에 해당하는 권한과 기능을 갖고 있다.
- Committee: 한시적인 역할을 하는 기구에 사용된다.

ex 1 Fair Trade Commission(FTC: 공정거래위원회), Financial Supervisory Commission(FSC: 금융감독위원회). FTC, FSC 모두 장관급이 운영하는 독립된 상설행정기구임.

ex 2 Regulatory Reform Committee(규제개혁위원회), South-North Exchange Promotion Committee(남북교류추진위원회). Committee는 일정기간 주어진 역할과 기능을 끝내면 해체되는 한시적기구로 위원장은 다른 직에 종사하면서 겸직하는 예가 많다.

Council, Counsel, Councilor

- Council: 회의, 심의회, 평의회, 지방의회, 시의회 등의 의미.

An assembly of persons convened for consultation or deliberation. A body of persons elected or appointed to assist in the administration of the government.

ex 국가안전보장회의: **National Security Council.**

The government's decision to offer fertilizer to North Korea was reached during a meeting of the National Security Council. Details related to fertilizer aid will be discussed in the South-North Exchange Promotion Committee.

(북한에 비료를 제공하겠다는 정부의 결정은 국가안전보장회의에서 정해졌다. 비료원조에 대한 세부사항은 남북교류추진위원회에서 논의될 것이다.)

- Counsel: 의논(하다), 협의(하다).

• Counselor(-llor, 英): 자문역, 상담역, 고문, 대사관의 참사관.
Counsel implies consultation for exchange of advice, opinions.

• Councilor(-llor, 英): 시의회 등의 의원, 고문관, 대사관의 참사관.
※ The house of councilors: 일본의 참의원.

Consuls General, Directors General, Secretaries General, Prosecutors General

"General"이 뒤에 붙는 직책은 일반적으로 "총체적으로 감독하는 의미"가 부여된 감독직일 때 쓰인다. 이들의 복수형은 "Generals"가 아니고 앞에 "s"가 붙는다.

Wrong	Consul Generals, Director Generals, Secretary Generals, Prosecutor Generals.
Right	Consuls General(총영사), Directors General(국장, 감독), Secretaries General(비서실장), Prosecutors General (검찰총장).

Condolences, Consolation

Condolence는 "애도"(종종 ~s)의 뜻으로 사용된다. 사망할 경우 유가족 또는 관련 친지에게 애도의 뜻을 표할 때 쓰인다.

Consolation은 위로, 위안의 의미로 어려운 상황에 있는 사람에게 용기를 북돋아주는 행위를 말함.

• Condolences: They expressed (or presented) condolences to me on my father's death. Please accept my sincere condolences.
• Consolation: Consolation money(위자료), Consolation Prize(감투상).

Draft Bill, Bill, Motion

- Draft Bill: (법안의) 초안

> *ex* The governing party has written a draft bill on the trade law.

- Bill: (의회에 상정된) 법안

> *ex* They will lay a reform bill before the National Assembly(Congress, Parliament, Diet).

Note

한국의 경우 법률제정안과 개정안은 정부 혹은 국회의원 들이 제출한다.

- Motion: 동의안

국무총리 해임안건이나, 해외파병 안 등 단순한 국회의 동의를 필요로 하는 안건을 지칭할 때 쓰는 용어.

> *ex* **1** The National Assembly approved a troop dispatch motion.

> *ex* **2** The National Assembly failed to pass a motion for dismissal of the premier proposed by the opposition camp.

Information, Intelligence

정보(情報)의 의미로 사용되나 용도가 다르다.

- Information: 지식, 견문, 자료 등 일반인들이 공유할 수 있는 정보를 말함.

Information applies to facts that are gathered in any way, as by reading, observation, hearsay, etc. and does not necessarily connote validity(for inaccurate information).

> *ex*   The Information-Communication Ministry: 정보통신부.
> Information Technology(IT): 정보기술.
> Super-Highway Information Network: 초고속 정보통신망.

- Intelligence: 넓은 의미에서의 정보를 뜻하지만 군이나 정보기관
  에서 다루는 Secret Information인 첩보(諜報)의 의
  미가 강함.

Intelligence implies information that is gathered secretly for military or police purpose.

> *ex*   The Central Intelligence Agency: 중앙정보부.
> The National Intelligence Service(NIS): 국가정보원.(중앙정보부
> 의 변형된 이름)
> Intelligence Agent: 정보부요원.

Misinformation, Disinformation

- Misinformation: 誤정보(False or Misleading Information).
- Disinformation: 逆정보(특히 적의 간첩을 속이기 위한).

Law, Act

새로 제정 혹은 개정된 법을 말할 때 쓰이며, 일반적으로 한국에서는 "Law", 미국에서는 "Act"를 쓴다.

National Assembly, Diet, Congress, Parliament

"국회"를 말할 때 나라에 따라 표현이 다르다.

- The National Assembly: 한국, 프랑스.
- The(National) Diet: 일본, 스웨덴.
- Parliament: 영국.
- Congress: 미국.

> **ex** The National Assembly conducted a parliamentary inspection of the administrative agencies, while the House is in session.
> (국회는 회기 중 행정부처에 대한 국정감사를 실시했다.)

Note

Congress와 Parliament 앞에는 The가 안 붙는다.

국가에 따라 국회의원을 "Assemblyman", "Lawmaker", "A member of the National Assembly", "A Diet member, Dietman", "A member of Parliament", "A Congressman" 등으로 표기함.

Headline(제목) 또는 본문 중 중복을 피하기 위해 국회를 "House"라고 표현할 수도 있다.

Boycott, Refuse, Reject

- Boycott: 불매(不買)동맹을 하다. 배척하다. 거부하다. 개인이 아닌 집단에 사용.

This word originated from a movement, led by a land agent named Captain Boycott in Ireland in 1880 and his aim was to persuade people not to buy certain goods. This word should be used to describe the refusal by a certain group of people engaging in a certain activity as a form of protest. It should be used for a group of people, not for a single individual.

> **ex 1** Civic groups yesterday launched a nationwide campaign to boycott Japanese goods in protest against Tokyo's authorization of history books that whitewash Japan's wartime atrocities.
> (민간단체들은 일본의 전쟁 잔악상을 속이려는 내용을 담은 역사교과서의 인준에 항의하는 표시의 일환으로 일본상품의 불매운동을 벌였다.)

> **ex 2** They boycotted the newspaper.
> (그들은 신문불매운동을 벌였다.)

• Refuse: (부탁, 요구, 명령 등을) 거절하다. To decline to do.

He refused to comment on that issue. I refused to discuss the question.

• Reject: (계획, 제안 등을) 거절하다, 거부하다, 각하하다.

The company rejected a merger offer.(그 회사는 통합 안을 거부했다.)

Note

Refuse가 주로 사람을 의식하고 거절하는데 반해 Reject는 사물을 염두에 두고 거부하는 뜻으로 사용된다.

Recruit, Scout

• Recruit: (신병, 새 회원을)모집하다. 신당원, 신입생, 신입회원.

To enlist new personnel for service, as in a military and other organizations. Recruitment Advertising: 모집광고.

> *ex* The Korea Times recruits reporters.
> (코리아타임스는 기자모집을 한다.)

• Scout: 찾으러 가다. 정찰하다.

To look for. To find new talent.

> *ex* The team scouts for a few promising players.

Sign, Placard, Picket

국문기사에서 시위에 관한 기사나 사진설명을 영문으로 쓸 때 "피킷" "현수막" 이라고 표기하곤 하는데 이러한 단어들을 영문으로 직역함에 있어 잘못 사용하는 경우가 종종 있다.

• Sign: 표지, 길잡이, 도표, 간판(Signboard), 도로표시판(Street Signs).

Information, directions, advertising, etc., publicly displayed. A structure on which such information is printed or posted.

- Placard: 간판, 벽보.

A printed or written notice, publicly displayed.

- Picket: 뚝, 경계 초, 감시병.

A pointed stick, tent peg, bar, fence paling, or stake.

Wrong	The members of a civic environmental organization hold up a picket reading "Let's Keep the Han River Clean".
Right	They demonstrated in front of the National Assembly yesterday, holding up a sign calling for opening the plenary House session at an early date. (그들은 국회 본회의 조기개최를 요구하는 표지판을 들고 국회 앞에서 시위를 했다.)

Note

Avoid using a "picket" in place of a "sign" or a "placard".

Confederation, Federation

두 단어 모두 영한(英韓) 사전에 "동맹" "연합" "연맹"으로 번역되어 일반인들은 구별해서 사용하지 않으나 외교문서 특히 남북한간의 문제에서는 정확하게 용도에 맞게 써야 한다.

- Confederation: Nations or states which joined in a league or union for a common purpose.

국가와 체제를 유지하면서 공동의 이익을 추구하기 위해 만든 연맹. 각 구성국이 대외적으로 독립성을 유지함.

ex The Confederation(아메리카 식민지동맹): The union of the American States(1781-1789) under the Articles of Confederation.

The Confederate States of America: 1861년 미국 남북전쟁의 발단 이 된 합중국으로부터 분리된 남부 11개 주의 연합. 11개 주인 Alabama, Arkansas, Florida, Georgia, Louisiana, Mississippi, North Carolina, South Carolina, Tennessee, Texas, Virginia는 The Confederate Army(남군)을 만들어 남북전쟁을 하게 됨.

- Federation: The union of states by agreement of each member to subordinate its power to that of the central authority in common affairs.

각 구성국이 Confederation 같이 독립성을 유지하는 것이 아니라 중앙 정부에 국가공동 업무에 대해서는 권한을 위임하는 형태.

> **Note**
>
> 한반도에 있어 정치통합을 하고 궁극적으로 통일을 위한 준비체제의 첫 단계로 남한은 "Confederation"을 북한은 "Federation"을 제안하고 있다. 남한은 "2국가, 2체제"형태의 Confederation을, 북한은 "1국가, 2체제"의 Federation을 제안하고 있어 정치적으로 예민한 문제로써 표기에 조심해야 할 부분이다.

Consist of, Comprise, Composed of

다같이 "구성하다, ~되다"라는 의미로 사용될 경우 전치사의 유무에 주의를 요한다.

- Consist of: Water consists of hydrogen and oxygen.(=is made of)
- Comprising: The United States comprises 50 states.
- Composed of: The troop is composed of Korean soldiers.

> **Note**
>
> The committee consists of(comprises, is composed of) seven members.

Family, Family Members, Relative

"가족"의 의미로 쓰일 경우 Family와 Family members의 올바른 사용이 요구된다.

- Family: 가족, 가정(부부와 자녀들), 가구(Household)의 개념으로 사용됨. A family consists of parents and their children.

- Family Members: 가족의 구성원 "식구"의 개념으로 초심자들이 쓰는 경우가 있다.
  "식구"의 정확한 표현은 members of a family이다.
  너의 가족은 몇 식구냐? 라고 물을 때 How many members are there in your family? 하면 되고, 여섯 식구라고 할 때 We are a family of six 라고 하면 된다.

  ex   Five members of a family were killed in a fire at a Seoul restaurant. (서울에 있는 한 식당화재로 일가족 5명이 불에 타 죽었다.) 유가족을 표현할 때 bereaved family 라고 하면 충분하다. bereaved family members 라고 하면 의미가 중복(redundant)되게 된다.

Improper   I have family members to look after.
Proper   I have a family to look after.

- Relative: "친척", "인척", "친족"의 의미를 가진 단어.

Relative applies to any person who is related to another by birth, marriage. Uncle, aunt, and cousin are one's relatives.

Shuffle, Reshuffle, Shakeup, Replace, Shift

내각개편, 광범위한 개각의 의미로 Cabinet Shuffle, Cabinet Reshuffle, Cabinet Shakeup 이라고 한다. 개개인의 자리바꿈은 Replace 또는 Shift를 쓴다.

- Shuffle: To mix(playing cards, positions) so as to change their order or arrangement.
- Reshuffle: Shuffle과 비슷한 뜻으로 쓰이나 개편한데 뒤이어 재개편의 의미로 쓰임.
- Replace, Shift: Individuals may be replaced by others or shifted to other post, but not shuffled or reshuffled.

> *ex*   The President yesterday conducted a major Cabinet shuffle(or reshuffle) affecting 10 ministers.

Improper   Foreign Minister Lee was reshuffled or shuffled.
Proper   Foreign Minister Lee was replaced(or shifted) in the Cabinet shakeup.

Father, Priest

종교적으로 신부를 지칭할 때 쓰이는 단어들.
- Priest : 이름 없이 신부라는 독립된 단어로 쓰일 때 사용됨.

> *ex*   He was ordained a priest.(그는 신부가 되었다.)

- Father: 이름과 같이 표기할 때 또는 대화 중 상대방을 호칭할 때 쓰임.

> *ex*   Father Brown(브라운신부), Father Hong(홍 신부).

Sir, Mr., Mrs., Dr.

사람 이름 앞에 쓰여 …경(卿: 영국의 나이트 작 또는 준 남작의 지위에 있는 사람에 붙임), …씨, …부인, …박사의 호칭으로 쓰일 때 주의를 요한다.

- Sir: This is used either with the full name or with the given name alone, but never with the family name alone. If John Smith is made a knight, he is to be called Sir John Smith or(more informally) Sir John.
- Mr., Mrs., Dr.: Use either with the complete name or with the family name.

ex   Mr.(Mrs., Dr.) Park, Lee, Kim.

Wounded, Injured

"부상"의 의미로 쓰일 때 용도가 다르다.

"Wounded" is used in battles or wars, but "Injured" is used in such accidents as car collisions and fires.

- Wounded: 전투, 전쟁에서 얻은 부상인 경우에 쓰임.

ex   Many soldiers were wounded in the Korean War.

- Injured: 교통사고, 화재 같은 사고에서 입은 상처를 말할 때 쓰인다.

ex   Many citizens were injured(or hurt) in a traffic accident.

Rob, Steal

"…에(게)서 훔치다"의 뜻으로 Rob, Steal을 사용할 때 논리적 오류를 범하기 쉽다. 전치사 위치와 사용이 다르다.

- Rob: rob a person of something.

ex   He robbed a student of money.

- Steal: steal something from a person.

ex   He stole money from a student.

Note

Rob는 폭력, 협박 등을 해서 물건을 강탈하는 것이고, Steal은 몰래 훔치는 의미로 사용된다.

Swindle, Embezzle

Both mean to take by fraud for one's own use.

• Swindle: 사취하다, 속이다.

ex He swindled money out of a woman.

• Embezzle: 유용(착복)하다.

ex He embezzled a lot of money from his company.

Mobilize, Use

전자는 "동원하다", 후자는 "사용(이용)하다"의 의미인데 잘못 혼용되는 경우가 있다.

• Mobilize: This is a military word. Its strict meaning is to place troops in a state of readiness for battle. By extension, one may also mobilize people and equipment for purposes other than military. But it is not a synonym for "use" or "prepare". Moreover, it does not apply to single individuals or small groups.

• Use: To put into service, to avail oneself of, to take advantage of, 개인 or 소수에 이용.

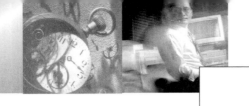

Apartment, Flat

자주 "아파트"의 의미로 쓰이는데 주의를 요한다. 공동주택 내의 한 가구 분의 주택.

- Apartment: A room or suite of rooms to live in.
  한 세대 주거를 위한 아파트 한 채를 말함.
- Flat: "아파트"의 영국식 표기법.

  Note

  Don't say "apartment flat" because it means "apartment apartment".

  몇 개의 아파트로 구성된 빌딩을 나타내는 "Apartment House"와 구별을 요함.

Forecast, Predict

"예상하다", "예언하다"라는 의미로 사용될 때 동사 "may"와 함께 쓰는 것은 바람직하지 않다.

Improper He forecast(or predicted) that it may be necessary.
Proper   He forecast(or predicted) that it would be necessary.

  Note

  The word "may" implies possibility or likelihood, a meaning which is already contained in the word "forecast" or "predict".

A Total Of

"총계"의 뜻으로 쓰인다.

- A total of 5,000 people: 전체 5,000명의 사람 또는 여러 분야의 숫자를 합산 처리할 때만 "total"을 사용하고, 단일 사항을 표기할 경우는 total 없이 숫자만 표기한다.

This phrase is not necessary unless the figure cited is a combination of other figures. Thus, if you would like to say the populations of various areas and then add them up, it is proper to say that this makes "a total of" of so and so. But when the figures are simply quantities that have not been combined, there is no need to use "a total of". This phrase is sometimes used to avoid spelling out the figures at the beginning of a sentence. Don't do it. Spell out!

Improper	A total of 98 people responded to the questionnaire.
Proper	Ninety-eight people responded to the questionnaire.

New, Newly

"신임 장관", "신축 건물" 등 "새로이" 임명되거나, "새로이" 지은 건물을 나타낼 때 "new" or "newly"의 단어를 남용(?)하는 것을 많이 보게 된다. 대부분의 경우 국문으로 표기 된 것을 "직역"하는 데서 오는 일종의 단어 "남용"으로 과감히 삭제해야 한다.

These words are, in most cases, redundant and unnecessary. When, for example, structure is built, it is certainly not necessary to say that it is "newly built". Obviously, a building constructed where there was no such building before is "new". When an old building is extensively repaired or remodeled, it is not "newly built". It is just "repaired or remodeled". The same is true of elections and appointments. Don't say "new president" or "new premier" because there is no such position as "new president", "new premier" or "new minister".

Improper	He was elected(or appointed) the new president(or new prime minister).
Proper	He was elected(or appointed) the president(or prime minister).

Trip, Tour, Visit, Travel, Journey, Voyage

"여행," "방문"의 의미로 사용되는데 정확한 용법에 유의할 필요가 있다.

- Trip: (짧은)여행, 출장. A honeymoon trip to Hawaii.
- Tour: (관광)여행, 유람여행. He is now on an Asian tour.
- Visit: (사교, 용건, 여행 등을 위한) 방문. He is on a visit to Seoul.
- Travel: (거리가 먼) 여행. Gulliver's Travels.
- Journey: (육상)여행. journey around the world.
- Voyage: (긴 바다)여행, (우주)여행. The Voyages of Marco Polo.

ex　U.S. Secretary of Sate Colin Powell plans to make a visit to East Asia, including South Korea, in early May. If realized, it will mark his first trip to this region since taking office in January. During his stay in Korea, he is going to make a tour of a frontline area.

From

"From" is often redundant and sometimes misleading or nonsensical.

Improper　The program will start from Sept. 10. The law will be effective from Oct.1.

Proper　The program will start on Sept.10. The law will be effective on Oct. 1.

ex　The meeting will last from Sept.1 to Oct.30.

Note

"From" is often used correctly when both the end and the beginning of a process are specified.

Prime Minister, Premier, Chancellor

총리, 수상의 뜻으로 각국 정부형태에 따라 차별화하여 쓰고 있다. 그러나 많은 영문 작성자들은 혼용하여 쓰고 있다.

- Prime Minister: Throughout the Commonwealth, formerly the British Commonwealth.

> **Note**
>
> Prime Minister is the traditional translation from most other languages.

- Premier: France and its former colonies, former Communist nations of East Europe and Asia. Provincial Governments in Canada, Australia.
- Chancellor: Austria, Germany.

> *ex* German Chancellor Gerhard Schroeder has endorsed the creation of a European Government.

The United Kingdom(UK), Britain, England

"영국"을 잘못 표기해서 영국정부나 대사관으로부터 항의를 받는 예가 있다.

- The United Kingdom of Great Britain and Northern Ireland: 영국의 공식명칭.
- (Great) Britain: England, Wales, Scotland로 이루어진 영국영토의 대부분을 이루고 있음.
- England: 수도 London이 위치한 주 행정 관할 구역.

Wrong	Korea maintains diplomatic relations with England. Ambassador to England.
Right	Korea maintains diplomatic relations with the U.K. British Ambassador to Korea.

Note

Don't use England in place of the U.K. or Britain.

the Netherlands, Dutch, Holland

"네덜란드"를 나타낼 때 쓰이는 국명으로 유의해야 한다.

- the Netherlands: 네덜란드의 공식 국명으로 일반적으로 통용됨. 수도는 Amsterdam.
- Dutch, Holland : the Netherlands의 다른 국명이나 외교적인 표현으로는 부적합하다.

Note

Dutch treat(각자 부담하는 회식) 등의 부정적인 인식 때문에 공식 외교문서에 Dutch의 사용을 삼가고 있음.

Snake, Rat

미국의 신문들 중에는 Snake(뱀), Rat(쥐) 같은 단어의 사용을 "Barred Words"라 하여 가급적 사용을 삼가고, 특히 조간신문의 Front Page에 Snake나 Rat가 들어가 있는 사진의 사용을 금한다.

Whisky, Whiskey

영국, 캐나다 산은 "Whisky", 미국, 아일랜드산은 "Whiskey"라고 표기한다.

Gas, Oil

- Gas: 원래 공기 이외의 가스 또는 기체를 말한다. 예를 들어 Tear Gas(최루가스), Natural Gas(천연가스) 등을 말할 때 쓰인다. 그러나 신문을 비롯한 Journal 등에서 Gas는 Gasoline(휘발유)의 줄인 말로 더 많이 쓰인다.

- Oil: 기름의 뜻으로 식용유(Cooking Oil), 등유(Lamp Oil), 중경유 (Heavy, Light Oil)를 표기할 때 사용하나, 미국에서는 엔진오일, 즉 윤활유(Lubricant)의 의미로 더 많이 쓰인다.

> *ex*   We are all set but we have to put some gas in our car and go to a gas station.
> (준비가 다 되서 기름을 넣기 위해 주유소로 가야겠다.)

Toward, Towards

Wrong	Towards, Afterwards.
Right	Toward, Afterward.

Half A Mile, A Half Mile

Wrong	A Half Mile, A Half Dozen.
Right	Half A Mile, Half A Dozen.

Words Commonly Confused

- accept: to receive
- except: to exclude

- access: approach
- excess: superfluity

- affect: to influence
- effect: to execute

- aisle: passage
- isle: island

- alley: lane
- ally: associate

- all ready: entirely prepared
- already: at this time

- all together: grouped
- altogether : completely

- allude: indirectly refer to
- elude: evade

- allusion: indirect reference
- illusion: deceptive appearance

- altar : table
- alter: vary

- angel: spiritual being
- angle: corner

- assure: to reassure
  (requires indirect object)
- insure: to obtain or supply
  insurance
- ensure: to make certain

- barbarous: almost savage
- barbaric: showy, lacking
  restraint

- berth: sleeping compartment
- birth: beginning

- beside: by the side of
- besides: in addition to

- boarder: one who takes meals
- border: margin

- Calvary: site of Christ's crucifixion
- cavalry: horsemen

- canvas: cloth
- canvass: to solicit

- capital: principal
- capitol: statehouse

- censor: examine
- censure: condemn

- centrifugal: proceeding from center
- centripetal: proceeding toward center

- chord: combination of tones
- cord: small rope

- cite: summon, quote
- site: position

- clothes: garments
- cloths: fabrics

- coarse: common, harsh
- course: route

- complement: addition, to add
- compliment: to praise

- congenial: kindred in taste
- genial: cheerful

- conscience: moral faculty
- conscious: cognizant

- consul: commercial representative
- council: assembly
- counsel: advice, attorney

- contemptible: despicable
- contemptuous: insolent

- continual: in close succession
- continuous: uninterrupted

- corps: unit of organized establishment
- corpse: dead body

- credible: trustworthy
- creditable: deserving of praise
- credulous: inclined to believe

- currant: raisin
- current: motion

- dairy: place for milk and its products
- diary: daily record

- desert: arid region; v.t, to leave, to abandon
- dessert: course at end of meal

- discreet: prudently silent
- discrete: separate or distinct

- disinterested: uninfluenced by personal advantage
- uninterested: apathetic

- dual: twofold
- duel: combat

- elegy: lament
- eulogy: commendatory oration

- emigrant : one who leaves
- immigrant: one who enters

- eminent: conspicuous or prominent
- imminent: ready to take place

- euphemism: softened statement
- euphony: pleasant sound
- euphuism: artificial statement

- exceptional: uncommon
- exceptionable: objectionable

- factious: dissentient
- factitious: artificial
- fictitious: false
- fractious: unruly

- faint: swoon
- feint: pretense

- farther: applied to distance, space
- further: applied to extent, degree

- forceful: possessing power
- forcible: violent

- feat: deed
- feet: terminals of legs

- formally: conventionally
- formerly: heretofore

- forth: onward
- fourth: ordinal of four

- hanged: executed
- hung: suspended

- healthful: wholesome
- healthy: well, vigorous

- ingenious: clever
- ingenuous: candid

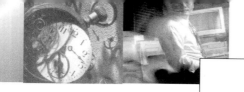

- indict: to charge
- indite: to write

- inhumane: lacking in human kindness
- inhuman(also unhuman): savage

- later: afterward
- latter: the second of two

- lay(also past of lie): to place
- lie: to recline

- liable: responsible, obliged
- libel: defame

- lightening: relieving
- lightning: flashing of light

- loose: unattached
- lose: to miss

- luxuriant : profuse
- luxurious: costly, ornate

- mantel: shelf
- mantle: cloak

- misogamist: marriage hater
- misogynist: woman hater

- noted: renowned
- notorious: disgraceful

- observance: act of custom
- observation: attentive consideration

- passed: crossed
- past: bygone

- persecute: to afflict
- prosecute: to carry on

- personal: private
- personnel: group collectively employed

- plain: level land
- plane: level surface

- practical: useful, skillful
- practicable: feasible

- precedence: priority
- precedents: antecedents

- principal: chief
- principle: doctrine or belief

- prodigy: wonder
- progeny: offspring

- propose: to offer
- purpose: to resolve

- prophecy: prediction
- prophesy: to predict

- quiet: undisturbed
- quite: wholly

- raise: to erect
- rise: to ascend

- recipe: formula
- receipt: written
  acknowledgment

- respectful: deferential
- respective: individual

- sciolist: pretender
- scholiast: commentator

- sensual: fleshly
- sensuous: pertaining to the
  senses

- sentiment: feeling
- sentimentality: excessive feeling

- stationary: fixed
- stationery: paper

- statue: mage
- stature: height
- statute: law

- specie: coin
- species: variety

- suit: apparel
- suite: set

- therefor: for that
- therefore: hence

- venal: mercenary
- venial: excusable

- waive: to relinquish
- wave: to swing

- wont: accustomed, habitual
- won't: will not

(2000 Webster's Pocket Grammar, Speech Style Dictionary, pp.193-197)

Korean-Derived Etymology 9

본란에서는 한국어에서 유래된 영어(Korean-derived etymology)를 다루어 보기로 한다.

한국의 국력이 신장되고 경제대국으로 성장함에 따라 "은둔의 나라 (Hermit Kingdom)"로부터 세계 속의 국가로 위치를 확고히 하게 되었다.

1988년 서울올림픽 개최, UN가입, OECD(Organization for Economic Cooperation and Development)가입, 세계무역의 10위권 진입 등으로 한국은 명실공히 국제무대에서 선진국들과 어깨를 나란히 할 수 있는 위치에 놓이게 되었다.

삼성, 현대를 위시한 몇몇 기업들은 이미 세계기업이 되었으며, 자동차, 철강, 반도체, 조선분야는 세계에서 이미 선두의 자리를 차지하게 되었다.

국제사회에서의 한국의 위치와 걸맞게 몇몇 한국의 토속어는 국제적으로 통용되는 영어가 되었다. 이들 중 일부는 이미 Oxford 사전이나 Webster 사전에 올라있다.

김치(Kimchi)는 2001년 정식으로 국제음식으로 공인되었고, 태권도 (Taekwondo)는 2000년 Sydney Olympics에서 정식 경기종목으로 채택되었다. 재벌이란 용어도 사용된 지 오래다.

다음은 Oxford, Webster사전에 올라 있는 한국어가 영어화 된 것에 대해 어떻게 표기되어 있는 지 원문 그대로 실어 보기로 한다.

■ Kimchi: spicy pickled cabbage, the national dish of Korea. (Page 1009, The New Oxford Dictionary of English) —: a vegetable pickle seasoned with garlic, red pepper, and ginger that is the national dish of Korea.(Merriam-Webster's Collegiate Dictionary, Tenth Edition)

- **Chaebol:** a large business conglomerate, typically a family-owned one. (Page 300, The New Oxford Dictionary of English)

- **Tae kwon do(Taekwondo):** modern Korean martial art similar to karate. origin, Korean, literally 'art of hand and foot fighting,' from tae "kick"＋kwon "fist"＋do "art" method.(Page 1887, The New Oxford Dictionary of English)

  —: often capitalized T&K&D, etymology: Korean taekwondo, from tae-to trample＋kwon fist＋to way, 1967: a Korean martial art resembling karate. (Merriam-Webster's Collegiate Dictionary, Tenth Edition)

- **Hangul:** often capitalized, 1946: the alphabetic script in which Korean is written. (Merriam-Webster's Collegiate Dictionary, Tenth Edition)

- **Kisaeng:** a Korean professional singing and dancing girl.(Merriam -Webster's Collegiate Dictionary, Tenth Edition)

- **Sijo:** an unrhymed Korean verse form appearing in Korean in 3 lines of 14 to 16 syllables and usually in English translation in 6 shorter lines.
  (Merriam-Webster's Collegiate Dictionary, Tenth Edition)

- **Moonie:** etymology: Sun Myung Moon born 1920 Korean evangelist, 1974: a member of the Unification Church founded by Sun Myung Moon.
  (Merriam-Webster's Collegiate Dictionary, Tenth Edition)

- **Won:** one hundred "chon".(Merriam-Webster's Collegiate Dictionary)

이들 단어들은 기사 작성시 특별한 설명없이, 그대로 사용해도 좋다.

ex 1 Kimchi has been formally certified as an international food. It has satisfied the standards on food safety and hygiene, required by the Codex Alimentarius Commission(CAC) which is the world's highest authority of food, CAC officials said during their 24th annual conference in Geneva, Switzerland.

ex 2 The chaebol have been defiant of the government's request for restructuring.

Note

위에서 기술한 바와 같이 정식으로 영어사전에 올라 있는 단어 이외에도, 외국인들(특히 주한 외국인들) 사이에 많이 통용되는 용어들이 있다. Pulgogi, Kwaoe, Hakwon, Yogwan, Ajumma, Naengmyon, Soju, Makkolli, Chige 등이 그것들이다.

oint :

한국어에서 유래된 단어들의 복수에는 S를 붙이지 않는다.

Wrong   Taekwondos, Chaebols, Kimchis, Chiges, Ajummas, Hakwons, Kwaoes, Pulgogis.

Right   Taekwondo, Chaebol, Kimchi,···

Faulty Words 10

한국인이 잘못 쓰는 영어 모음

Wrong	Right
Handphone(핸드폰)	Cellular Phone, Cell Phone, Mobile Phone
Handle(자동차핸들)	Steering Wheel
Fighting!(파이팅)	Go!
Vinyl House(비닐하우스)	Plastic Greenhouse
Gas Range(가스레인지)	Gas Stove
Golden Time(골든타임)	Prime Time, Prime Hour
Condo(콘도)	Condominium
Hotchkiss(호치키스)	Stapler
Ball Pen(볼펜)	Ballpoint Pen
One Shot(원샷)	Chug-a-lug, Bottoms Up
Bomb Drink(폭탄주)	Boilermaker
After Service(아프터서비스)	After-Sales Service, Warranty Service
Accel(악셀)	Accelerator, Gas Pedal
Punk or Punc(빵꾸, 펑크)	Puncture, Flat Tire
Running(난닝구)	Sleeveless Undershirts
Side Brake(사이드브레이크)	Hand Brake
Sign Pen(사인펜)	Felt-tip Pen
Super(슈퍼)	Supermarket
Back Mirror (백미러)	Rear-View Mirror(차 안), Door Mirror(차 밖)

Wrong	Right
Chou Cream (슈크림)	Cream Puff
Castella (카스텔라)	Sponge Cake
I am a single (싱글이다)	I am a single handicap player.
Ray Ban (라이방)	Sunglass
Klaxon (클랙슨)	Horn, Honk
Salary Man (샐러리맨)	Salaried Worker
Season Off (시즌오프)	Off-Season
Enquete (앙케트)	Questionnaire
Katyusha (카추샤)	KATUSA
Hot Cake (핫케이크)	Pancake
Panty Stocking (팬티스타킹)	Tights, Pantyhose
Hiking Course (하이킹 코스)	Hiking Trail
Hearing Test (히어링테스트)	Listening Test
Benz (벤츠)	Mercedes Benz
Baby Car (베이비카)	Baby Carriage, Baby Buggy, Pushchair, Pram
Symbol Mark (심벌마크)	Logo
Home Doctor (홈 닥터)	Family Doctor
Ice Coffee (아이스커피)	Iced Coffee
Table Charge (테이블차지)	Cover Charge
Training (추리닝)	Sweatshirt, Sweat Suit
Cheer Girl (치어걸)	Cheerleader
Free Dial (프리다이얼)	Toll Free, Toll-Free Number
Coordi (코디)	Coordination, Coordinator
Combi (콤비)	Combination
Open Car (오픈카)	Convertible (Car), Ragtop
White Shirt (와이셔츠)	Shirt
Hard (아이스캔디, 하드)	Popsicle
Room Salon(룸 살롱)	Saloon (Bar)
Dead Ball(데드볼)	A Walk

Wrong	Right
Four Ball(포볼)	A Walk, A Base on Balls
Home In(홈인)	Return to Home Base, Home Plate
Home Ground Playing	Home Playing
Trans(도란스)	Transformer
X-mas(엑스마스)	Christmas
Name Card(네임 카드)	Business Card, Calling Card
Cunning(칸닝구, 컨닝)	Cheating
Slow Video(슬로우 비디오)	Slow Motion
White(문구용 화이트)	White Out
Window Brush(윈도우브러시)	Windshield Wiper, Wiper
Narrator Model(나레이터모델)	Pitch Girl
Diary(메모장, 수첩)	Date Book, Appointment Book
Burberrys(바바리)	Trench Coat
Mustang(무스탕)	Bomber Jacket
Classic Music(클래식 뮤직)	Classical Music
Agit(아지트)	Agitation Point
Eye Shopping(아이 쇼핑)	Window Shopping
Arbeit(아르바이트, 독일어)	Part-Time Job
CF, Commercial Film(씨에프)	Commercial
Sticker(스티커)	Ticket
Infra(인프라)	Infrastructure
Illust(일러스트)	Illustration
Fan(후앙)	Ventilation Fan
Free Madonna(프리마돈나)	Prima Donna
Stain(스덴)	Stainless Steel
Shorber, Shober(쇼바)	Shock Absorber
Sign(싸인)	Autograph
Bonnet (본네트, 엔진덮게)	Hood (미국), Bonnet (영국)
Vacances (바캉스, 불어)	Vacation
Perma (파마)	Permanent Wave, Perm

Wrong	Right
Mission (밋숑, 자동차 부속)	Transmission
Machine (미싱, 재봉틀)	Sewing Machine
Meeting(미팅, 남녀 만남)	Blind Date
Ment(한마디의 말)	Comment
Manner(매너, 예의범절)	Manners

Note

■ Handphone 기사를 포함한 정통문장에서는 Handphone으로 표기하지 않고, Cell Phone, Cellular Phone, Mobile Phone으로 표기한다.

그러나 Singapore, Malaysia, Indonesia, 일부 Europe 국가에서는 일반 회화체에서 Handphone이란 용어를 사용하기도 한다.

■ X-mas "X"는 그리스어에서 "크"로 발음되고, 그리스도의 첫 글자이기 때문에 광고나 카드에서 공간을 줄이기 위해 사용되는 경우가 있으나, 정통영어에 사용하는 것은 잘못이다.

■ Bomb Drink 폭탄주의 의미로 올바른 표현은 Boilermaker이지만 Time지에서 한국인의 술 문화를 다루면서 "Bomb Drink"라고 표기한 적이 있다.

■ KATUSA Korean Augmentation Troops to United States Army 의 약어로 "미국육군에 파견 근무하는 한국군인"을 뜻함.

■ Castella Portugal어로 Spain 중앙 북부의 Castilla 지방에서 만

든 빵에서 유래됨. 영어의 Custard(우유와 계란을 섞어 만든 케이크 일종)로부터 온 단어라는 설도 있다. <가짜영어 사전/안정효/현암사 p. 575>

■ Mustang

사전적 의미는 야생마, 포드제 승용차의 일종, 제2차 세계대전 당시의 미 공군 전투기를 뜻한다. 한국에서는 "무스탕"이 "털 달린 두꺼운 겨울외투"로 사용되고 있다. 이는 아마도 제2차 세계대전 당시 미 공군전투기 "Mustang"조종사 들이 추위를 이기기 위해 두꺼운 양가죽과 양털로 만든 외투를 입었는데 그래서 나온 말이 "Mustang Jacket"이고 이것이 몇몇 유럽국가에서 사용된 것에서 유래된 것으로 보인다. 영어에서는 잘 쓰이지 않고 Bomber Jacket으로 표기한다. 사전에는 다음과 같이 설명하고 있다.

Bomber Jacket: A jacket made of leather resembling those worn by World War II bomber crews. <Konglish 22/문화일보, 박현영>

■ Sign

"Sign"과 "Autograph"는 두 단어 모두 "서명"의 의미를 가지나 Sign은 기관이나 조직에서 이루어지는 "결재 성격"의 서명을 말하고 "Autograph"는 가수, 배우 등 유명인들이 지지자들에게 해주는 "기념 성격"의 서명을 말한다.

American vs. British English 11

미국영어(American English)와 영국영어(British English)에는 같은 의미지만 다른 철자 또는 단어를 쓰는 경우가 있다.

그러나 오늘날 영어는 미국영어에 많은 영향을 받고 있다.

미국계 통신인 The Associated Press(AP), The United Press International(UPI), 그리고 The New York Times, The Washington Post지 등은 미국영어를 따르고 있고, The Reuters, Financial Times 같은 영국계 통신과 신문 등은 영국영어를 사용한다.

그 외 여타 지역에서 발행되는 신문의 경우는 미국영어를 보편적으로 사용하고 있다.

한국의 영어신문 The Korea Times, The Korea Herald는 미국 영어 스타일을 따르고 있다.

Internet상에서 이루어지는 Data, Text들은 거의 모두가 미국영어로 이루어지고 있다.

다음에 열거한 것은 철자, 어휘에서 미국영어와 영국영어의 차이를 비교한 것이다.

Spelling

American English	British English
Analyze	Analyse
Catalog(ue)	Catalogue
Center	Centre
Check	Cheque
Color	Colour
Defense	Defence
Jewelry	Jewellery
Labor	Labour
Organization	Organisation
Pajamas	Pyjamas
Program	Programme
Tire	Tyre
Whiskey	(Scotch)Whisky, (Irish)Whiskey

Vocabulary

American English	British English
Apartment	Flat, Apartment
Attorney	Solicitor, Barrister
Can	Tin
Candy	Sweets
Cookie, Cracker	Biscuit
Corn	Sweet Corn, Maize
Diaper	Nappy
Elevator	Lift
Eraser	Rubber, Eraser
Fall, Autumn	Autumn
First Floor	Ground Floor
French Fries	Chips
Garbage, Trash	Rubbish
Gas(Gasoline)	Petrol
Highway, Freeway	Motorway, Main Road
Intersection	Crossroads
One-Way Ticket	Single Ticket

온라인신문 & 12
홈페이지

컴퓨터 보급의 증가, 방대한 정보의 양, 그리고 정보교류의 확대 등으로 인해 온라인신문은 점차로 많은 독자층을 확보해 가고 있다.

특히 젊은 세대에게 있어 온라인신문은 그 이용도가 급증하는 추세이다.

전자신문은 보통 14~17인치내의 작은 면이다.

온라인신문은 기존의 오프라인 신문과 어떻게 다른가?

한마디로 온라인신문은 동적이고 오프라인 신문은 정적이다. 온라인 신문에서는 공간, 색채, 소리, 움직임의 사용 등이 다양하다.

그러나 두 신문 모두 News Writing, Headline, Layout 등 지면 구성면에서 비슷한 원리가 적용된다.

온라인 신문에서는 초기화면을 여러 부분으로 나누어 간단한 헤드라인이나 뉴스요약, 안내 등을 먼저 제공한 후, 독자가 그 기사를 선택하면 더 자세한 본문을 볼 수 있도록 한다.

오프라인 신문에 강조된 것 중에서 온라인 신문에서 유념해야 될 원칙들을 반복강조, 간략하게 제시한다.

① Modular 형(직사각형 편집) 으로 편집한다.
② 헤드라인 충돌을 피한다. (Avoid butting headlines)
③ 헤드라인은 간결하게 처리한다.
④ 단신 정보성 기사는 꾸러미로 처리 한다.
⑤ 기사 및 사진설명은 5W's＋1H 원칙에 의거 오프라인에서의 일반기사와 같은 요령으로 처리한다.

해외홍보원에서 발행하는 국정뉴스 홈페이지(Figure 1)와 World Cup 조직위에서 발행하는 월드컵 뉴스 홈페이지(Figure 2)는 위의 원칙들을 따르고 있음을 잘 보여 주고 있다.

About KOIS [English / Kor

KOREA.net

Korean Government Homepage

Korea Today

Nation | Foreign Relations | Business | Arts / Events | Science / Tech | Living / Travel / Sports | Opinion

more news...

Focus

July-Augus

Governmen
US Traffic
Report

Government

Executive Branch
Legislature
Judiciary
President
Independent Organizations

Background

Statistics
Facts about Korea
National Symbols
Hangeul [*Korean Alphabet*]
Images of Korean Culture
World Cultural Heritage

Additional

Japanese Textbook Issue
South-North Relations
Human Rights in Korea
Events & Entertainment
Laws & Regulations
Visa & Immigration

Call Rate Cuts Have Positive Impact on Economic Growth: BOK
The Bank of Korea (BOK) predicted on Friday that a call rate cut of 1 percentage point would increase the nation's economic growth rate by 0.2 percentage point.

'Korean Firms Can Participate in Kazakh Oilfield Development'
A senior Kazakh lawmaker said on Friday that Korean firms could participate in the development of oil fields in petroleum-rich Kazakhstan.

7 Pro-Pyeongyang Activists Formally Arrested
The Seoul District Court on Friday allowed prosecutors to arrest several pro-Pyeongyang activists and one professor who allegedly engaged in pro-Northern activities during their recent trip to the communist country.

Find by

Arts/Cult
Busines
Cities/Pr
Compute
Educatio
Govern
News/Me
Referenc
Science/
Society/
Sports/R
Travel

World Fam

Find Error
Prizes!
Survey on I
July Winn
Classes on
and Cultur
Essay Cont
Korean Cul
Informatio
Publication
Magazines

Government Policy Updates   more...

Presidential | North | Foreign | Economy...Society...Information...People
Activities | Korea | Affairs

- Briefing Session on WTO New Round to Tour in Provincial Cities [August 25, 2001]
- Culture Ministry Opens Content Development Center [August 25, 2001]
- Song of Seoul [August 24, 2001]
- Gov't to Issue Bonds Abroad to Privatize Tobacco Corp. [August 24, 2001]
- KNTO Offers English-subtitled Korean Movies for Free [August 24, 2001]
- Korea, Iran Hold Consular Chiefs Meeting in Seoul [August 24, 2001]
- President Kim Won't Dismiss Unification Minister 'Cause of Controversy [August 24, 2001]
- APEC Meeting Under Way in Dalian Preparatory to APEC Summit [August 23, 2001]

Busines
Region:
Name:
SEARC

2002 FIFA WORLD CUP
KOREA JAPAN

The 14th Asian Games
BUSAN 2002

YeoSU World Expo 2010

VISIT KOREA
YEAR 2001

World CERAMIC

Weather

Seoul
23°C (73.4°F)
~ 30°C (86°F)

Exchange Rate [w/ $]

Buying	Selling
1,303.42	1,258.58

Stock Quotations

KOSPI	569.31	-0.76
KOSDAQ	67.78	-0.16

Figure 1

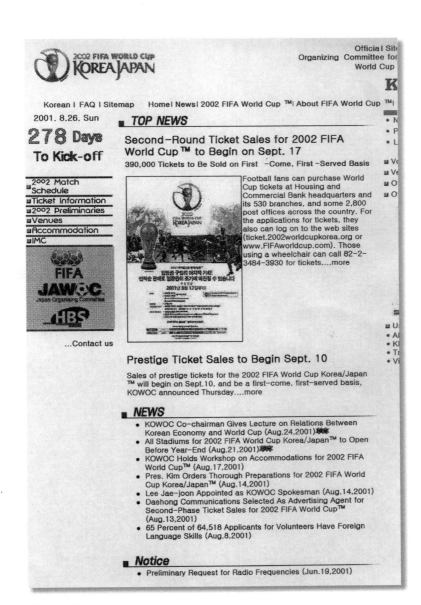

Figure 2

전문용어 13

온라인, 오프라인 불문하고 영문 뉴스기사 작성시, 직함이나 의전에 관한 용어를 한국식으로 잘못 직역함으로서 오류를 범하여 논쟁 또는 분규의 대상이 되는 수가 있다. 이 경우 관련된 사람이나, 기관으로부터 정정 보도(Correction)를 요청 받아 기사작성자의 신뢰도가 떨어지기도 한다.

본란에서는 국제적으로 통용되거나, 한국의 공식기관에서 인정 통용 되는 전문용어 들을 소개하기로 한다.

시대가 변천함에 따라 기구와 직함이 변하게 되고 용어표기도 달라지 고 있다.

외교관련 용어

외교용어는 1961년 비엔나에서 채택된 "외교관계에 관한 비엔나협약 (Vienna Convention on Diplomatic Relations")의 규약에 의거 사용하는 것이 국제적 관행이다. 한국을 비롯한 대부분의 나라들이 비엔나협약을 준수한다. 홈페이지, 신문, 잡지 기사작성시 비엔나협약에 기준한 용어 를 사용하는 것이 바람직하다.

외교사절(diplomatic envoy)

외교교섭 및 기타 직무를 수행하기 위해 상주 또는 임시로 외국에 파 견되는 국가대표를 외교사절(diplomatic envoy)이라고 함.

공관장(head of the mission)

공관장은 비엔나협약에 의거 국가원수에게 파견된 외교사절을 말하며 보통의 경우, 대사 및 공사, 대리대사를 말함.

The "head of the mission" is the person charged by the sending state with the duty of acting in that capacity.

공관직원(members of the staff of the mission)

공관직원은 파견국(sending state)의 임명에 의하여 직원으로서의 지위를 가지게 된 사람을 말하며 외교, 행정, 기술, 노무직으로 구분됨.
접수국(receiving state)의 인정에 의해 특권, 면제(diplomatic privileges and immunities)의 범위와 내용이 상이함.

The "members of the staff of the mission" are the members of the diplomatic staff, of the administrative and technical staff and of the service staff of the mission.

공관원(members of the mission)

공관장과 공관직원.

The "members of the mission" are the head of the mission and the members of the staff of the mission.

외교직원(members of the diplomatic staff)

공사, 참사관, 서기관 등 외교직명(diplomatic rank)을 가진 자를 뜻함.
외교직원은 파견국이 발행하는 외교여권을 소지함.

The "members of the diplomatic staff" are the members of the staff of the mission having diplomatic rank.

외교관(diplomatic agent)

관례적으로 공관장만 지칭하였으나, 비엔나협약에서는 외교직원을 포함함. 외교관이라 함은 파견국 국가원수의 대리인(agent)임을 의미하며, 외교관(diplomat)으로 통칭함.

The "diplomatic agent" is the head of the mission or a member of the diplomatic staff of the mission.

주재관(attache)

외교영역의 확대에 따라 국방, 경제, 재정, 교육, 문화, 공보, 조달 등 전문부서에서 파견되어 공관에 근무하는 주재요원으로 무관(military attache), 상무관(commercial attache) 등. attache에 대해서도 외교직원에 준하는 외교특권이 주어짐.

행정 및 기능직원(members of the administrative and technical staff)

외교사절의 사무기능 직무에 종사하는 행정보조원, 비서, 타자원, 통역원 등을 말하며 파견국 국민인 행정, 기능직원은 파견국이 발행하는 관용여권을 소지함. Personnel employed in the administrative and technical service of the mission.

노무직원(members of the service staff)

공관의 가사에 종사하는 자로 파견국이 고용한자. 수위, 운전원, 요리사, 경비원 등.

Members employed in the domestic service of the mission.

외교관의 계급(diplomatic rank)

대사(Ambassador)

대사는 파견국의 원수가 접수국의 원수에게 파견하는 외교사절임. 동등한 계급을 가진 기타 공관장의 구체적인 예로서는 영 연방 제국간에 파견, 접수되는 "고등 판무관"(High Commissioner), 리비아가 파견하는 People's Bureau의 Secretary를 들 수 있음.

대한민국은 재외공관의 장으로서 특명 전권대사(an ambassador extraordinary and plenipotentiary) 또는 특명 전권공사(a minister extraordinary and plenipotentiary) 제도를 인정하고 있음.

대사 내정자(Ambassador-designate)

대사 내정자로서 아직 주재국의 신임장(Letter of Credence, Credentials)을 못 받은 상태에 있는 대사를 말함.

공사(Minister)

원칙적으로 공사는 파견국의 원수가 접수국의 원수에게 견하는 특명 전권공사를 말함.

최근 대사의 상호교환이 상례가 되고 있어 특명 전권공사제도는 사실상 소멸되고 있음. 다만 대사 밑에 차석을 공사로 두는 경우가 많음.

Minister-Counselor

공사(Minister)와 참사관(Counselor) 사이의 직급으로 Latin America

지역과 기타 몇 나라에서 쓰는 호칭으로 정식 외교직책은 아니다.

간혹 부 공관장(Deputy chief of the mission)역할을 한다.

대리 대사, 대사대리

대리대사는 외무장관에게 파견된 사절로서 국가원수에게 파견된 대사 또는 공사와는 구별된다.

"대리대사(Charge d'Affaires en pied 또는 en titre)"는 공관장이라는 점에서, 대사가 질병이나 기타사유로 임시 대사직을 수행하는 "대사대리(Charge d'Affaires ad interim)"와 구별된다.

참사관, 1등(2등, 3등) 서기관, 주재관

diplomatic rank에 따라 통상적으로 대사, 참사관(Counselor), 1등 서기관(First secretary), 2등 서기관(Second secretary), 3등 서기관(Third secretary), attache의 순서임.

아그레망(agrement)

공관장(대사, 공사, 대리대사)을 파견할 때 주재국에 동의를 구하는 외교적 행위.

persona non grata(불만인 인물)

접수국이, 파견국이 공관장으로 파견하고자 하는 외교관에 대해 agrement을 요청할 때 자국에 불만이 있는 인물이라고 규정짓는 사람을 지칭함. 이 경우 접수국은 공관장의 접수를 거부할 수 있다.

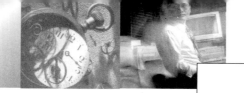

기타 기관 용어

1) 군대용어

□ 군인	Military Personnel, Armed Forces Servicemen, Military Servicemen.
□ 국군(한국)	ROK Armed Forces.
□ 육군(한국)	ROK Army.
□ 공군(한국)	ROK Air Force.
□ 해군(한국)	ROK Navy.
□ 해병(한국)	ROK Marines.
□ 장교	Officer.
□ 사병	Soldier.

Note

일반용어 표기로 육군사병: Enlisted Men,
공군: Airmen,
해군: Sailors or Seamen.

2) 계 급

 육 군

□ 원수	General of the Army, Five-Star General.
□ 대장	General, Gen.
□ 중장	Lieutenant General, Lt. Gen.

- □ 소장   Major General, Maj. Gen.
- □ 준장   Brigadier General, Brig. Gen.
- □ 대령   Colonel, Col.
- □ 중령   Lieutenant Colonel, Lt. Col.
- □ 소령   Major, Maj.
- □ 대위   Captain, Capt.
- □ 중위   First Lieutenant, 1st Lt.
- □ 소위   Second Lieutenant, 2nd Lt.
- □ 준위   Warrant Officer, W.O.
- □ **주임상사(원사)**   Sergeant Major, Sgt. Maj.
- □ 상사   Master Sergeant, M. Sgt.
- □ 중사   Sergeant First Class, Sfc.
- □ 하사   Staff Sergeant, S. Sgt.
- □ 병장   Sergeant, Sgt.
- □ 상병   Corporal, Cpl.
- □ 일병   Private First Class, Pfc.
- □ 이병   Private.

> **Note**
> 해병대 계급은 육군과 같다.

공군

- □ **상병-대장** 육군과 동일.
- □ 이병   Airman.
- □ 일병   Airman First Class, Afc.

해군

- □ 대장   Admiral, Adm.
- □ 중장   Vice Admiral, Vice Adm.
- □ 소장   Rear Admiral, Rear Adm.

- □ 준장 　 Commodore, Commo.
- □ 대령 　 Captain, Capt.
- □ 중령 　 Commander, Cmdr.
- □ 소령 　 Lieutenant Commander, Lt. Cmdr.
- □ 대위 　 Lieutenant, Lt.
- □ 중위 　 Lieutenant Junior Grade, Lt.j.g.
- □ 소위 　 Ensign, En.
- □ 주임상사 　 Master Chief Petty Officer, M.C.P.O.
- □ 상사 　 Chief Petty Officer, C.P.O.
- □ 중사 　 Petty Officer First Class.
- □ 하사 　 Petty Officer, P.O.

3) 경찰 계급

- □ 치안총감 　 Commissioner General, Com. Gen.
- □ 치안정감 　 Chief Superintendent General, Ch. Supt. Gen.
- □ 치안감 　 Senior Superintendent General, Sen. Supt. Gen.
- □ 경무관 　 Superintendent General, Supt. Gen.
- □ 총경 　 Senior Superintendent, Sen. Supt.
- □ 경정 　 Superintendent, Supt.
- □ 경감 　 Inspector, Ins.
- □ 경위 　 Lieutenant, Lt.
- □ 경사 　 Sergeant, Sgt.
- □ 경장 　 Assistant Sergeant, Asst. Sgt.
- □ 순경 　 Patrolman, Pat.
- □ 의경 　 Private, Pvt.

4) 행정부 조직

□ 대통령	President.
□ 청와대	Chong Wa Dae, Office of the President, or the Blue House.
□ 대통령 경호실	Presidential Security Service.
□ 국무회의	Cabinet meeting or State Council.
□ 국가경제자문회의	National Economic Advisory Council.
□ 국가안전보장회의	National Security Council.
□ 민주평화통일자문회의	Advisory Council on Democratic and Peaceful Unification.
□ 대통령과학기술자문회의	Presidential Advisory Council for Science & Technology.
□ 감사원	Board of Audit and Inspection.
□ 국가정보원	National Intelligence Service.
□ 총리실	Prime Minister's Office.
□ 행정조정실	Office for Government Policy Coordination(총리실산하).
□ 비상기획위원회	Emergency Planning Committee(총리실산하).
□ 기획예산처	Ministry of Planning and Budget.
□ 법제처	Government Legislation Agency.
□ 국정홍보처	Government Information Agency.
□ 해외홍보원	Korean Information Service.
□ 국가보훈처	Patriots and Veterans Administration Agency.
□ 공정거래위원회	Fair Trade Commission.
□ 금융감독위원회	Financial Supervisory Commission.
□ 청소년보호위원회	Commission on Youths Protection.

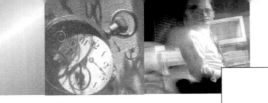

□ 재정경제부	Ministry of Finance and Economy.
□ 국세청	National Tax Service.
□ 관세청	Korea Customs Service.
□ 조달청	Public Procurement Service.
□ 통계청	National Statistical Office.
□ 교육인적자원부	Ministry of Education and Human Resources Development.
□ 통일부	Ministry of Unification.
□ 외교통상부	Ministry of Foreign Affairs and Trade.
□ 법무부	Ministry of Justice.
□ 검찰청	Public Prosecutor's Office.
□ 국방부	Ministry of National Defense.
□ 병무청	Military Manpower Administration.
□ 행정자치부	Ministry of Government Administration and Home Affairs.
□ 경찰청	National Police Agency.
□ 과학기술부	Ministry of Science and Technology.
□ 기상청	Meteorological Administration.
□ 문화관광부	Ministry of Culture and Tourism.
□ 문화재관리국	Cultural Properties Administration.
□ 농림부	Ministry of Agriculture and Forest.
□ 농업진흥청	Rural Development Administration.
□ 산림청	Forest Service.
□ 산업자원부	Ministry of Commerce, Industry and Energy.
□ 중소기업진흥청	Small Medium Business Administration.
□ 특허청	Intellectual Property Office.
□ 정보통신부	Ministry of Information and Communication.
□ 보건복지부	Ministry of Health and Welfare.

□ 식품의약청   Food and Drug Administration.
□ 환경부   Ministry of Environment.
□ 노동부   Ministry of Labor.
□ 여성부   Ministry of Gender Equality.
□ 건설교통부   Ministry of Construction and
                    Transportation.
□ 철도청   National Railroad Administration.
□ 해양수산부   Ministry of Marine Affairs and Fisheries.
□ 해양경찰청   National Maritime Police Agency.

5) 입법부

□ 국회   National Assembly.
□ 국회의장   Speaker.
□ 국회부의장   Vice Speaker.
□ 상임위원회   Standing Committee(위원장: Chairman).

6) 사법부

□ 대법원   Supreme Court.
□ 대법원장   Chief Justice.
□ 고등법원   High Court.
□ 지방법원   District Court.
□ 가정법원   Family Court.
□ 행정법원   Administrative Court.

7) 독립기관

□ 헌법재판소   Constitutional Court.
□ 선거관리위원회   National Election Committee.

(Citation Source: http://www.korea.net)

Romanizaton: 14
로마자표기법

Pusan or Busan? Inchon or Incheon? Kimpo or Gimpo? Mr.Kim or Mr.Gim? Mr.Park or Mr.Bag?

위에서 열거한 바와 같이 한국말 고유명사를 로마문자로 표기하는 데는 현재 여러 방식이 쓰이고 있는데 통일된 방식이 필요하다.

Romanization이란 알파벳으로 자국어 및 문자를 표기하는 방법을 말한다.

한글의 경우, 현재 여러 종류의 표기법이 제기되어 무질서하게 사용되고 있다.

정부관련 자료나 홍보물은 정부에서 제정한 표기법을, 외국인을 상대로한 신문이나 잡지 등에서는 주로 매큔-라이샤워 체계(McCune-Reischauer Sysytem)를 사용하고 있으며 일원적 표기체계를 이루지 못하고 있다.

한글의 로마자 표기에는 몇 차례에 걸쳐 개정 시행하고 있는 정부안과 McCune-Reischauer System("M-R방식") 이외에, "람슈테트" 방식, "예일방식"(The Yale System) 등이 있다.

어느 나라나 자국의 언어를 로마문자로 규격화하여 표기하기에는 여러 가지 어려운 점이 있는데 특히 한글인 경우 그 어려움은 더하다. 태생적으로 다른 음운구조와 언어구조를 가진 한글을 로마자로 표기함에 있어 그 어떤 표기법도 완전할 수는 없으며 다만 얼마나 가깝게 근접하여 표현하느냐 하는 것이 문제일 뿐이다.

각 표기법 마다 많은 예외규정을 두고 있으며 본서에서는 영어신문과 민간단체들이 발행하는 홍보물 등에 많이 사용되고 외국인들이 선호하는 M-R방식과 최근 정부가 개정 발표하여 정부기관지 홍보물 등에 범용 되고 있는 문화관광부안(2000년, 7월)에 대해서만 다루기로 한다.

M-R System

McCune-Reischauer 방식은 1939년 당시 평양 숭실전문학교 교장이던 미국인 선교사 George McCune과 Harvard 대학교 출신 Edwin O. Reischauer가 공동으로 만든 로마자 표기법이다.

McCune은 서울에서 태어나 연희전문의 최현배 선생 밑에서 한글을 공부했고, Reischauer는 도꾜에서 태어나 하버드 대학교에서 동아시아의 역사와 언어를 공부한 "동양문학사"의 저자로 일본대사도 역임하였다. M-R방식은 1937년 고안 발표되어 국내외에서 널리 사용되어 왔다.

M-R방식은 한글을 로마자로 표기할 때 한 자, 한 자 따로 떼어서 표기하는 것이 아니라, 발음될 때 겪는 활음적 변화(滑音的變化, Euphonic Change)를 고려하여 표기하는 방법으로 문자를 구성하는 각각의 자음, 모음대로 발음하는 것이 아니라 그것들이 연결되어 실제로 발음되는 대로 표기하는 방식이다. 특히 소리구조가 다른 외국인들이 발음하기 쉽도록 참작하여 고안된 것이다.

1) 자음 표기

자음의 표기는 초성(Initial Sound), 종성(Final Sound), 유성음(Voiced Sound), 무성음(Voiceless Sound), 자음(Consonant)과 자음, 자음과 모음(Vowel)이 연결되어 발생하는 활음적 변화에 따라 표기형태가 달라진다.

예를 들어 ㄱ, ㄷ, ㅂ이 초성과 종성으로 사용되는 경우는K, T, P로 표기 되지만, 중간에 모음과 연결되어 유성음으로 될 경우는G, D, B로 표기된다.

초 성

자음이 단어의 처음에 시작될 경우 다음과 같이 발음된다.

ㄱ:k, ㄴ:n, ㄷ:t, ㄹ:r, ㅁ:m, ㅂ:p, ㅅ:s, ㅈ:ch, ㅊ:ch, ㅋ:k, ㅌ:t, ㅍ:p, ㅎ:h (ㄱ, ㄷ, ㅂ과 ㅋ, ㅌ, ㅍ은 처음 시작하는 초성인 경우 같은 k, t, p로 표기한다).

> *ex* 가리봉동 : Karibong-dong   난지도: Nanjido
> 동작동   : Tongjak-dong   라면 : Ramyon
> 마포   : Mapo   변산 : Pyonsan
> 사당동   : Sadang-dong   종로 : Chongno
> 창동   : Chang-dong   키다리: Kidari
> 탑골(공원) : Tapkol   파주 : Paju
> 효자동   : Hyoja-dong

 종 성

받침으로 사용될 경우 위에서 언급한 초성의 원칙을 따르나 반드시 그렇지는 않다. 예외를 두고 있다.

> *ex* 중학동: Chunghak-dong   이천 : Ichon
> 굳   : Kut   청담동: Chongdam-dong
> 신답   : Sindap   고합 : Kohap

2) 유성 자음(Voiced Sound)

모음과 연결된 자음에서 유성음으로 발음되는 경우 ㄱ, ㄷ, ㅂ은 G, D, B로 표기한다.

> *ex* 창경원   : Changgyongwon
> 신당동   : Sindang-dong
> 가리봉동: Karibong-dong

3) 변별부호(辨別符號)

실제로는 사용되지 않으나, M-R표기법의 초안에는 辨別符號 (Diacritical Mark)를 사용토록 했다.

한글음과 로마자음과의 현격히 다른 音을 표기하기 위해 변별부호(辨別符號: Diacritical Mark)를 사용할 것을 권장하였으나 불편하여 실제로는 사용되지 않고 있다.

M-R방식에서 사용되고 있는 辨別符號는 반달표(˘)와 어깻점(')이다. 반달표(Breve)는 단음 위에 붙혀 상이한 音을 나타내도록 하고 어깻점 (Apostrophe)은 有氣音 위에 붙혀 구별하여 音을 내도록 하고 있다.

로마자로 표기하기 어려운 <ㅓ>와 <ㅡ>는 반달표(˘) 를 사용, <ŏ>와 <ŭ>로 표시하여 <ㅗ:O>와 <ㅜ:u>와 구별토록 하고 있다. 어깻점 (Apostrophe)은 유기음에 붙혀 썼다(ex: p'=ㅍ, t'=ㅌ). 그러나 Computer의Keyboard(글쇠판)에서 辨別符號가 없어 실제로 사용되지 않고 있다.

4) 연결음

앞서 열거한 원칙에도 불구하고, 자음간, 자음과 모음간의 연결음에 대해서는 소리나는 대로 표기하는 것을 원칙으로 한다.

<Figure 1>은 McCune, Reischauer가 고안한 로마자 표기법을 J. 하비가 마련한 실용위주로 바꾼 간소한 표다.

원래의 간소표(簡素表)에는 변별부호가 있는데 실제로 사용되지 않아 표기를 생략하였다.

<도표 1>에서 종성은 받침에 해당 된다. 연결음이 되는 경우, 종렬(縱列)에 표기된 ㄱ,ㄴ,ㄹ,ㅁ,ㅂ,ㅇ의 받침이 다음에 오는 ㅇ,ㄱ,ㄴ,ㄷ,ㄹ,ㅁ,ㅂ….과 연결될 때의 연결음이 <도표 1>에 표시되어 있다. 모음간의 결합은 비교적 간단하며 <Figure 2>를 보면 쉽게 이해된다.

ex　도표참조

ㄱ＋ㄱ＝kk(국기원, Kukkiwon)　ㄴ＋ㄹ＝ll(천리마, Chollima)

ㄹ＋ㅈ＝lch(울진, Ulchin)　　ㅂ＋ㄹ＝mn(왕십리, Wangsimni)

ㅂ＋ㅈ＝pch(갑자, Kapcha)　　ㅇ＋ㄹ＝ngn(청량, Chongnyang)

Write It Sounds!

Common Errors in M-R System

	Right	Wrong
금 강 산	Mt. Kumgang	Mt. Gumgang
설 악 산	Mt. Sorak	Mt. Solak
속 리 산	Mt. Songni	Mt. Sokri
절 두 산	Mt. Choltu	Mt. Choldu
백 두 산	Mt. Paektu	Mt. Paekdu
백 록 담	Paengnoktam	Paeknokdam
낙 동 강	Naktong River	Nakdong River
백 령 도	Paengnyong-do	Paekryong-do
정 　 주	Chongju	Jongju
울 　 진	Ulchin	Uljin
철 　 원	Chorwon	Cholwon
천 리 마	Chollima	Chonrima
전 민 련	Chonminnyon	Chonminryon
조 총 련	Chochongnyon	Chochongryon

M-R표기의 간소표(簡素表), <자음>

종성 ＼ 초성	○	ㄱ	ㄴ	ㄷ	ㄹ	ㅁ	ㅂ	ㅅ	ㅈ	ㅊ	ㅋ	ㅌ	ㅍ	ㅎ
	*	k	n	t	®	m	p	s	ch	ch	k	t	p	h
ㄱ k	g	kk	ngn	kt	ngn	ngm	kp	ks	kch	kch	kk	kt	kp	kh
ㄴ n	n	ng	nn	nd	ll	nm	nb	ns	nj	nch	nk	nt	np	nh
ㄹ l	r	lg	ll	lt	ll	lm	lb	ls	lch	lch	lk	lt	lp	rh
ㅁ m	m	mg	mn	md	mn	mm	mb	ms	mj	mch	mk	mt	mp	mh
ㅂ p	b	pk	mn	pt	mn	mm	pp	ps	pch	pch	pk	pt	pp	ph
○ ng	ng	ngg	ngn	ngd	ngn	ngm	ngb	ngs	ngj	ngch	ngk	ngt	ngp	ngh

Figure 1

*<쉬> is romanized *"shwi."*

모음

ㅏ	ㅑ	ㅓ	ㅕ	ㅗ	ㅛ	ㅜ	ㅠ	ㅡ	ㅣ	ㅘ	ㅝ	ㅚ	ㅟ	ㅢ	ㅐ	ㅔ
a	ya	o	yo	o	yo	u	yu	u	i	wa	wo	oe	wi	ui	ae	e

ㅖ	ㅒ	ㅞ	ㅙ
ye	yae	we	wae

Figure 2

2000년 문화관광부 로마자 표기법

문화관광부는 2000년 7월 4일 새 국어의 로마자 표기법을 발표했다. 이로써 지난 1984년1월13일에 고시된 정부제정 로마자 표기법은 16년 만에 개정을 보게 된 것이다.

국어의 로마자 표기법은 원칙적으로 고시한 날부터 시행토록 되어 있으나, 기존의 도로표지판 및 문화재 안내판 등은 2005년 12월 말까지는 모두 새 표기법에 따르도록 하고 있다. 기존의 교과서 등 출판물은 2002년 2월 말 까지는 새 표기법에 따르도록 하였다.

문화관광부 로마자 표기법의 특징

새 로마자 표기법의 주요 특징은 다음과 같다.

첫째, 반달표(˘) 와 어깻점(')같은 辨別符號(Diacritical Mark)를 없앴다.

1984년 1월 13일 고시되어 정부제정 문화관광부 안이 나오기까지 16년간 사용되어 왔던 정부의 로마자 표기 안은 M-R표기법과 같이 辨別符號(Diacritical Mark) 사용을 권장해 왔는데, 컴퓨터와 인터넷에서 특수부호 표기가 어려운 점을 고려하여 이들의 사용을 폐지했다. (M-R안은 실용화 단계에서 특수부호 사용이 없어졌다)

둘째, 자음 표기에서 유성음과 무성음을 구별하지 않고 'ㄱ, ㄷ, ㅂ, ㅈ'을 g, d, b, j로 통일하였다. (종전 표기법에서는 '도동'을 Todong로 적었으나 새 표기법에서는 Dodong임)

주요 내용

새 표기법에서의 자음, 모음의 표기를 보면 다음과 같다.

① 'ㄱ, ㄷ, ㅂ, ㅈ'은 g, d, b, j로 한다.

종전에는 'ㄱ, ㄷ, ㅂ, ㅈ'을 어두에서는 k, t, p, ch로 단어 가운데서는 g, d, b, j로 적었는데, 위치에 상관없이 g, d, b. j로 적도록 하였다.

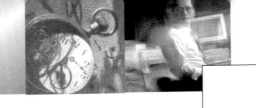

ex 광주: Gwangju, 대구: Daegu, 부산: Busan, 제주: Jeju

② 'ㅋ, ㅌ, ㅍ, ㅊ'은 k, t, p, ch로 한다.

'ㅋ, ㅌ, ㅍ, ㅊ'은 종전에 k, t, p, ch 또는 k', t', p', ch'의 두 가지로 표기하던 것을 k, t, p, ch로 통일하고 어깻점 사용을 없앴다.

ex 태안: Taean, 충주: Chungju

③ 모음 '어, 으'는 eo, eu로 한다.

종전에는 '어'를 <ŏ>로 '으"를 <ŭ>로 표시하였다. 새로운 문화관광부 안에서는 이 같은 특수부호의 사용을 폐지하였다.

새 표기법에서는 '어, 으'를 eo, eu로 표기한다.

'어'를 eo로 하는 것은 1959년부터 1983년까지의 표기법이었다. 로마자의 모음 은 a, e, i, o, u 뿐이어서 한국어의 '어', '으'는 특수부호를 사용하여 표기해 왔다.

ex 성주: Seongju, 금곡: Geumgok

④ 'ㅅ'은 항상 s로 적는다.

종전에는 'ㅅ'을 뒤에 'ㅣ'가 올 때에는 sh로 그 밖의 경우에는 s로 적었는데 새 표시법에서는 s로 통일하여 표기하기로 했다.

ex 신라: Silla, 실상사: Silsangsa

⑤ 자음과 자음

자음과 모음과의 연음으로 인해 음운이 바뀌는 경우는 구개음화 등 국어의 표준발음법에 따라 "발음되는 대로" 표기하는 것을 원칙으로 한다.

- **한라**(할라) Halla
- **종로**(종노) Jongno
- **국민**(궁민) Gungmin
- **신문로**(신문노) Sinmunno
- **독립문**(동님문) Dongnimmun
- **법문** (범문) Beommun

⑥ 'ㄱ, ㄷ, ㅂ'은 어말이나 자음 앞에 올 때에는 k, t, p로 적는다.

ex 곡성: Gokseong, 무극: Mugeuk

⑦ 관용을 허용한다.

　새 표기법의 실시에도 불구하고 그 동안 써 온 인명, 회사명, 단체명은 원래대로 쓸 수 있도록 하였다.

　세계적으로 널리 알려진 '삼성(Samsung), 현대(Hyundai)' 등의 회사명을 새 표기법에 따라 바꾸는 것은 현실적으로 어렵기 때문이다. 인명의 경우도 마찬가지이다. 그러나 새로이 만드는 인명, 회사명, 단체명은 정부안 로마자 표기법에 따를 것을 권장하고 있다. 새 표기법에서 인명의 성씨 표기만은 추후 별도로 정한다고 명기하였다.

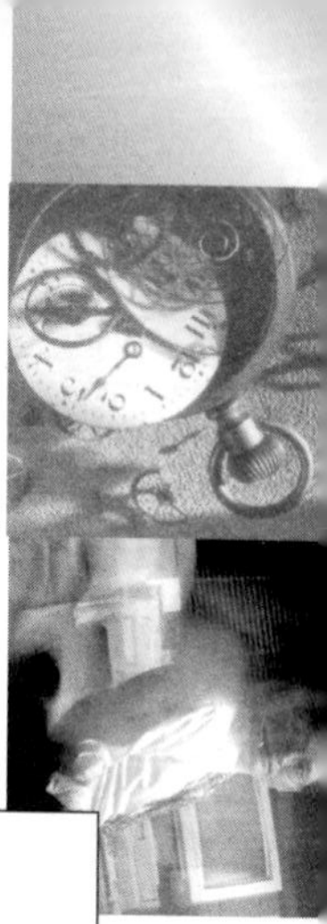

문화관광부 안의 로마자 표기법

<모 음>

ㅏ	ㅓ	ㅗ	ㅜ	ㅡ	ㅣ	ㅐ	ㅔ	ㅚ	ㅟ	ㅑ	ㅕ	ㅛ	ㅠ	ㅒ	ㅖ	ㅘ	ㅙ	ㅝ	ㅞ	ㅢ
a	eo	o	u	eu	i	ae	e	oe	wi	ya	yeo	yo	yu	yae	ye	wa	wae	wo	we	ui

Figure 3

<자 음>

ㄱ	ㄲ	ㅋ	ㄷ	ㄸ	ㅌ	ㅂ	ㅃ	ㅍ	ㅈ	ㅉ	ㅊ	ㅅ	ㅆ	ㅎ	ㄴ	ㅁ	ㅇ	ㄹ
g, k	kk	k	d,t	tt	t	b,p	pp	P	j	jj	ch	s	ss	h	n	m	ng	r,l

Figure 4

✔ 주요 용례(도표3, 4에 의한 예)

강원도	:Gangwon-do
강화도	:Ganghwado
거북선	:Geobukseon
거제도	:Geojedo
경기도	:Gyeonggi-do
경복궁	:Gyeongbokgung
경상남도	:Gyeongsangnam-do
경상북도	:Gyeongsangbuk-do
경주	:Gyeongju
경포대	:Gyeongpodae
고구려	:Goguryeo
고려	:Goryeo
광주	:Gwangju
광화문	:Gwanghwamun
국새	:Guksae
금강	:Geumgang
김포	:Gimpo
김해	:Gimhae

낙동강	:Nakdonggang
남대문	:Namdaemun
남태령	:Namtaeryeong
내장산	:Naejangsan

다보탑	:Dabotap
대관령	:Daegwallyeong
대구	:Daegu
대동강	:Daedonggang
대전	:Daejeon
대한민국	:Daehanminguk
덕수궁	:Deoksugung
독도	:Dokdo
독립문	:Dongnimmun
동강	:Donggang
두만강	:Dumangang

무궁화 :Mugunghwa

백제 :Baekje
부산 :Busan
불국사 :Bulguksa

서울 :Seoul
석가탑 :Seokgatap
설악산 :Seoraksan
속리산 :Songnisan
신라 :Silla

압록강 :Amnokgang
애국가 :Aegukga
영산강 :Yeongsangang
완도 :Wando
울릉도 :Ulleungdo

울산 :Ulsan
인천 :Incheon
임진강 :Imjingang

전라남도 :Jeollanam-do
전라북도 :Jeollabuk-do
전주 :Jeonju
제주 :Jeju
종로 :Jongno
종묘 :Jongmyo
지리산 :Jirisan
진도 :Jindo

창경궁 :Changgyeonggung
창덕궁 :Changdeokgung
창원 :Changwon
첨성대 :Cheomseongdae
청주 :Cheongju
춘천 :Chuncheon
충청남도 :Chungcheongnam-do
충청북도 :Chungcheongbuk-do

태극기	:Taegeukgi
태백산	:Taebaeksan
태종대	:Taejongdae

한강	:Hangang
한글	:Hangeul
한라산	:Hallasan
홍도	:Hongdo
화랑	:Hwarang

판교	:Pangyo
포항	:Pohang
포천	:Pocheon

Point :

한글의 로마자 표기는 M-R안이든 정부안이든 일일이 이론을 복잡하게 암기하는 것
보다는 실제 용례를 반복 활용하는 것이 습득의 지름길이다.

Citation Sources 15

Books

- Ames, Steven. E.(1989) Elements of Newspaper Design. N. Y.: Praeger.
- Barnhust, Kevin G.(1994) Seeing the Newspaper. N. Y.: St. Martin Press.
- Harrower, Tim(1995). The Newspaper Designer's Handbook. Wm.C. Brown Communications, Inc.
- Howard B. Taylor & Jacob Scher. Copy Reading and News Editing. N.Y.: Prentice-Hall Inc.
- Outing, Steve(1996). "Newspapers 온라인: The Latest Statistics". Editor & Publisher Interactive.
- The new International Webster's Pocket Grammar, Speech Style Dictionary of the English Language. Trident Press International.
- The Associated Press Stylebook and Libel Manual(1989).
- The Korea Times Stylebook.
- The Poynter Institute for Media Studies(1991). Eyes on the News.
- The Society of Newspaper Design(1996). The Best of Newspaper Design. 17.
- Utt. Sandra H. & Pastermack, Steve(1989, Autumn), "How They Look: An Updated Study of American Newspaper Front Pages", Journalism Quarterly.
- 동아 세계 대백과 사전(1982).
- 민경우(1995). 디자인의 이해. 미진사.

□ 박선의, 최호천(1989). 시각 커뮤니케이션 디자인. 미진사.
□ 송지연(1998). 영자신문이 영어를 끝내줘요. 도서출판 신나라.
□ 스기모토 쿄코(1999). e-mail 영어. 시공아카데미.
□ 안정효(2000). 가짜영어사전. 현암사.

Newspapers

□ Financial Times
□ International Herald Tribune
□ Los Angeles Times
□ Mainichi Daily News
□ South China Morning Post
□ Taipei Times
□ The Asian Wall Street Journal
□ The Japan Times
□ The Korea Herald
□ The Korea Times
□ The New York Times
□ The Washington Post
□ USA Today
□ 문화일보
□ 조선일보

Periodicals

□ 남북정상회담 외신 기사집: 국정 홍보처 해외 홍보원(2000)
□ 로마자 표기 용례: 문화관광부-국립국어연구원
□ 신문정리연구(1994): 일본 신문협회
□ 뉴미디어시대 신문디자인(1996) 언론실무서 ③: 한국언론연구원
□ 미국 신문업계의 뉴미디어 진출현황과 과제: 한국언론연구원(1996)

〈著者紹介〉

■ 박 창 석

에듀타임즈 편집인, 주필(현)
코리아타임스 수석옴부즈맨(현)
한국외국어대학교, 경희대학교 ENIE 담당 겸임교수(현)
코리아타임스 편집국장, 편집인, 상무이사 역임
미국 하버드대학교 GSAS 국제정치전공
연세대학교 언론홍보대학원 졸업
경희대학교 졸업

영어야, 논술로 말할래?

2007년 8월 20일 인 쇄
2007년 8월 27일 발 행

著 者　朴　　昌　　錫

發行人　(寅製)秦　旭　相

發行處　白山出版社

서울시 성북구 정릉3동 653-40
등록 : 1974. 1. 9. 제 1-72호
전 화 : 914-1621, 917-6240
FAX : 912-4438
http://www.baek-san.com
edit@baek-san.com

값 12,000원
ISBN 978-89-7739-536-7